# Teaching Kids to Care

## Exploring Values through Literature and Inquiry

**Sharon Vincz Andrews**

Clearinghouse on Reading, English, and Communication

EDINFO PRESS

© 1994 by EDINFO Press

Co-published by

Indiana State University (Terre Haute)

and

EDINFO Press

and

ERIC Clearinghouse on Reading, English, and Communication

Carl B. Smith, Director

Indiana University

P.O. Box 5953

Bloomington, Indiana  47407

Editor: Warren Lewis
Design and production: David J. Smith
Cover design: David J. Smith

This publication was funded in part by the Office of Educational Research and Improvement, U.S. Department of Education, under contract no. RR93002011. Contractors undertaking such projects under government sponsorship are encouraged to express freely their judgment in professional and technical matters. Points of view or opinions, however, do not necessarily represent the official view or opinions of the Office of Educational Research and Improvement.

**Library of Congress Cataloging-in-Publication Data**

Andrews, Sharon Vincz.
    Teaching kids to care  :  exploring values through literature and inquiry / Sharon
    Vincz Andrews.
        p.     cm.
    Includes bibliographical references.
    ISBN  0-927516-41-1  :  $19.95
    1. Moral education (Elementary)--United States.  2. Moral education
(Secondary)--United States.    I. ERIC Clearinghouse on Reading, English, and
Communication.    II. Title.
LC311.A49    1994
370.11'4--dc20
                                            94-19040

# ERIC/REC Advisory Board

# Dedication by the author:

*To Jason and Dale, with love.*

**Dedication by the Floyd family:**

*The Everett I. Brown Company supported this research in honor and memory of Everett I. Brown, its founder.*

## Dedication by the Floyd family:

*Mr. and Mrs. Karl H. Kettelhut supported this research in honor and memory of Charles T. Stallard, father of Mrs. Kettelhut.*

# Table of Contents

# Acknowledgments

I wish to acknowledge my early mentors, Jerome Harste, Carolyn Burke, and Anabel Newman at Indiana University, whose vision and demonstration of what teaching can be, what inquiry can do for learner and teacher alike, provided me with a framework for thinking about the kind of curriculum that could support the teaching of values. I read what they write, see their students produce beautiful and moving pieces about teaching and learning, and continue to feel a kinship with their ideas. Pat Wheeler, my friend and colleague at Indiana State University, has been a great collaborator in thinking through theme cycling with our graduate classes.

Many other colleagues, students, and friends have contributed their insights. Donna Martin, a former student, now teaching in Houston, Texas, worked in many different capacities on this project. She served as a researcher, worked diligently with me on developing the children's literature bibliography organized according to the values taught, and became a sister-learner and co-thinker on the subject of values and how they are taught.

Jean Harris, the sixth-grade teacher whose work on the AIDS project is reported in chapter one, was a great support and an embodiment of the caring, compassionate teacher that I believe is necessary for the teaching of values in today's classroom. Shelley Harris Roembke, the teacher in chapter two who challenged her third-graders to new views of compassion in an inquiry project on the homeless, also expanded my concept of the kind of teacher that the future will demand. The work of both of these teachers and their students is gratefully acknowledged.

Other graduate students in reading, counseling, and educational psychology—Laura Reynolds, Lionel Matthews, Kennedy Vanderpool—did much of the initial data gathering from the old textbooks. My son, Jason Vincz, read textbooks, edited, and checked references in the initial research report. Many other students served as raters of values in the modern textbooks.

Judy Peckam, a children's bookstore owner and children's librarian in Houston, Texas; Shirley Mullin, owner of a children's bookstore in Indianapolis, Indiana; Pat Smith, a fifth-grade teacher from Terre Haute, Indiana; Margaret Leiberman, the media specialist at West Vigo Elementary in Terre Haute; and Pat Riley from the Jasper, Indiana public library provided input for the children's literature bibliography.

I am grateful, too, to David Vancil, for his description of the Floyd Collection of old textbooks in the Appendix. As the curator of the rare-book collections at Indiana State University, Dave provided insight and perspective on the project. I thank David Gilman, Professor of Curriculum, Instruction, and Media Technology at Indiana State

University, who developed the original grant proposal and helped gather data from the old textbooks.

This book has evolved out of a research study funded by a small grant that was intended to provide a researcher with the means to investigate the values taught in old textbooks. Therefore, a great debt of gratitude is owed to Mr. and Mrs. William Floyd, both for having collected the textbooks that were the basis for the research portion of this book as well as for gathering the funds for the grant that made it possible. I wish also to acknowledge the Everett I. Brown Company who supported this research in honor of their founder, Everett I. Brown, and Mr. and Mrs. Karl H. Kettelhut who supported this research in honor of Mrs. Kettelhut's father, Charles T. Stallard.

Although I have read many articles and books on the teaching of values and the functions of textbooks, I want to acknowledge two people in particular who have given me wonderful ideas and provided me with an expanded theory of teaching through their work. Thomas Lickona's book, *Educating for Character*, was inspirational. Nel Noddings's book, *The Challenge to Care in Schools*, has been a great influence on my thinking about the true goals of education.

I gratefully acknowledge the time and efforts of my editor, Warren Lewis, who acted as a literary midwife in helping to bring this volume to birth.

Finally, I thank my dear husband, Dale, who allowed "Floyd" to move into our lives and take over for the past three years. He gratefully acknowledges this book as the end of the lease.

*Sharon Vincz Andrews, Shelli Roembke, and Jean Harris*

# Introduction

There are many ways to make your classroom an exciting, thoughtful, challenging place to be. You are probably already giving your students the opportunity to choose some of their reading materials and topics for writing. You may be doing an "authoring cycle" or some other form of process writing, culminating in the publishing of the students' work. You may be having guest speakers regularly as resources for learning in the social studies and science areas. You may be integrating traditional subject areas to form a more cohesive and meaningful curriculum. However, unless your curriculum provides a personal and caring connection between the students and the content, the potential for educating students to the rights and responsibilities of living in a democracy is limited. To provide a curriculum that deals with the moral dilemmas of everyday life is to give students the opportunity to consider and practice the decision making that is required of every citizen. The inquiry approach to developing curriculum with students (demonstrated in chapters one and two) and the strategies for establishing democratic teaching and the bibliography of children's literature (provided in the last chapter of this book) provide you with some sound ideas and powerful books for developing a caring and democratic classroom.

For many students in primary schools in the past (and, perhaps, today), textbooks were the most important books (not to mention the *majority* of books) that they read. The pictures and concepts they formed in their minds as a result of reading textbooks and "readers" contributed to the formulation of their ideas about social justice, public ethics, private morality, personal etiquette, and the social relations and conflicts involving race, class, and gender issues. The questions that now plague our era to a greater extent than in past eras are not only **what** should be taught in the way of values (though that, too, is in dispute) but also **who** should teach those values, and **when**, **where**, and **how** those values should be taught. Should teachers, textbooks, and schools be the arbiters of values or even provide a forum for values development in the young?

In this book, I argue not only in the affirmative that public schools *are* and ought to be an appropriate social context for development of values in the young but also in the negative that textbooks and curriculum guides can do little in and of themselves to inculcate values in children. I argue, further, that a curriculum of direct teaching of values must be redirected to an emphasis on the context and environment of the learning that the students and teachers are constructing, giving the learners themselves a voice in the knowledge and values they are developing, and giving teachers and students alike a methodology that is democratic and conducive to development appropriate to a free and democratic people. The current emphasis on values teaching must encompass a broader array of concerns and a deeper commitment to humanity and the natural environment as a whole than it has done in the past.

This book is divided into chapters that reflect the "How-To" of future values teaching and the "What" and "Who" of past, present, and future values. In chapters one and two, I present examples of a context and structure for values teaching that are occurring in a few classrooms today; these examples adequately represent what I advocate for the future. In both of the examples offered, the basis of the learning is inquiry—study that grows out of the students' own interests, curiosity, and personal questions. Issues of great social import addressed in these examples—AIDS and homelessness—were formulated all the more clearly for the simplicity in which the children—third graders and sixth graders—asked their hard questions and demonstrated their remarkable insight, understanding, and compassion.

Future values teaching will likely occur best in classroom environments such as those described in chapters one and two in which values are not only read about and discussed but also demonstrated and practiced. Future curricula will ideally provide opportunity for expanding choices, the hearing of individual voices, personal decision-making, confrontation of real issues, and the pondering of consequences—a "values-possible" curriculum.

Chapter three briefly outlines the methodology of the historical research portion of this book. Chapter four is a modest attempt to provide an historical overview of the evolving context for values teaching, and a close look at values teaching in the textbooks of the past and present. Chapter five is a statistical study of old and new textbooks. Chapter six discusses the results of these studies. Chapter seven provides some interpretation of the impact of changes in values teaching as reflected in the first five chapters. Chapter eight is devoted to the "Who" of values teaching—the participants in constructing the moral environment and context for teaching today's children to live with a tenable structure of values. Chapter nine contains some "getting started" strategies for teachers who want to pursue a limited school democracy in their classrooms. Chapter nine is also an invitation to parents and teachers to use children's literature as a starting point for values discussions, and some suggestions for using that literature. The bibliography of current children's literature categorized by the values embodied in the stories may serve as a starting place for classrooms full of children ready to collaborate on constructing their democratic future.

# 1 The Values-Centered Classroom: An AIDS Project with Sixth Graders

**F**ew school teachers are pessimists—that's not what we're about. We are cheerleaders for the past, present, and future of children and the adults they will become. The examples shared in this chapter and chapter two show ways in which some cheerleaders for children have helped to construct classroom environments and facilitate research projects that provided rich soil for growth in values. These narratives attest to the truth that children exhibit moral and ethical standards when a learning community has been developed and nurtured and when teachers respect students' questions and inquiry topics.

## An AIDS Project with Sixth Graders

*AIDS is a serious disease, so I am going to watch my step for the rest of my life. AIDS is a killer. But it won't attack you or me if we think straight and act right. I know the risks of AIDS, and you should too.*

David, 6th grader

*It is terrible.*
*It is scary.*
*It is ruining the world.*
*It is AIDS.*

Mitch, 6th grader

Mitch and David wrote about a topic they chose to study as a part of the sixth-grade health curriculum. It is doubtful whether either the students' parents or their teacher, Jean Harris, would have chosen this topic for thorough study, although it is "covered" in the health curriculum for their school corporation. Why avoid it? Because AIDS is sensitive, risky, personal, and terrifying. Why did these sixth graders choose it? For exactly those reasons.

Jean had not been comfortable with teaching the topic of AIDS to her sixth graders the previous year, and she felt that she had not done a very good job. She explained:

*Jean Harris*

**Last year I was forced to teach this unit. I didn't want to. A thick curriculum guide was given to all the 6th-grade teachers, and they said "You will teach this." I did teach it, but I wasn't comfortable.**

She was surprised and apprehensive when, after a brief discussion of alternatives, this year's new group of students unanimously chose AIDS as the topic of prolonged study. Jean wondered if they could cope with a topic that required maturity to come to grips with. Were they old enough? During the brainstorming session on the first day, one of the children shouted out, "I know it's sexually transmitted." Giggles followed, with wide eyes and embarrassed faces. They stopped and had a long talk about the seriousness of the subject and the maturity they would need to deal with it well. The children made their own decision to continue. After that, there were no problems. Jean was pleased at her students' pride at behaving maturely.

Next, she wondered whether she would get negative reactions from parents in her small Midwestern town. To her surprise, Jean received no negative responses, and many parents specifically thanked her for their children's opportunity to study the critical health issue carefully. They also appreciated their children's excitement about, and dedication to, the project. Here is the letter Jean wrote to parents before starting the study:

**Dear Parents,**

**I would like to share what will be happening in our classroom these next two weeks in case your child doesn't share it. Because of a college class I am taking that emphasizes student choice, I am letting my students choose something for in-depth study that they are really interested in and that they want to know more about. After much brainstorming, they came up with the topic of AIDS. Since the corporation curriculum guide requires that I teach AIDS anyway, I felt that this was a wise choice made by my sixth graders.**

**However, being a parent myself, I thought you might be a little in awe if you happened to look at this week's spelling vocabulary and see such words as "intravenous," "blood," "exposed," "sexually transmitted," etc. Therefore, I would like to share with you a few of my lesson plans for the upcoming two weeks. I will be reading several pieces of literature dealing with AIDS. Two of these are _Losing Uncle Tim_ and _Friends for Life_. We will also read and discuss the story of Ryan White to try to relate to his feelings at having to live and die with AIDS. We'll be writing several of our own stories, doing some role playing, commercials, debates, and reporting.**

In social studies, we'll be mapping the spread of AIDS throughout the world and graphing the statistics we find in the almanac. The children will do research with many articles from periodicals and pamphlets, and they will report their findings. We will be doing much videotaping of the many things we are learning.

I want to have several resource people come in to speak about AIDS to further the children's knowledge about this widespread disease.

We're excited about starting this unit. I like the topic that the children chose, and I feel that they believe, as I do, that their generation is the one that must find a way to stop the AIDS virus. Be sure to ask your child what he or she is learning about AIDS.

Mrs. Harris

## Getting Started

The students began the study by brainstorming their current information and ideas about the topic. Jean wrote on the board while the students generated ideas for over an hour. The diagram below is a "cleaned up" web from the first day of brainstorming.

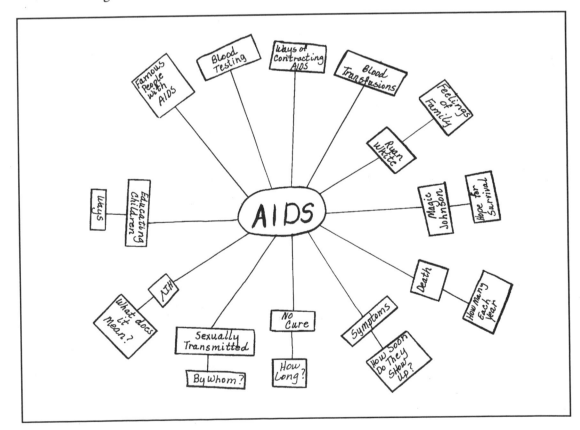

As the children participated in this group process, they engaged in considerate turn-taking and a group-generated excitement about the topic and possibilities for study. At the end of the semantic webbing, the students reorganized their current knowledge and questions, and they generated two lists:

## Things we already knew about AIDS

- There is no cure for AIDS.
- AIDS is sexually transmitted.
- A person must have direct contact to acquire AIDS.
- Famous people can get AIDS.
- A baby can be born with AIDS.

## Things we want to know about AIDS

- All the ways possible to get AIDS
- How long before a cure is found?
- How do they test for AIDS?
- Why do people take the risks?
- What are scientists doing to find a cure?
- Why do some people live longer than others?
- What kind of blood testing is being done?
- What testing is done to be sure that blood is safe?
- How safe is the blood testing process?
- What do they do with the HIV blood at hospitals?
- Can HIV persons give blood?
- How do people who have AIDS survive daily?
- How does AIDS destroy the immune system?
- Would AIDS victims ever want to commit suicide?

The process of student-centered research and developing lists of known and unknown information naturally operationalized *curiosity* even in students who were ordinarily difficult to engage. Jean discovered that one of her most needy and difficult students had visited the city library one evening during the beginning of this unit; he was looking for information to contribute to the class's knowledge base. He checked out five books and brought them to class. She said it was probably the first time in his educational career that he had been interested enough actually to initiate a library visit on his own. Because he felt that this project belonged to him—he had helped to choose it, and some of his ideas were in the web and on the charts—he was motivated to work on his own out of pure interest and curiosity. He wanted to contribute meaningfully to a class discussion. The structure and the process were helping him to develop *independence*. He was gaining *respect* for himself as a learner, a researcher, and a thinker.

## Theoretical Memo: Questions Express Values

Not only was Jean operationalizing curiosity in her students but also she was providing an initial opportunity for students to express their values. Reread their questions: Though most of them are information-seeking, factual questions, they also imply analytical and reflective concerns.

- *Why do people take the risks?*
  A very thoughtful question for a sixth grader. This inquirer was trying to understand other people's motivations, trying to step outside of the relatively safe 11/12-year-old world into the thinking of a people who had put themselves at risk for AIDS.

- *How do people who have AIDS survive daily?*
  The essence of the question is more than the mechanics of treatment and response; it is a question related to the mental and spiritual resources of living when one knows that one is dying with a terminal disease.

- *Would AIDS victims ever want to commit suicide?*
  This question may be appropriately explored in a sixth-grade classroom; it is not an unusual question coming from students of this age. The suicide rate of children in the United States has tripled since 1960 (National Center for Health Statistics, cited in Lickona [1991], p. 19).

At this point in their study of AIDS, the students lacked knowledge. Their lack of knowledge produced fear and desperation; suicide seemed a logical response to the disease. Later in the study, they read about the courage of Ryan White and his family and of others who have successfully fought the disease and are outliving the predictions of their demise. Hope, faith, trust, and positive outlook come to seem possible, even in the face of this mortal plague. The empathy and understanding that the students later expressed are not evident in these initial questions. These questions were just the beginning of a variety of "higher order" inquiries.

# Doing Research

The lists of things that the students wanted to know pointed them in several directions. They gathered information from a variety of resources: the public and school libraries, the classroom teacher, videos, and outside speakers. Because they were interested in blood transfusions and blood testing ("That's how you find out if you have it."), they decided to contact the county hospital to see if someone there would talk to them about these procedures. A laboratory technician agreed to speak with the class about blood testing, and the class took a field trip to the hospital. Several letters from the students show what they learned and that they took this study seriously.

Dear Mrs. Mathis,

You taught me alot today about AIDS and how it destroys the immune system and that kind of stuff. I would really like to come and see your laboratory. I think that would really be fun. I would appreciate that. You know alot about blood and AIDS. I didn't know that the AIDS virus usually doesn't kill the person. Some other illness usually kills the person.

Your friend,
Mitch

YOU'RE A WINNER

Dear Mrs. Mathis,
I really appreciate you coming and talking to us. I really learned alot, but didn't understand a little bit of it about DNA and antigens. I know your equipment is pretty geeky, but at least they protect you! Thanks for coming. I'm looking forward to seeing you at our trip to the hospital. We made our commercials about AIDS. We've also did our reports. We are going to present them pretty soon. Well, Thanks again!

Shawnee

RX

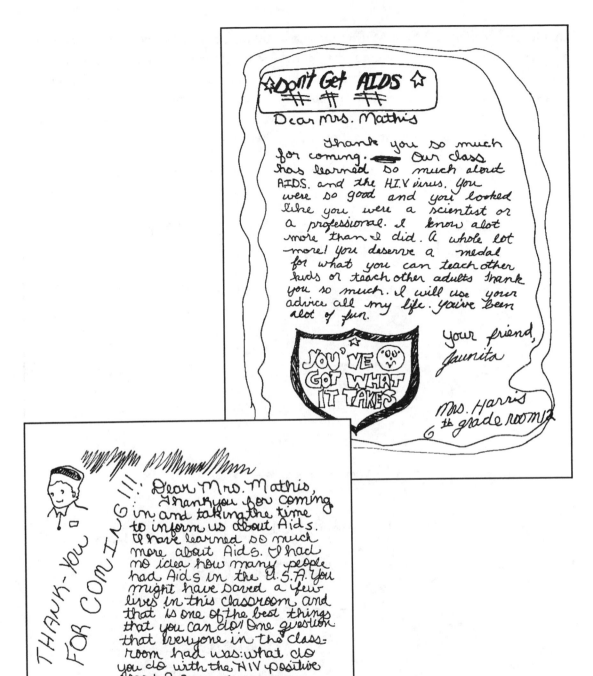

☆ Don't Get AIDS ☆

Dear Mrs. Mathis

Thank you so much for coming. Our class has learned so much about AIDS. and the H.I.V. virus. You were so good and you looked like you were a scientist or a professional. I know alot more than I did. A whole lot more! You deserve a medal for what you can teach other kids or teach other adults thank you so much. I will use your advice all my life. You've been alot of fun.

YOU'VE GOT WHAT IT TAKES

Your friend,
Jaunita

Mrs. Harris
6th grade room 12

THANK-YOU FOR COMING!!!

Dear Mrs. Mathis,
Thank you for coming in and taking the time to inform us about Aids. I have learned so much more about Aids. I had no idea how many people had Aids in the U.S.A. You might have saved a few lives in this classroom and that is one of the best things that you can do! One question that everyone in the classroom had was: what do you do with the HIV positive blood? I thank you for clearing that up. THANK-YOU
Sincerely,
Julie

RX

BEWARE OF AIDS!

*The Values-Centered Classroom: An AIDS Project with Sixth Graders*

In addition to visits by Mrs. Mathis and a local dentist, current journal and newspaper articles provided information and issues for the students to synthesize and organize into coherent graphs, charts, and reports. They worked in teams, focusing on different areas of interest. Some teams were responsible for statistical information. They made charts and diagrams which were displayed in the hallway. One of these teams focused on "Pediatric AIDS." The information they gathered was displayed on the chart below.

Pediatric Aids: Distribution by Patient group.

Aug. 31, 1987

(N= 571)

Patient Group:

▨ Hemophilia/coagulation Disorders (5%)

▢ Parents with Aids or at increased Risk for Aids (78%)

▨ Transfusion with Blood or Blood Products (12%)

▨ Undetermined (5%)

Other teams explored the feelings and emotions of AIDS victims. They used the computer to complete this report.

"AIDS Victims Feelings"

*When people are threatened with death from a fatal disease, such as AIDS, it is essential to cope with the emotional problems. People often need help in dealing with them. They [articles] have talked about group therapy and AIDS support groups, which can be of great help. If more help is needed, they could go into psychotherapy available through high school and college guidance counselors. When people become very depressed, they may need antidepressive drugs available from physicians.*

*If someone you care about has AIDS, it can hurt you emotionally as much as it hurts him or her, maybe more.*

*When a person keeps AIDS a secret, it builds up inside them. Then they get stressed and don't know what to do. Instead of getting stressed, you can talk about it and get those feelings out. Some stories of people with AIDS are stories with love and pain, hope and sorrow, acceptance and despair. There are stories of people just like me and you who have lived with and loved someone with AIDS. People with AIDS feel lonely, sad, uncomfortable and angry. As an example, Ryan White had bad feelings and was afraid he was going to die. He was interviewed, and one of the questions was, "What was the worst feeling when you got the virus?" He said he was afraid, but "It wasn't so bad when I knew I couldn't do anything about it." He was afraid to die, but he said, "I'm never going to give up."*

Aleska, Jaunita, and Ina

Despite the fear generated by the topic, the students' compassion for the victims of AIDS was evident throughout the study. Jean read a number of novels aloud to the class. These fictional accounts provided another perspective on the study—the human cost, the emotional ordeal, and the personal and family grief that occurs when someone contracts this disease. Here is the class bibliography of fiction:

Hermes, Patricia (1989). *Be still my heart*. New York: Pocket Books.
Jordan, Mary Kate (1989). *Losing Uncle Tim*. Niles, Illinois: Albert Whitman and Co.
Humphreys, Martha (1991). *Until whatever*. New York: Clarion Books.
Miklovitz, Gloria (1987). *Goodbye, Tomorrow*. New York: Delacorte Press.
Shulman, Jeffrey (1988). *Friends for life*. Frederick, Maryland: Twenth-First Century Books.

They responded in many ways to the plight of AIDS victims—posters, poetry, and letters. Both the fictional accounts of AIDS victims and real-life stories, e.g. Ryan White and Magic Johnson, contributed to the students' growing awareness and compassionate response to the plight of AIDS victims. The students were most concerned with Ryan White's battle with the disease; they chose to write letters to his mother after reading an article about her in *Indianapolis* magazine. Some examples show their heartfelt concern:

Dear Mrs. White,

Hi, my name is Nick. I am 12 yrs. old. Our class is trying to find articles on people who have AIDS. We just finished an article about Ryan White. I am very sad that your son died from the AIDS virus. Your son sounded like he was very popular because of being with all those people. Your son was a very strong boy. He lived for a long time, even with the AIDS virus. I know how you feel but I know since he was strong you can be strong too. I think his sister misses him too as well as his dad. But you and your family can hang on for a long time. I'm glad that you are trying to do something about AIDS

Your friend,
Nick

P.S. You have a really nice family.

Dear Mrs. White,

Hi, my name is Jaunita. I am in the sixth grade. I hear a lot about Ryan. I heard he was an active kid. He was lucky to live the way he lived. He didn't let AIDS ruin his life! I think Ryan is a nice and understandable person! I think teaching kids about AIDS would be fun. But the sad part about life is all the sicknesses and the diseases there are. I just want to wish you good luck with teaching kids to stay away from AIDS. Good LUCK!!!

P.S.
Go for IT!!.

Your friend,
Jaunita

Another team investigated the risks of acquiring AIDS. Their report showed that they were trying to dispel the myths about acquiring AIDS.

### "Risks"

*AIDS stands for Acquired Immune Deficiency Syndrome. This disease kills the immune system, allowing sickness into your body. Without an immune system, nothing fights the germs out of your body, so you stay sick.*

*There are many ways to acquire AIDS. Fifty percent of all small children who have AIDS get it from the mother passing it on to them during pregnancy. The biggest risk to adults is unprotected sex. Also, unsterile needles can spread AIDS. There are a lot of people who are afraid of AIDS victims because they think you can get the HIV virus from being near an AIDS victim. But it is safe to be friends with a person infected with AIDS. You can't get AIDS from drinking out of the same water fountain, hugging, using the same shower and toilet facilities, playground equipment, or using the same cups, plates, and silverware.*

*Sometimes, parents don't like their children going to the same school as a child or teacher who has AIDS, but you can't get the virus from chairs or desks either. Eating food that has been prepared by someone with AIDS is safe, just as swimming in the same pool is safe. Also, mosquitoes can't pass the HIV virus by biting an infected person and then biting a person without the virus.*

Carrie, Jennifer, Julie, and Shawnee

---

## *Theoretical Memo: Group Processes as a Context for Building Values*

The processes of group inquiry, teamwork, and process writing developed compromise, notions of consensus building, mutual support, shared decision making, interpersonal reasoning, and perseverance. Encouraging and supporting group work and discussion in the elementary classroom will go a long way towards fostering cooperation rather than competition, supportive critique of peers rather than criticism, and a sense of belonging to a working democracy.

Current literature is full of talk about "cooperative" learning. I prefer to refer to this kind of curriculum structure as *collaborative* because no idea fostered through group work belongs exclusively to one person. Learners are not merely working side by side on their separate tasks; they are working together on a common task. They are mutually engendering new thoughts, plans, projects, and actions that could not come about if the individual were working alone. The result is different from what it would have been if the group members were merely cooperating side-by-side. Though a specific idea may occur to one person who then shares it, the impetus and the environment for that idea is the group, and its working out and perfecting is the common property of all.

Emphasis of this point with students builds respect for group work and for themselves as they acknowledge and benefit from the ideas of their colleagues in collaboration.

# Demonstrating New Understandings

The structure of inquiry curriculum provides integration of normally separate subject areas. Jean's students studied AIDS across the curriculum: spelling, English, math, social studies, science, and health. Her students not only *learned* new information in a variety of areas but also decided to *display* their new understandings in a variety of ways: role-playing, debates, commercials, reports, poetry and informed conversations. This allowed them to demonstrate some previously unrecognized talents and skills. Some of the students chose the debates as the best part of the unit for them personally. Jean described this part of the study:

> **I have some students who hardly talk at all in class, but when the time came for debates, I couldn't get them to stop! They demonstrated that they had done a lot of good research, both at the library and in class, to back up their debate points. I was surprised at how much information they had gained and retained over time. Some of the debate questions were: Should a student with AIDS be allowed to attend our school? Should a woman who has AIDS be allowed to have a baby? Should dentists, doctors, and other health-care workers have to take regular tests for AIDS?**

The following is an excerpt of a debate on the question of whether or not Magic Johnson should have been allowed to play basketball since he had tested positive with the HIV virus.

> **Question (posed by the teacher):** *"Do you think Magic Johnson should be allowed to play basketball, knowing that he has the AIDS virus?"*
>
> **Bree:** *Yes, I think he should be allowed to because just because he has the virus doesn't mean everyone else can catch it.*
>
> **Carrie:** *Yes, I agree, you can't get AIDS just through casual contact. The only way you can get AIDS is through sexual contact, blood transfusions, and needles.*
>
> **Jennifer:** *If you had AIDS, you would still want to play basketball, wouldn't you?*
>
> **Mary:** *AIDS isn't a disease, it's a virus. You can't get it just by bumping into somebody on a basketball court.*
>
> **Kirk:** *But what if he scrapes himself. He might fall down on the basketball court and scrape his elbow—it would most likely be his arms or his hands because that's what he uses the most—and he starts to bleed. And then he runs into his team-mates and hits them in the mouth with his elbow and busts their lip against their teeth. Then the blood is mixed and the other guy could have AIDS.*

**Mary:** *First of all, what would he scrape his elbow on?*

**Kirk:** *He could scrape it on anything. He could scrape it on this desk right now, if you were to trip and fall and go across it.*

**Mary:** *This desk isn't rough enough to be scraped on.*

**Kirk:** *That edge is. But that's irrelevant, anyway. That could happen on the basketball court.*

**Carrie:** *I think he would know it, if he got cut.*

**Kirk:** *But it looks healed, let's say. It's scabbed over.*

**Mary:** *He should at least have a bandage over it where he got scraped.*

**Kirk:** *Well, he falls down and the bandage gets ripped off. AND the scab gets ripped off.*

**Mitch:** *If he's in the locker room before the game, and he hurried up and shaved, and the other guys are in the locker room and he put his razor back in a different place and somebody else used it, then the other guy's shaving with it and they both cut themselves because they're in a hurry, then he's transmitted to the other person.*

**Mary:** *That person should know that the razor is not his, and he should have shaved before he got there.*

**Shawn:** *Also if Magic Johnson is brushing his teeth in the locker room and using dental floss, and a guy comes by and thinks that the toothbrush is his and he has a cut in his mouth, it could transmit the AIDS virus to him.*

**Bree:** *Why would you be brushing your teeth in the locker room?*

**Kirk:** *It's an out-of-state game. You have to travel on a bus. The bus got delayed or something. You get there late and you're in a hurry. That could happen.*

**Mary:** *I still feel Magic Johnson should be allowed to play basketball. I think he will certainly be responsible enough to shave at home. The other guy should be responsible enough to have his own toothbrush at the locker room.*

**Kirk:** *If he was responsible enough, Magic Johnson wouldn't have AIDS.*

## Theoretical Memo:
## The Child as a Moral Thinker

Kohlberg (1976) posed "moral dilemmas" in his research on moral development, and he developed a "stage theory" of moral development. His research convinced him that people typically develop over time in their understanding of justice and morality, and that these stages are evident in this growth:

Stage 1: Avoid punishment.
Stage 2: Look for a reward.
Stage 3: Watch out, someone won't approve.
Stage 4: Consider the consequences for society.
Stage 5: Respect everyone's rights.
Stage 6: Act on your own principles of conscience.

Stages 1 and 2 dominate children's actions during the primary years, but after that, they vary. Some children progress more rapidly than others through the stages.

If we call Jean's debate question about Magic Johnson the "moral dilemma," we can see that several of the moral stages are evident in the students' debate. Because it was to be a debate, Jean had asked the girls to defend Johnson's right to play basketball and the boys to take the opposing position—the opposites, Jean predicted, of the positions that either group, unprompted, would normally have taken. This was an excellent way for the students to think through the reasoning of the "other side" and to appreciate another's position, though unfortunately in this case, it set up a "boys versus girls" mentality. The boys' position seems very much a Stage 4 argument—the consequences to society must be considered. The girls argument could be seen as a Stage 5 perspective—they wanted to respect Johnson's right to play, although the argument is a bit weak and legalistic. He **should** wear a bandage if cut, he **should** shave with his own razor, he **should** brush with his own toothbrush, and so **should** everyone else around him: sort of a "Mom's eye view" of behavior—Stage 3 in the values hierarchy.

The point here is not so much to determine which stage of moral development the children were demonstrating, but rather to appreciate that the curriculum was allowing for the practice of moral thinking and deliberation.

Although the boys' debate team in Jean's classroom took a hard line about Magic Johnson's right to play and his sense of responsibility, their letters reflect compassion. These excerpts are from some of the letters that class members wrote to Johnson:

> • *I think that you are showing a lot of AIDS victims that even if they have AIDS they can still do the same things that a normal person can do.*

> Shawn

• *I bet it is hard knowing that there is no cure for the virus. I wish I could play basketball like you, but no one will ever play like you do.*

Devin

• *I just finished reading your article in People magazine. I like the idea that you didn't keep all your feelings to yourself. Instead you told the public and even took the time to call the people who you'd had sexual contact with. I'm so glad you are still playing basketball. I'm glad you're not just giving up.*

Shawnee

• *Your story really touched my heart. I hope the new president will help doctors and scientists to find a cure for the AIDS virus. Always remember, never give up!!!*

Julie

Other students chose poetry as their favorite way to respond to the new information. Of Randy, whose poem appears on the following page, Jean wrote this:

**I have some kids in my classroom who normally struggle. Here is one of those kids. His mother cannot read or write, but during this project, he was really able to express himself. Here is the poem he came up with:**

# A.I.D.S.

By Randy

Having AIDS is tough.
Having AIDS is rough.
People with AIDS die.
People with AIDS cry.

Sometimes people live and sometimes they don't
Sometimes people care but some people won't.

When they are infected they may not guess.
Until they get a Western Blot and a HIV test.
So be smart and help stop AIDS and keep people
from going to their graves.

Other children in the classroom also responded to the study by writing poems and reflections.

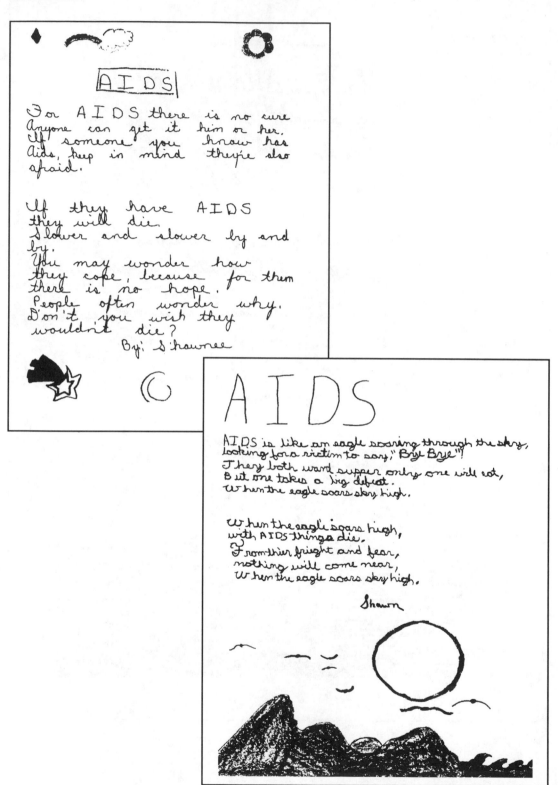

Teaching Kids to Care

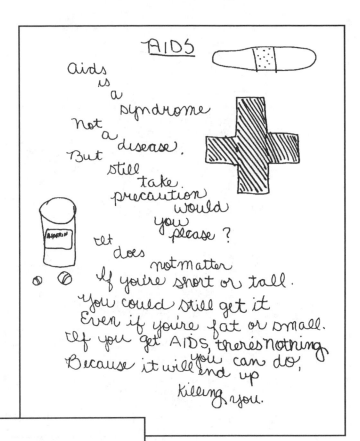

AIDS

Aids
is
a
syndrome
not
a
disease.
But
still
take.
precaution
would
you
please?
It
does
not matter
If you're short or tall.
You could still get it
Even if you're fat or small.
If you get AIDS, there's nothing
you can do,
Because it will end up
killing you.

AIDS

You must stop the spread of AIDS.
AIDS has the whole population worried and afraid.
Prevent it — don't use unsterile needles and abstain from sex,
Or your life will be nothing but a bunch of wrecks.

By: Mitch

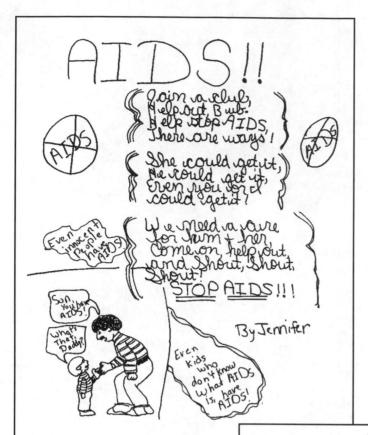

The children's work is powerful. They seem to have recognized their personal roles and responsibilities in helping to stop the spread of the virus. Their knowledge of the risks is reflected in their pleas to the reader to take precautions. The poems are full of heartfelt response to the plight of AIDS victims and the magnitude of the problem. When Jean asked Julie, "What did you learn from the AIDS unit?" she replied:

*I learned that if a person has AIDS, you can't just shut them off and push them to one side. You have to be their friend. You have to realize that they have feelings, too.*

Nick summed up the learning on this topic when he wrote this brief essay:

By Nick

Ever sinse my class and I were working on the AIDS unit, we now know almost everything there is to know about the AIDS virus, and how it travels from human to human. Here are the things I now know about AIDS-

There is no cure for AIDS. It travels from human to human by having sex with an infected person, or sharing a unsterile needle with an infected person.
There are ways that you won't get AIDS. Use a condom, don't take drugs, don't use unsterile needles. Ryan White got the HIV virus from the infected blood. I think Magic Johnson got the AIDS virus by having sex.

Help Stop AIDS!

Jean reflected on her class's experience in these words:

> The children found out so many things that they hadn't known about AIDS, I was amazed. The children started out knowing six facts about AIDS. When the unit was finished, they couldn't list all the things they knew. That speaks highly for a thematic study and it also shows how motivated and excited they were about learning.
>
> I felt that the students were highly motivated, interested, and enthusiastic about their unit on AIDS. Notice that I say *"their* unit." I feel that they took ownership in this unit because it was their choice. I saw a great improvement in their writing skills during this time as well. I feel that the improvement was due to their high interest and motivation for the subject. The greatest reward was in seeing and hearing the way the children worked together cooperatively for a common goal—to learn more about AIDS. I did give a written test at the end of study, similar to a test I would give on any topic we study in science or social studies. The grades were the best I can remember on any test I have given, but I was more pleased with their interest, dedication, and sense of compassion evident throughout the study. I'm sure that my students have acquired much valuable knowledge about AIDS. Maybe by teaching this unit, I've instilled an understanding of the risks of AIDS and kept at least one person from contracting this deadly virus.

## Teaching Values in Jean's Classroom

Jean's classroom experience with the AIDS study represents a number of things I want to say about the teaching of values in today's classrooms. First, the learning that occurred in the several weeks that Jean and her students spent on "The AIDS Project" generated not only important factual information about the virus but also a *compassionate understanding* of the victims and of their challenges and fears. The goals of schooling—knowledge and mastery of subject matter—as well as the goals of true education—understanding and compassion—were met. Moments of coming to grips with the dilemmas of the individual and society were filled with an earnest desire to solve the problems and deal compassionately with other human beings.

Second, *inquiry curriculum* sets the stage for moral growth. The processes inherent in an inquiry curriculum opened the door to new opportunities to live and to think as an informed moral community. When students ask their own questions, search for the answers, and grapple with tough issues, the motivation for learning and the quest for knowledge becomes real and firsthand.

Third, *democratic classroom practices* bring democratic values to life. Choice brings commitment and ownership of the curriculum—*my* topic, *my* questions, *my* research, *my* answers. The democratic classroom dynamic moves towards trust, caring, responsible social action. Because the study of AIDS was important to the students, chosen by the students, and well researched and debated by the students, they were highly motivated to learn. They willingly shared the commitment to be prepared for class, to find information from several sources to increase the group's knowledge, and to take responsibility for their own learning.

Fourth, *teamwork* and *collaboration* foster interaction and give students a stage for open expression of developing values and beliefs. Students learn to listen to what others think and to practice arguing a point of view in the relative safety of a small group. They have reasons to search for information to support their arguments. Students learn about shared decision making, shared work loads, and loyalty to the group. The "child as a moral thinker" emerges as students have opportunity to discuss and debate.

Fifth, the achievements of Jean's class demonstrate that valuable and meaningful learning can occur without a textbook. Adherence to textbooks and teacher's guidance would have inhibited students' choices, motivations, curiosity, and spontaneity of thought and purpose. Inquiry leads the mind to discover the new and unknown; textbooks constrain the mind within the known and predigested.

## Democratic Teaching

Democratic learning, such as occurred in Jean's classroom, is neither unbridled freedom to study any topic in any manner the students desire nor is it disregard for state requirements or local curriculum decisions. Just as in representative democracy, in which the authority of the law, the courts, and the Commander-in-Chief maintain order at both the national and local levels, so also the teacher's legal, moral, and intellectual authority to maintain the classroom as a safe and humane place of learning does not cause the classroom to cease to be democratic. In an inquiry classroom, students and teacher collaborate to agree on curriculum, with the teacher taking the lead.

Jean teaches values—democracy, understanding, compassion, and others—through demonstrating them and allowing for their expression in her classroom. She teaches values not through a prepackaged "value-a-week" curriculum but through grappling with tough issues, through fostering student inquiry, through debate and discussion. She trusts her students and cares enough about them to support their heartfelt efforts at understanding the issues and facts in their chosen areas of interest. In short, she shares her authority and upholds a democratic atmosphere for learning, acknowledging that students' choices and voices have equal importance with her own. Teachers like Jean are daily hammering out a working definition of democracy: freedom with responsibility, choice within an agreed-upon curriculum, voices that speak from individuals' experiences but that respect others' rights and feelings. It is this kind of learning context—complete with tough issues and multiple perspectives—that supplies the medium for refined and redefined values in school. Without the tough questions and multiple perspectives, teaching values would be little more than rote moralizing.

## Grappling with Tough Issues: The Heart of a Values-oriented Curriculum

Is conflict necessary for learning? The study of controversial issues becomes the engine for the development of values. Instead of pretending that we can eliminate conflict from teaching and learning, let us make use of it. Conflict and well-informed debate is applicable to any learning setting. A child of any age can be presented with problems that are identified and felt by the students themselves. If an issue is of sufficient interest to the students, they will tackle opposing viewpoints and meanwhile learn to think through their own and the differing perspectives. Noddings (1992) gave examples similar to Jean's debate questions:

> . . . caring for a pet can be a powerful component in moral education. Children learn to relieve pain and discomfort, not to inflict suffering, and to appreciate the range of responses in living things. Sharing the care of pets can bring delight as well as responsibility to parents and children.
>
> But our relations with nonhuman creatures are complicated, and many issues arise as we explore them. Should we wear furs, for example, or is the whole fur trade immoral? Contrary to simplistic defenses and attacks on the fur business, the question is a complex one. Some of us want to argue that suffering should be minimized or eliminated. That would outlaw steel-jaw traps. Others argue that naturally wild animals should not be raised just for their furs on farms or in cages. But can there be a sharp line between domestic and wild animals? What about the possibility of gradually domesticating useful species? . . . Is it wrong to engage in fur trade? . . . I hope that teachers concerned with "critical thinking" will stimulate our children to consider a long list of related questions: What happens to animals when their range is overpopulated? Is there a form of killing for fur

**that is more humane than the natural processes in a stressed population? What effects would an end of fur trade have on human beings? Should we use the furs of some animals but not others? . . . Should we stop killing and eating animals? Do animals have rights? Should they be used in research?"** (p. 56)

Teachers, like everyone else, do not have simple answers to these questions. Jean did not have ready-made answers to the questions she posed to the students. Complex problems worthy of study do not allow for simple black-and-white answers that can be learned and fed to students in incremental doses and then evaluated by a true/false test. Does that mean we should not study serious areas of moral and ethical concern in schools? Quite the contrary, these are exactly the substance of a curriculum in which enquiring students and compassionate teachers together can learn to honor honest differences of opinion—the essence of democracy. The classroom becomes a place in which participants learn the importance of coming to their task of decision making with informed perspectives. They learn the importance of negotiating ideas, of learning when to compromise and when not, and, then, of getting along with people with whom they seriously disagree. Where, if not in schools, will students learn that the complex issues that face us today are many sided, and that respect and responsibility for one another's words and actions are necessary components of our daily lives? Complex issues are usually uncomfortable ones for the classroom just as they are for society, but they provide hearty fare for learning. How do complex issues emerge for discussion? How do students develop a stake in learning about them? Inquiry projects chosen by the students energize that motivation.

## Inquiry: Springboard to Developing Positive Social and Personal Values

"All children can learn," we agree. Surely, all children can learn, but *what* will they learn and in what environments, and with what kinds of teachers and with what materials? In this chapter, I have suggested a way of sustaining schooling as a moral enterprise through student-centered and student-developed inquiry projects. Inquiry is not a new philosophy or method, though the emphasis on the *values potential* of student-centered inquiry is a new perspective. This approach has roots in many inquiry approaches: See Graves (1991), Harste, Watson & Burke (1989), Short & Burke (1992), Altwerger (in press), Tschudi (1991), Gamberg, et al., 1988), Wigginton (1986). Most of these researchers and practitioners would look to the thoughts of John Dewey for their philosophical base.

Early in this century, Dewey (1902) advocated students' involvement in the construction of their own objectives for learning; he recommended that they pursue their own questions and solve other than ready-made, teacher-made, publisher-made problems. Later, Dewey (1938) argued that teachers needed to start with the experiences of the students and draw the connections between the givens of the curriculum guide and the students' interests. Noddings (1992) took this argument further and said that although "there are a few things that all students need to know, it ought to be acceptable to reject some material in order to pursue other topics with enthusiasm." (p. 19) She advocated a form of education that not only concentrates on producing moral people but also that is in itself moral in purpose, policy, and methods.

The current crisis in our educational system, identified by Goodlad (1990), Sarason (1991), and others, may well be the result of several decades of politically expedient and socially safe curricular decision making that ignored the moral dimension of education. Kierstead & Wagner (1993) discussed the difficulty that teachers have in implementing anything other than the given curriculum:

> **Having no power, little say-so, and limited resources, teacher-educators continue to be blamed for failed plans of improvement they had no part in originating. While extolling the importance of the teacher, the states shackle classroom teachers with curricula that are politically expedient. Teachers are asked to socialize students; educate for AIDS; mainstream; prepare students for a job; propagandize against alcohol, drug use, sexual promiscuity, smoking, and a dozen other societal "don'ts"; enforce dress codes; reduce teen pregnancy; and ready students for citizenship. There has been no sign of prioritizing these "additional" goals for teachers, nor of making them educational goals rather than mere behavioral control.** (p. 164)

An inquiry-based curriculum can transform the emphasis on behavioral control to real educational goals that have the potential to promote moral values. When students collaborate with their teacher to make curricular choices (even first-grade students can choose which books they want to read, their writing topics, and their classroom learning centers) and develop their own questions for which to seek answers, they have the opportunity to live out the values of a democratic system in the classroom. A democratic curriculum has the potential to be a higher moral enterprise than old-fashioned transmission pedagogy because of the values potential inherent in the process. The traditional givens of basal textbooks, teacher's guides, and curriculum guides must give way to democratic processes and context-specific studies that reflect the interests and concerns of the participants.

Inquiry inevitably goes beyond textbooks. The health textbooks for Jean's class did not have a section on AIDS education, but the curriculum committee for the school corporation had developed a curriculum guide on that subject. The guide contained factual information, worksheets, tests, and some resource material. The guide had been approved by the local school board, and parents were mostly in agreement with the idea that children should be educated about the dangers of AIDS. This curriculum guide was not an in-depth curriculum, though many teachers taught from it, including Jean herself the previous year.

Textbooks and curriculum guides as currently conceived are useful as only one of many resources. The materials that can be physically bound between two covers or snapped into a loose-leaf folder can contain only the beginnings of an in-depth meaningful study—a study in which the students themselves develop the curriculum.

# 2 The Values-Centered Classroom: A Study of Homelessness with Third Graders

*Homeless people live on the streets. They are very poor. They need clothing and money. Homeless people are very lonely. They need shelter before they get cold. They need a family.*

Kara

*You should be grateful that you have a home.*

Melissa

*A home means someone loves me.*

Macky-Lynn

Shelli Roembke, a third-grade teacher, gave her students the opportunity to choose their own topic for study. They chose homelessness. Why would third graders choose that unhappy topic? Why not dinosaurs or space travel? Shelli answered this question in a memo to me:

*Shelli Roembke*

> **I believe that the children chose this topic for several reasons. First of all, we had discussed a hobo in a piece of literature that I was reading aloud to them earlier in the school year. Because of this, I think the curiosity was there. Also, all of these children have seen movies in which the homeless people are digging through the trash searching for food. Lastly, I think there was a general concern for these people: Why are they homeless and what can we do to help?**

Shelli judged that her students had a "T.V. perspective" on most issues, including homelessness. Without personal contact with homeless people or accurate information, they could rely only on their perceptions gained from news and movies. Shelli welcomed the opportunity to help her students demonstrate selflessness and to grow in humane values and concern for their fellow humans.

# Brainstorming and Webbing

After having chosen the topic, the students and Shelli brainstormed a web of the different issues they wanted to study about the homeless. Even though many of her students had never done any brainstorming, Shelli observed that they all seemed to become experts immediately because they were the ones making the decisions.

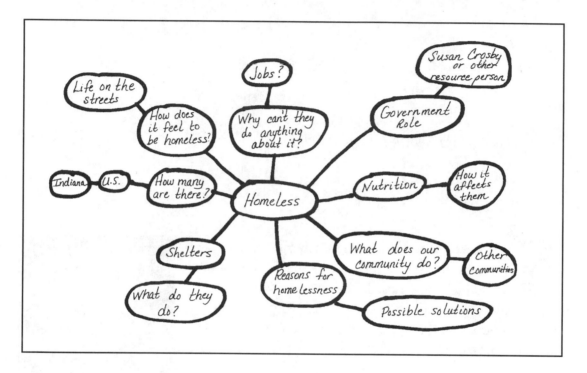

# Issues

Determining the issues to be studied is one of the aspects of their education in which students at any grade level can take some leadership, develop independence, and learn respect for themselves and others as thinkers and reasoners. They begin to ask themselves: What interests me? How can I connect with this topic? What is important to me? What do I already know? What would I like to know?

Shelli said of the brainstorming process:

> **Once the webbing was completed, the students made two lists: "What we already know" and "What we want to know." It became quite clear to me that the information they thought they knew came**

**from sources such as made-for-TV movies. The things they wanted to know more about dealt with the more personal issues of being homeless.**

Shelli wrote the two following lists on the chalkboard as the students dictated:

## What we already know

- Homeless people do not have a home.
- They dig through the trash for their food.
- They sometimes steal food to survive.
- Homeless people don't have any money.
- A lot of homeless people use drugs.
- Homeless people wear old clothes.

## What we want to know

- Do they have jobs?
- How do they get to be homeless?
- What do they eat?
- Why can't they do something about it?
- Where do they go to sleep and for shelter?
- Do they get a lot of diseases because of poor nutrition?
- Do they feel dirty?
- Do they travel a lot?
- Do they live with other homeless people?
- Why can't they get jobs?
- Do they have families that can help them?

# Doing Research

Before beginning this unit, Shelli gathered together all the materials she could find on homelessness and placed them in a designated section of the classroom for the students to use. The third graders researched the topic and gathered information through various note-taking exercises. Shelli began by reading articles aloud to her students. After listening to an article, they wrote down five things they had learned. As they became more experienced at identifying major points in the articles, the students read the articles themselves and wrote down important information. They also took notes from books and guest speakers' presentations. Not only was the note taking and the development of research skills challenging for third-grade students but also the subject matter, though of great interest, was full of tough concepts and information that the children had not previously encountered.

Shelli wrote the following about the visit of Rick Posson, director of the Indianapolis Day Center:

Ours is a rural community. The children are isolated. Although many realize what it's like to have little money, they had no idea that so many people were homeless, that people actually slept under bushes in the winter time. We had a resource person come from Indianapolis Day Center. He was excellent. He told us about what his center does in providing shelter and food for the homeless. It was a big eye-opener for my kids. In fact they were so solemn the rest of the day, we had to stop and talk a couple of times for at least a half hour just to discuss what they were feeling. He had told us that, last year, eighteen people had died at the center. The children wanted to know why. Some deaths were gang related and others were due to overexposure to the weather. It was a really tough thing for them to think about, but I think that emotionally they benefited from it. It made them even more caring and concerned about what other people were going through. Another thing that the speaker stressed was that the children should all go home that night and thank their parents for having a roof over their heads, thank them for going to work every day and bringing home a paycheck so that they can have food on the table.

The children developed so much gratitude. We made a bulletin board for Thanksgiving soon after that speaker came, and almost all of the children said that they were thankful for their homes. That's one of the ways I evaluated this unit—by how grateful these children became for their homes and families.

Other forms of research and classroom experiences raised "moral dilemmas" for the students. For example, the visit of Susan Crosby from the Indiana House of Representatives initiated a moral dilemma about public support of the homeless. When speaking to the class, she stressed that the government does not do enough for the care of the homeless. Although Crosby and other speakers provided insights on the issue, the students needed more information, information that was not available at their reading level, so Shelli decided to have them develop an interview for their families and neighbors. They brainstormed interview questions together as a class, then each student formulated his or her own list of questions. Through this activity, they learned something about idea generation, mutual support, shared decision making, interpersonal reasoning, and problem solving. Shelli talked about good questioning techniques and how interviewers can best conduct interviews.

The third graders' interview questions reflect their intense personal interest in the topic. The interviewees' answers show the diversity of attitudes about the homeless, and this led to the moral dilemma mentioned above. Here are two of the interviews:

## Macky-Lynn's Interview of her Mother

1. How would you feel if you were homeless?
   *I would be unhappy.*

2. How do you think we can solve the problem of the homeless?
   *You would have to build more houses they can afford and try to find jobs for them.*

3. Do you care about the homeless?

   *Yes, I do.*

4. What do you know about the homeless?

   *I know they suffer from the cold and go hungry most of the time.*

5. How do you think they feel?

   *They feel like nobody loves or cares about them.*

6. How do you feel about government shelters?

   *I think that is the only way that they can care for them now because there are so many.*

7. If a homeless person broke into your house, what would you do?

   *I would tell him it is wrong to break into a house, but I would feed him.*

8. What do you think the cause of homelessness is?

   *Some, because of no work.*

9. Do you think the homeless are like us?

   *Yes, I do.*

10. Why do you think so many veterans are homeless?

    *Some have no family, and some are not able to work.*

11. Do you think the government does enough for the homeless?

    *She does not think so.*

12. How many homeless people do you think there are?

    *300,000*

13. How many do you think have jobs?

    *1/3 have jobs.*

14. Do you know that 1/5 are kids? How do you feel about that?

    *Sad that they can't have a better life.*

15. Do you know that homeless women are having twice the amount of babies as other women? How does that make you feel that kids are going to come into the world homeless?

    *It is sad that babies are born in our great country without a home to live in. I think our government could do better.*


## Melissa's Interview with her Grandmother

1. Do you know about the homeless?

   *I know they are struggling harder to make it than some other people.*

2. Do you care about them?

   *Yes, I do because anyone could be homeless at any time.*

3. How do you think they feel?

*Alone, cold, afraid.*

4. How do you feel about government shelters? Why?

*Good. At least they have a warm place to stay and something to eat.*

5. If a homeless person would break into your house, what would you do?

*Probably give them something to eat, warm clothes, and take them to a shelter.*

6. What do you think the cause is?

*Not enough jobs.*

7. Do you think the homeless are like us?

*Yes. They are just someone who has lost everything and maybe doesn't know how to make it better.*

8. Do you think the government is doing enough?

*They think they are, but all they do is take everyone's money.*

9. How many homeless do you think there are?

*More than the world needs. About a million or more.*

10. Why do you think so many veterans are homeless?

*Maybe since the war, their life has been too terrible to get it straight.*

11. Do you think they have enough food?

*No, since they find most of it in store and restaurant trash.*

12. How many do you think have jobs?

*Not even half.*

13. How many homeless children are there?

*Probably more children than adults.*

After completing these interviews with adult friends and relatives, the students shared information in small groups and compared how people were alike and different in their responses. Many of those interviewed expressed the opinion that the government was already doing too much. In comparing the students' interviews with the responses of Susan Crosby from the House of Representatives, they saw two sides of the issue. It was especially beneficial to the students to see that when people's views diverge widely, it is important for both sides to defend their responses with facts and reasoned arguments to correct the feelings and unexamined opinions that people so readily express. The students began to recognize that, as good thinkers and researchers, their new insights could contribute significantly to class and home dialogues on the topic. It was also important for the children to note that adults did not always have the correct information, and that study and research can provide an accurate basis for opinions and problem solving.

Even though the students were learning factual information about the causes of homelessness, they were very concerned about how everyone *felt* about the issue. They had strong emotional responses themselves, and this permeated their work. Their heartfelt response made the learning meaningful, but it also stirred dissonances for some children and raised a moral dilemma. Shelli described the difficulties of one child whose stepfather offered less than a compassionate response towards the homeless. Also significant here is her fellow students' compassionate response towards their third-grade colleague.

**After we finished interviewing, the children brought their interviews and responses to small groups, and then small groups shared with the whole class. One of the hardest things for one of my students was trying to understand her stepdad's answers to her interview. She was so upset because he thought the homeless were disgusting, that they were lazy bums. He felt that it was their own fault that they were on the street and that we shouldn't do anything for them. She was just sick because she had developed all this compassion for the homeless, and he had none. I was glad to see that her group of students was so supportive and helped her to see that some people do feel that way and that there are at least two viewpoints.**

---

## *Theoretical Memo:*
## *Respect for Process of Knowledge Generation*

The students experienced some real anomalies in their study of the homeless issue. Parents, grandparents, legislators, and peers provided conflicting information and opinions that caused the students to question and do further research. They were dealing with primary-source information—their own interviews—in their quest to understand the issues. Typically, social-studies textbooks deal with "communities" as a topic of study in the primary grades, but the information is factual and unlikely even to mention the problems of the cities in dealing with crime, homelessness, and poverty. The information is sanitized by publishers so as to be safe, inoffensive, and considered appropriate for study by primary-school students; textbooks are, therefore, of such a general nature as to be beyond dispute and controversy. Conflicts of opinions and jarring dissonance among different groups in society are omitted—just the facts, ma'am, just the facts! Once students recognize that genuine differences of opinion exist about the sources of, and solution to, real problems in society, then there is opportunity for confusion, question, debate, critical thinking, analysis, revision, new ideas; this is a context in which values may emerge.

# Responding to New Information

The students spent several weeks gathering information, hearing speakers, listening to books read aloud on the topics, and responding in a variety of ways. They kept journals, wrote letters to speakers, wrote and illustrated poetry. The poems and journal reflections show their depth of response:

By Lindsey

The nightly hike

I am homeless.
I'm very sad.
Everyone stares at night
when I'm on my nightly hike
So when they stare at night,
I look at them what a sight.
Then I travel on my flight
to where I want to go.

What does a home mean to me?
It means I'm loved.
It means where I'm safe.
It means where I live.

Arthur

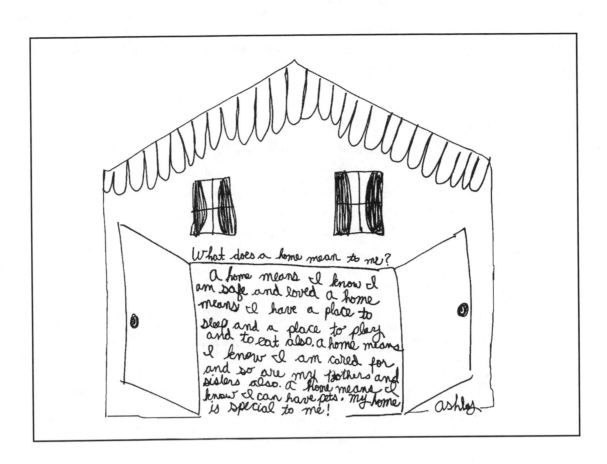

What does a home mean to me?

A home means I know I am safe and loved a home means I have a place to sleep and a place to play and to eat also. a home means I know I am cared for and so are my brothers and sisters also. a home means I know I can have pets. My home is special to me!

— ashley

Shelli read aloud to the class Eve Bunting's novel, *Fly Away Home*, about a homeless family living at an airport. One student responded as follows:

Fly away Home

This story made me scared and worried. This would not make me feel grateful to a homeless person. This is the saddest story I've heard of homeless people.

Amber

Other children responded in writing as if they were writing from the point of view of a homeless person.

Hi. my name is Kara. I am a homeless person. I walk 25 miles. People treat me like dirt. I ask for food but I don't get any. So I walk on. I have to sleep on streets. Sometimes I go to a shelter. They give me money and food. Some people say I look ugly I don't care and I just walk on. I wish I had a home and family. I have no friends or a mom or dad. I am just a kid.

By
Kara

## The Road

By: Lindsay

I was scared when I slept under a bridge. I thought someone might harm me. So next when I woke up I went to my sister's house. I asked her if I could stay there until I get settled. She said I could only stay for three weeks because her husband didn't care for me a whole lot. After my sisters kids went to bed, my sister suggested for me trying a shelter. I just left and said thanks a whole lot so I stayed all night in a bush and the next day I got thinking and I went to the shelter And they gave me everything I needed so they got me on my feet again

Teaching Kids to Care

My name is Melissa
It is hard to live on the streets by yourself wondering every night where you
are going to be. You always
want to know if you are going
to be killed I lost my family
because I am homeless. I wonder
sometimes if I will ever get a home
again. My dream is to have
a home. Maybe it will come
true.

Some students responded out of their religious convictions, as did Susan, putting this prayer into the mouth of a homeless person:

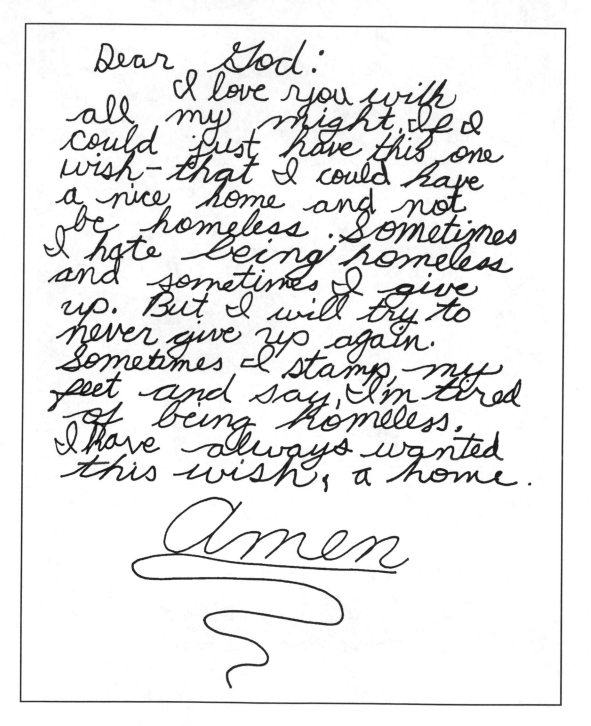

Dear God:
I love you with all my might. If I could just have this one wish—that I could have a nice home and not be homeless. Sometimes I hate being homeless and sometimes I give up. But I will try to never give up again. Sometimes I stamp my feet and say, I'm tired of being homeless. I have always wanted this wish, a home.

Amen

Responses to the theme, such as these, were ongoing throughout the project in journal writing, poems, letters, and stories. The sharing of new knowledge was continuous, and presentations of information were not reserved for "the end" of the project; however, more elaborate presentations and culminating activities did help to bring closure and give the students an opportunity to use talents and skills other than purely academic ones. Shelli described these activities:

> **We did two main culminating activities. First, the students did group projects. They were allowed to do any type of presentation that would show something they learned about the homeless. We had two plays, two newscasts, and a puppet show. Also we had a sleep-over and baked cookies which we delivered the next day to the shelter. This made the issue of homelessness real for the children.**

Making an issue "real" for students can often be accomplished through social and civic action that allows participants to use their heads, hearts, and hands in contributing to the betterment of their physical community or their neighbors.

# Social and Civic Action

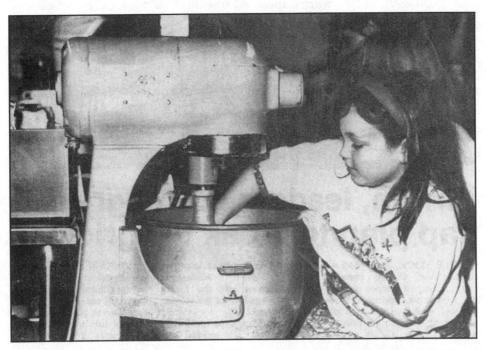

*Nine-year-old Kara, a third grader in Shelli Roembke's elementary school class, stirs cookie batter for one of six batches of chocolate chip cookies baked for Indianapolis homeless residents Friday night. Kara and her fellow classmates baked the cookies during an overnight sleep-in at the school as part of a two-week thematic lesson on the homeless selected by the children. Saturday morning the kids took the cookies to the Indianapolis Day Center for homeless people where Roembke said they were greeted with applause. Mrs. Roembke said the children have learned to appreciate their own homes more, particularly during the Thanksgiving season.*

Part of the demonstrated learning involved in this inquiry project was social action taken by the students. Shelli discussed this experience in a graduate seminar:

We did two different projects for the Indianapolis Day Center. First we had a school-wide drive for hygiene items. The children in my class talked to all the classes in the school, and I sent a letter to all the teachers. The kids throughout the school brought items, and we delivered those to the shelter. Our final project was a sleep-over at which we made six dozen cookies. The next day, two parents and I drove the children to Indianapolis and went to the shelter. It was full—probably 75 people. At first the children were afraid; the people there looked unhealthy and their clothes were mostly ragged. But immediately, everyone came up to us and began talking—saying things like, "I haven't talked to anyone your age in such a long time." The children lost their fears and began talking with them. The director let us pass out cookies, and we got a standing ovation. I heard one child say, "They were supposed to take two cookies, and that man took four. I bet he hasn't had chocolate chip cookies in a long time." My kids had worked so hard to prepare for this—I don't think they realized how important it was to the people there, how much it meant to them. They applauded and thanked us over and over. They took us upstairs and let us interview one of the homeless men. Among others things, he told us that he had children, but that he hadn't seen them for ten years. It made my kids realize the importance of family life and to be grateful for their families.

Roger wrote this in his journal after the field trip:

> I learned a lot about the homeless. I talked to a homeless guy. He told us a lot about him. He had two children and a car. The car would not run. He got all he could take with him and packed his things. He thought he would not need anything for November. He was wrong. I felt sorry for this man.
>
> By: Roger

Macky-Lynn summarized her learning at the end of the project:

> The Homeless
>
> During the homeless unit, I learned a lot about the homeless. Do you know 1,000,000 kids are homeless? I learned that sometimes homeless sleep in carts and some live in airports and sometimes during the day they go to shelters. Did you know most homeless are veterans because they went to war and when they came back they did not have jobs. Also sometimes they got injured and they could not work. I will help them when I get big.
>
> By Macky-Lynn

## Theoretical Memo: Social Activism and the Development of Moral Classroom Communities

Moral growth requires action, a practicing of the precepts that lead to just-community endeavors. Kohlberg (1976) and his followers began with the notion of "moral dilemmas" in discussion groups in schools. Students were to hypothesize the consequences of particular actions for themselves and others in the community. A number of "just-community" school sites, generally at the secondary level, have developed around the country. These have moved beyond the hypothetical situation to the application of ethical and moral principles to school and community problems.

Textbooks begin to address the workings of government and charitable institutions, but it is difficult for a textbook by its very nature to provide the immediate context and situation for a discussion of problems that brings home the need for action and a high sense of service to one's neighbor and community. Textbooks can give teachers and students only a broad overview of any issue. In a textbook, there is no immediacy, no community heartbeat, no pressing dilemma that can give rise to student commitment in their own neighborhoods. Shelli's class's inquiry into homelessness was a culminating activity that embodied the responsiveness of our society toward human suffering. Shelli's comments about her work with students and their own written work on this project highlighted their heartfelt yearning to understand and to do something for the homeless. Unlike either the didactic approach of old textbooks or the "core-values" approaches that focus on named values and then teach about the values, Shelli's approach allowed the students to recognize the values within themselves and then act upon them. Through their guest speakers and interviews with friends and relatives, the students saw that the government does not, and perhaps cannot, shoulder the burden for all citizens in need. They demonstrated, with their own brand of third-grade activism—collecting supplies for the shelter and baking cookies—that everyone can act upon his or her highest individual sense of right in a given situation.

Shelli later wrote to me:

> **The students now have a greater understanding of the society in which they live. They had no idea of the reasons for homelessness nor how large the homeless population was. I have seen a greater appreciation of home aroused in all of my students. I would like to do this unit every year with my class. I hope I can help develop "future adults" who will work to end the problem of homelessness.**

I have seen the development of a theme cycle in my classroom from beginning to end, and have been amazed with its effects! As I think and write about this experience, I believe that it is virtually impossible not to mention a very dull way of teaching: Can a child get excited about worksheet after worksheet with the same standard materials that they have seen year after year? I have seen that the children need to take ownership of what they are studying before they really dive into the learning process. I believe this to be one of the most important reasons for choosing to use a theme cycle in my classroom. Since the children feel such great ownership, they want every piece of work to be their best. The pride is seen on an individual as well as a group basis.

Using a theme cycle also generates a high level of student involvement. I believe this can be attributed to the many different activities and projects. Because of the variety of projects, students with different learning styles are still able to remain actively involved. One doesn't achieve that kind of involvement through traditional teaching.

Theme cycles also promote social skills. Students learn to cooperate within their group and work toward a common goal. Theme cycles also promote self-esteem because students with different ability levels work together, and everyone contributes to the process.

When the class participates in a theme cycle, the inquiry process is taught as they work. This is an important life-skill that the students can use throughout their future as students and adults, making positive contributions to their world. Inquiring minds in children mean inquiring adult minds later on. Because a theme cycle never really ends, a spark for extended learning is ignited which goes with each child, even into the home. This kind of excitement is what every teacher should strive for in his/her classroom.

## Teaching Values in Shelli's Classroom

Because each teacher, each classroom full of students, and each moral project is unique, different focus points in the teaching of values can be highlighted from classroom to classroom. As in Jean's classroom, so also Shelli's class embodied democratic processes—choice of topic, raising questions, working with partners, sharing information in multiple ways and in multiple modes of responding. Both classrooms provided fertile ground for emergence of the students' moral stance on issues. Even though Shelli's students were younger than Jean's, and not so ready for debate, defense of their positions, or extensive pursuit of independent inquiry, their interest, compassion, and desire to help solve problems were evident and heartfelt. Shelli's classroom work demonstrates what I want to say about the classroom as a place not only to master the facts of an issue but also to develop compassion for the situation and the people involved. Shelli fostered a classroom context that allowed for the development of a moral classroom community through compassionate thinking and doing. Her classroom also highlighted a natural, integrated approach to teaching values that emerged from an issue chosen by the students.

## An Integrated Approach to Values Teaching

Students who do not know justice, compassion, and altruism by experience cannot internalize those values simply by hearing about them or reading about them in pre-planned values lessons. Decades of teaching values in schools through the McGuffey readers (see chapters four and five) worked relatively well because places of worship and the home were equal partners in producing children educated morally to the same values taught in the readers. Those traditional values of honesty, justice, bravery, and the work ethic that were preached in the readers found practical moral application in the spiritual and familial laboratories of actual of living. Many students today do not attend places of worship and parents who work outside the home are often hard pressed to keep families economically viable, let alone spend the time necessary to maintain a strong, demonstrated values base. The mutually supporting influences of school, home, and place of worship in the teaching of values is gone; something must take its place if a similar effect is to be achieved.

An integrated approach to values teaching in the classroom provides the missing piece in today's moral education of students. It combines processes that demonstrate values through the actual development of values, so that students can experience the values they are learning about. Shelli did not set out to teach "gratitude for home and family," but it quickly became apparent to her that the students' responses were indicating the emergence of this quality of thought. Lesson plans did not reflect an objective: "The student will be grateful." However, the classroom environment—complete with student choice, motivation for the subject, knowledgeable speakers on the topic, field trips that involved the children's attempt to improve the lives of some homeless people, and some independent student research—was a ripe one for changes in thinking and values recognition among the students. Shelli's classroom teaching in this project embodied the theories of Thomas Lickona (1991) who believed that schools can offer a setting for developing values:

**Children will need lots of practice at being moral persons: many opportunities to solve problems, act upon their best moral reasoning, be in social roles that give them real social responsibilities, and otherwise participate in a moral community.** (p. 68)

Shelli also did not set out to teach "altruism," "social responsibility," or "care for one's fellow citizens," but the outcomes in student work and reactions reflect those qualities of thought in many of the students. That the students chose this topic of study may well indicate their natural moral urge to understand and alleviate suffering. The context developed by the inquiry process gave the students the opportunity to voice their moral stance. Whatever the catalyst, the students demonstrated Nel Noddings's (1992) concept of the classroom as a moral community of those who care about others. The development of the personal values of gratitude and altruism emerged from the students' personal experiences and was an authentic outcome of their learning.

## Social Action as a Catalyst for Values Development

Moral growth requires action, a practicing of the precepts that lead to just-community endeavors. In New York, two schools are experimenting with values teaching through a "just-community" concept that encourages moral growth. The directors of those schools believe that it has taken a long time for our society to admit that all teachers are moral educators whether they want that responsibility or not. In these schools, there are environments where issues are debated openly with adolescents who are also given a say about how the rules are enforced. They have town meetings where representatives of students, teachers, support staff and custodians discuss issues of common concern. Students learn to reason about issues of justice and fairness. Although the directors of the school say that it's a reasoning process that students come out with rather than a particular stand on a particular moral issue, they allow that the community does come out with decisions that are more fair and more just than if participants didn't go through this process ("Moral Crisis, Moral Courage," interview broadcast June 5, 1987, MONITORADIO weekend edition). In a similar way, Shelli's third graders moved from the reasoning and learning processes of the inquiry curriculum to action.

In Shelli's classroom, students were eight- and nine-year-olds. Their chocolate-chip social action was different from the older, more sophisticated decision-making groups in the New York schools, but their actions—contributing their time and effort to a community activity, helping others, and participating in a group effort for kindness and compassion—were similar and logical end products produced by students who are in touch with their own values. Teachers like Shelli need support and ideas for helping their students achieve the goals they set for social action; a variety of resources is available to teachers who want to help their students take action in community and world problem-solving.[1]

# Respect for the Processes of Knowledge Generation

Where does knowledge come from? Who has the actual answers to the questions posed by students? Shelli's students asked many good questions in the course of their study on homelessness. Through their own research, interviews, and knowledge-seeking, they began to recognize that differing opinions are possible, that "right answers" may not be easily forthcoming, that the process of seeking answers for oneself must supersede hearsay information or "common knowledge," and that inquiry gives the learner a more sound basis for opinion and fact. These are not easy lessons for third graders. No information on homelessness in the United States was included in the social-studies book, and some of the primary source information from speakers and others interviewed by the students yielded conflicting opinions. The solution for the students was to continue to gather information, arrange fields trips, interview homeless people, and come to their own conclusions. The process of knowledge generation in Shelli's class was far different from the traditional classroom settings in which the assigned textbook determines the information to be learned. The inquiry process generated students' interest, responsibility for their own learning, some confusion, dissonance, more questions, and ultimately critical thinking about the sources of knowledge. Good questions foster the process for getting to the answers, and meanwhile encourage some critical thinking about the construction of knowledge itself.

---

# Endnotes

[1] Some recently published guides for teachers and parents in helping children pursue social-action goals include this group compiled in the September, 1993, issue of *Booklinks* :

*ABC Quilts: Kids making quilts for kids* (1992). The Quilt Digest Press, P. O. Box 1331, Gualala, California 95445.

Adams, P. & Marzollo, J. (1992). *The helping hands handbook*. New York: Random House.

Goodman, B. (1991). *A kids' guide to how to save the planet*. New York: Avon.

Hoose, P. (1993). *It's our world, too!: Young people who are making a difference*. Boston: Little, Brown and Co.

Hopkins, S. & Winters, J. (eds.) (1990). *Discover the world: Empowering children to value themselves, others, and the earth*. Philadelphia: New Society Publishers.

Howard, T. & Howard, S. (1992). *Kids ending hunger: What can we do?* Kansas City, Missouri: Andrews and McMeel Publishers.

Lewis, B. (1991). *The kid's guide to social action: How to solve problems you choose & turn creative thinking into positive action.* Minneapolis: Free Spirit.

Logan, S. (1992). *The kids-can-help book: Lend a hand, volunteer, share a skill, make a difference.* New York: Putnam.

McVey, V. (1993). *The Sierra Club kid's guide to planet care and repair.* Boston: Little, Brown Publishers.

Terrell, R. (1992). *A kid's guide to how to stop the violence.* New York: Avon.

# 3 The Research of Values in Textbooks, Old and New

I began the historical study that undergirds this book by looking for values teaching in old textbooks. At some point during that research, I recognized that what made my own teaching and the teaching of my students worthwhile, meaningful, and exciting was the teaching of values wherever and however it occurred. Those important connections informed the beginning of this volume: the "how-to" of values teaching as I currently see it. The research study that describes the "what" of values teaching as it has occurred in textbooks over the past two hundred years follows this chapter on methodology. The road from that historical study of old textbooks to inquiry curriculum is shorter than may at first appear. In this chapter, I map that road and outline the methodology of the study and the connection between the historical study and inquiry curriculum.

## Questions that Drove this Study

As American society, founded in cultural compromise among its many regions and interests, continues the trend from earlier, relatively simpler multiculturalism to the current exploding diversity of ethnicities, lifestyles, and cultures, the American patchwork of values demands expression in the nation's classrooms and textbooks. In the face of this change in our culture, the school teacher must find an answer to the question: How ought the multitude of values to be taught so that the learning process will prepare students for life in a democratic, just, orderly, and yet diverse society? Additional questions arise: To what resources can the teacher turn? What is and has been the role of textbooks in values teaching? Can textbooks today carry the major burden for the teaching of values in school as they seem to have done one hundred years ago? These questions entail a considerable range of subsidiary issues.

### What are "values?"

The major charge to me as a researcher funded by the grant that made this study possible was this: How have the values taught in textbooks changed over time? There was an assumption on the part of the funders and myself that values in textbooks have indeed changed. We set out to discover the nature and extent of that change. I must admit that my first question was not: What is a "value?" However, as I have continued the research and the applications in today's classrooms, acknowledging the diversity of groups in many schools, that question has loomed somewhat larger, not because I think values are fundamentally different among differing social and ethnic groups or between old and new textbooks, but because of the perceived constraints on public-school teaching and textbooks in regard to the teaching of values.

Here is the definition of "value" from *The Reader's Digest Encyclopedic Dictionary* (1966): 2) "Something regarded as desirable, worthy, or right, as a belief, standard, or moral precept: the values of democratic society."

Other dictionary definitions are similar, and none is particularly helpful because they are all so general. "Something regarded as right or worthy as a standard" seems very open-ended and subject to varieties of interpretation. To look for "values" in children's textbooks is to look for "the moral of the story." To look for values in today's class-rooms is to look for the moral of the project, the debate, the field trip, the poem. What is "the moral of the story?" What does the story try to teach? What does the story mean to the reader? What is the message from the author to the reader? What does the story teach about harmonious and successful interactions among groups and individuals *or* about disharmonious and unsuccessful interactions? Many children's stories one hundred years ago and some of today attempt to capture a sense of right thinking and doing. It is that "moral of the story" that is the "values" component. It is that "moral of the story" that I and other researchers on this project looked for in rating and ranking the "values" in stories for children published over a two hundred-year period.

Do one's personal background and belief systems blind one to what others may see as values? Do they enable one to see values that others do not see? Probably. However, I believe that the basic values found in elementary-school textbooks are not so veiled in abstract worldviews, nor are they so shrouded in ignorance of the common codes of fairness, justice, and morality which undergird American law, that the average Ameri-can could not detect them. I invite the reader to peruse the story on page 55 from a children's reading textbook of one hundred years ago. When you have finished, ask yourself, "Was that story attempting to teach any values? If so, what values might it be teaching?"

If you said, "Yes, the story teaches values, and the value is probably *integrity* or *honesty*, then you might be a middle-class American Christian, Jew, or Moslem, agnostic, male or female, parent, teacher, college student, book publisher, or college professor. Most of those categories, in various combinations, were represented by the raters of reading selections in textbooks in this study. The stories, such as this one from the McGuffey Readers, were overtly moralistic. It is possible that an adult American would neither recognize that this story teaches values nor recognize the value being taught, but that is highly unlikely.

## LESSON XIII.

| said | steal | kinds | words | flow′ers |
| does | shalt | house | ro′ses | moth′er |
| pick | print | found | a-fraid′ | blush′ed |
| card | fence | blown | pret′ty | thank′ed |
| yard | large | bloom | stŏl′en | walk′ing |

### THE ROSE.

1. ONE day, as Ann was walk-ing with her moth-er, she found a large card.

2. On the card, in large print, were the words, "Thou shalt not steal."

3. As Ann held the card in her hand, they came to a house with a neat yard.

4. In the yard were all kinds of flowers in bloom.

5. "O moth-er," said Ann, "see the ro-ses, see all the pret-ty flowers!

6. "This is the house that Jane lives in, little Jane, who sells flowers."

7. A half-blown red rose hung just o-ver the fence.

8. "See," said Ann, "what a fine rose! Would I not like to have it?

9. "Moth-er, may I pick this rose, just this one? Jane can not miss it."

10. "What does that card say to you?" said her moth-er.

11. Just then, Jane came out, and ran up to Ann.

12 "I am so glad to see you," said Jane. "See this rose. I kept it for you. I was a-fraid it would be stol-en."

13. She then cut off the very rose, and gave it to Ann.

14. Ann blushed; but she took it, and thanked Jane for it.

15. As they went a-way, her moth-er said to Ann: "What if Jane had seen the rose in one hand, and the card in the oth-er?"

McGuffey *Second Eclectic Reader* (1865), pp. 36–37.

*The Research of Values in Textbooks, Old and New*

I am not arguing for an unquestioned and uncritical use of the term "values" in this study, but I am suggesting that there is a general understanding (though not a 1.0 correlation) among literate Americans of any subculture or ethnicity about what a traditional value is and when it is present in a piece of literature.

So, how did we recognize a value when we saw one? How did you as the reader recognize the value in the story above? I have wrestled considerably with this question, attempting at several points during the research to find out how students, teachers, parents, peers, and publishers recognize and label values in stories. I have attempted to establish that the term "values" does not represent a personal definition on my part, but rather a common understanding of the qualities that define the harmonious behaviors and just functioning of groups of people.

It is not difficult to rate the values in textbooks, but for purposes of research there needs to be a general agreement on what those values are and whether or not one is present in a piece of literature. I acknowledge that I am using the term to refer to qualities of character, to moral qualities, to those qualities that enable human beings to live and work harmoniously and bravely with each other and the natural world. I have established to my own satisfaction through interviews and "blind" rating of reading selections that others (including college professors, college students, parents, and textbooks publishers) also use the term in that way.

"Values" does not represent any and all emphases in stories—no one involved in the research on this topic suggested that enjoyment, entertainment, and informational stories on content areas such as science and social studies represented "values" in and of themselves. A limitation? The reader may view it as such. The charts in chapters four and five show a large category of selections in readers that is labeled "Entertainment" and "Informational." That category contains selections focused on humor, science and social-studies topics. If one wishes to assign the label "values" to those categories of selections and think of them as modern cultural values, one may do so. I and other researchers in this project did not do so.

To establish a view of values among those involved in this project, I interviewed sales representatives, editors, and authors of the major basal-reader publishing companies, and the president of one major basal-reader publishing companies. My initial question was this: *How are selections chosen for inclusion in your basal-reader series?*

The second interview question concerned values: *What are the most important values taught in your basal-reader series?* By neither specifying what a value is nor giving examples, I hoped for three results. First, if indeed the term "value" had some commonly accepted meaning, the interviewee would probably not ask, "What do you mean by 'value?'" Second, the response to the second question would give me some sense of the value *labels* that might be attached to stories in the readers. I was also interested in determining whether the publishers viewed selections about science, art, music, social studies, and other informational selections as teaching some values. I reviewed sales materials from several companies, and found incidental comment in interviews that gave me information on this question.

The raters of the selections in the modern readers were college students, teachers, and parents of elementary school children. Two interrater reliability figures were established. The first represented how reliably two raters picked a selection as containing a major values thrust; the second represented how reliably two raters chose the *same* value(s) for that selection. The raters of selections in the old textbooks were college professors, teachers, and college students.

The interviews with publishers and the interrater reliability figures satisfied me that the term "values" had a common meaning among the raters, and that the resulting research results reflected some measure of reliability, given that definition. I concluded that the intended values stated in the literature under examination, i.e., "the moral of the story," are sufficiently explicit that the raters—of whatever ethnicity, class, gender, or age—could recognize an explicit value when they saw one in a story. Whether the raters might agree or disagree with the teaching of the values in school or elsewhere is a different matter. Whether or not implicit values were also being expressed is likewise a different matter.

## The Research Study: Values in Textbooks

Once the question of a definition of values had been answered to my satisfaction, I wanted to establish that some reasonable measure of cultural values through the use of past and current documents was possible. I initially thought that I could not use the selections in the textbooks themselves as representative of the values or literature choices of parents and society, except in a general way. Although the authors of textbooks for children do represent a certain segment of society that has its own interest in pedagogical methods, children's literature, and the education of children, these authors' contributions to textbooks are affected not only by their own beliefs and values but also by parents' group demands, the marketplace, religious groups, and the forces for censorship.

Some precedent exists for using children's readers to analyze cultural values. McClelland (1958, 1975) argued that content analysis of cultural documents can give a measure of the values of that culture if the researcher uses many authors of similar materials. He reasoned that the use of children's readers was ideal because they are written with the intent of transmitting cultural values. Moreover, information on how widely these materials were used is available, which gives some sense of the culture's acceptance of the values portrayed in the readers and hence the extent of the books' influence. De Charms & Moeller (1962), in their study of old texts, also assumed that cultural values can be extrapolated from children's readers. Given these studies, I concluded that we could identify the values that have been taught in public schools via textbooks and that these values were some measure of the cultural values present in the era in which the books were written.

My next questions became these: How are the values in today's textbooks different from the textbooks of a hundred to two hundred years ago? How can those differences be categorized and accounted for? To answer these and related questions, my colleagues and I undertook the study of old textbooks at the Indiana State University library.

## The Sources

The primary sources of our research were the 1,100 volumes of the Floyd Family Collection in the Department of Rare Books and Special Collections at Indiana State University's Cunningham Memorial Library. The collection now has grown to include 1,500 books. The credibility of these sources as authentic texts used in the classrooms of the past two hundred years has been established by the painstaking work of the curators of this collection.

The collection contains publications from companies and authors from the State of Indiana and texts used in the schools of Indiana. A number of the texts were used not only in Indiana but also in many parts of the United States—for example, the McGuffey Readers and Ray's arithmetics were used widely in this country from the mid-1800s to the early 1900s. Therefore, the collection is representative of textbooks that were in use across the country a hundred and fifty years ago. The size of the collection is not so overwhelming that it necessitated random samplings of pages from individual books, as has been the method in most of the past studies of old textbooks (de Charms & Moeller, 1962; Lystad, 1980). My research associates and I actually read a large sample of entire books from all time periods represented in the collection.

A second data source for this study is the collection of basal readers currently used across the country in elementary schools. Copies of all of the grade levels of ten basal series representing the top publishers of school textbooks in the country are housed in the Instructional Resource Center in the School of Education at Indiana State University. This collection provided an excellent resource for study of the reading textbooks currently in use.

## The Analysis

Pursuing ways to analyze old textbooks in terms of the values communicated to the children who read these texts, I considered a variety of techniques. Some researchers have taken random samplings of pages within a range of old texts (Perkins, 1921; de

Charms & Moeller, 1962; Lystad, 1980). Others have done topical/content analyses (Schmidt, 1983; Vitz, 1986). Still others have viewed the historical study of old textbooks as a way of analyzing the evolution of curriculum (Walker, 1976).

Although a number of interesting aspects of the old texts were considered (illustrations, for example), it seemed likely that the vocabulary and the content of the old texts would yield some measure of the values teaching. Four graduate students—two master's candidates in Reading and two African doctoral students in Counseling—undertook the task of analyzing the texts according to topic and vocabulary expressive of religious, moral, or values orientations. The majority of the books in the collection was analyzed by the four research assistants; by David Gilman, a professor of Curriculum, Instruction, and Media Technology; and by myself, a professor of Reading and Language Arts. We read approximately 80% of the books in the collection; we took extensive notes on content and vocabulary.

## Vocabulary Analysis in the Old Textbooks

In content analysis studies, researchers may merely describe the surface characteristics of content, for example, frequency of occurrence of specific data in the document. That is where we began. Frequency-counts of vocabulary provide a simple statistical level of analysis. Vocabulary use can give some clues to the beliefs and emphases of authors of textbooks and to the prevailing sentiments in the culture. The vocabulary used to impart the beliefs and values of the authors, expressed qualities of thought and character that produce subsequent actions in human life.

The analysis of the old textbooks included frequency counts of values-laden vocabulary such as "honesty," "justice," "courage," and "fairness." We charted the changes in vocabulary use over time. Some of those charts are included in chapter five. Because of the more technical nature of the sciences and mathematics texts, the vocabulary in selections in those books did not generally focus on religious, moral, or values issues. For that reason, we have not included vocabulary data from those texts.

## Content Analysis in the Old Textbooks

Frequency counts of vocabulary provide one level of analysis; I was also interested in the content as a reflection of the phenomenon of values teaching. Analysis of the content in the texts of the Floyd Collection revealed three major genres of material whose authors sought to influence values: 1) Biblical stories and references, 2) short biographies of American leaders focused on their moral standards and qualities of character, and 3) stories with explicit moral values.

I was interested in what inferences could be drawn from the story content that would illuminate various aspects of the culture and cultural change. Therefore, content data was analyzed in conjunction with independent indices—cultural eras or norms. I correlated the eras of education as identified and described by Walker (1976) and others with the content of textbooks published during those eras, attaching to each some actual stories and references. The eras of education as characterized by Walker are "Education for Salvation," "Education for Democracy," "Education for Patriotism," "Education for the American Way," "Education for Survival," and "Education for Defense." (p. 1)

An additional component of the content analysis was a ranking from the most-prevalent to the least-prevalent values in the McGuffey Readers of 1879. Because the McGuffey Readers are well represented in the Floyd collection, and because they were so widely used (from 1836–1920, half of America's school children learned to read from McGuffeys), we did a separate analysis of those readers. It was reasonable to assume that the values content of McGuffey Readers was more influential than any other readers during that eighty-year period. Because the McGuffeys are better represented in the Floyd collection than any other reader, we could analyze a complete series for a particular publishing year in the same way that we analyzed the modern readers. For that reason, and because they were the most widely used and influential readers for eighty years of the one-hundred-and-fifty-year period in our analysis, it is the McGuffeys therefore that were compared to the modern readers in chapter five. Also included are content analyses of some readers that were less values-laden and other readers that were more values-laden than the McGuffeys. These readers were not so widely used; therefore, they cannot be viewed as equally influential.

## Content Analysis in Modern Reading Textbooks

In order to judge the values content of the modern basal readers, three or four basals (grades 2–5) from a number of the major publishing companies were read by two or three raters. If a reasonable interrater reliability figure could be established, then there would be a logical reason to conclude that the value was present for that group of raters, most of whom were Midwestern school teachers and parents. I, as the primary researcher, read all of the textbooks; a variety of other raters read one or more texts. The other raters included parents of school-age children, undergraduate Education majors, and American Literature majors. The readers were of both genders and a variety of ages. There was one African-American rater in the group; the rest were Caucasian and from the Midwest.

Directions given to the raters were sparse so as not to affect the rating. The major question for each rater to answer about each selection in his/her basal was this: *What value(s) is (are) being taught in this selection?* Directions included this point of specificity: *The value observed and recorded for a selection must be a major thrust of the piece, rather than an incidental mention only.* For example, a character's saying "thank you" would not justify assigning the value of "gratitude" to the selection.

I note that this methodology is different from other values studies that have been done. In this study the entire selection was the unit of analysis rather than a random selection of pages. This was purposeful: Much of the furor over censorship of children's books results from taking passages out of the context of the selection and attempting to determine the worth of the book based on small passages. My belief is that the values thrust of a selection cannot be judged by a random sampling of a few lines from a few pages from the piece. Children read the story as a whole; "the moral of the story" is gleaned from the whole; the values content of the story must be researched as a whole.

We established two interrater reliability figures: One represented how reliably two raters picked a selection as containing a major values thrust; the second represented how reliably two raters chose the *same* value(s) for that selection. The overall interrater reliability figure for choosing selections that contained values teaching in all series was 0.78. The overall interrater reliability figure for choosing the *same* value in each selection was 0.75. Dr. Walter Sullins, Director of the Center of Educational Research at Indiana State University, in private conversation suggested that an interrater reliability figure of 0.60 is considered good for this type of rating by many experts in the field of statistical research.

## An Application of Values Teaching Today

As I completed the first round of data collection, and it appeared that the traditional values evident in the old textbooks were much reduced in quantity in the modern readers, I began to look for examples of values teaching in today's classrooms. I reasoned that if the overt moral teaching of the nineteenth century was no longer apparent in textbooks, and selections in today's readers reflected a felt need by publishers for entertainment, humor, and informational pieces, perhaps a more subtle method of teaching values existed in some classrooms today. As I reflected on today's values teaching, the following questions emerged:

- What is the best way of teaching the values we want taught?
- What approach to values education, what instructional method, is consistent with the principles of an ideally just and democratic society?
- What is appropriate for purposes of educating the young to take their place among a just and compassionate citizenry?
- What are the current approaches to teaching values?

As I researched the literature on values teaching, I found that there exists a spectrum of values and methods used to teach them, from incidental discussion to packaged programs. I organized the typical instructional approaches under two headings: the "process" and the "product" approaches to values education. Product approaches generally comprise prepackaged programs aimed at transmitting lists of moral basics. Process approaches consist of values-clarification models and integrated approaches. The more I read, the stronger became my conviction that one such integrated approach to values teaching, the "inquiry approach" to curriculum in elementary schools, is a viable approach to values teaching for today's classroom. The inquiry approach supported the two exemplary teachers and classes described above in chapters one and two.

Those two teachers were also two of my graduate students who shared their classrooms, their students, and their work with me in the investigation of inquiry curriculum as a vehicle for values teaching. We met weekly during the course of the semester in which they were teaching the units outlined in the first part of this book. At that time, we did not focus on values teaching or the values that their students were learning. We focused on good teaching practices that we also considered to be "democratic," resources, student motivation, and the theoretical basis for inquiry curriculum. Later, while I was writing the research report in chapters four and five, I asked their permission to exhibit their work as examples for building a moral classroom community. I offer their examples as inspiration for teachers who wish to promote democratic processes and a values-possible curriculum within an inquiry process.

When I began the study of values in textbooks, I was not consciously aware of the close connection between the inquiry approach and the values that lie at its heart or of their combined attractiveness. I might have known this had I thought to apply to education the now proverbial dictum of Marshall McLuhan: "The medium *is* the message." It all became clearer to me as I looked for instances of values teaching in my own experience and that of my graduate students who are teachers. As we observed the students' responses to important topics of their choosing, their values emerged within the process and were shaped by the process. We could see the potential for providing a forum for discussion of moral dilemmas.

The structure for inquiry projects can vary considerably. For example, sometimes a fictional novel sparks the more extensive study of an issue. Sometimes questions follow from one study and lead to the development of another. Because each moral project is unique to its time, place, and people, the content chosen for study by the students, their teachers, and parents, will also vary. The most important phases are at the beginning because they set the tone for the entire project. When students choose the topic, they take ownership of the curriculum. When the questions come from the students, they find motivation for learning. When students work together, they learn respect, tolerance, and understanding. By learning democratically, students learn to be democratic.

# 4 Historical Study of Textbooks

*All students should be engaged in a general education that guides them in caring for self, intimate others, global others, plants, animals, and the environment, the human-made world, and ideas. Moral life so defined should be frankly embraced as the main goal of education.*

> Nel Noddings, *The Challenge to Care in Schools* (1992): 173.

*If there is a single piece of the educational process that is vulnerable to attack from all sides, it is the pubic school textbook.*

> Dan Fleming, "Ethical Issues in the Classroom" (1987).

These two seemingly unrelated quotations address the common denominator of educational research: What are the means through which the goals of a worthy education are achieved? School textbooks have been one means. They have encouraged and supported the values of the "moral life" (in Noddings words) to some degree throughout our nation's history. The "moral life" of seventeenth-, eighteenth-, and nineteenth-century America was defined by the Judeo-Christian heritage of the Western European settlers, and the Bible was often the only book in the home of rural Americans. Many historical accounts of educational materials used in the United States begin with a discussion of the *hornbook*, in popular use in schools of the seventeenth century. A sheet of paper containing the Lord's Prayer, the alphabet, and phonic elements, such as the vowel and consonant combinations, was attached to a wooden paddle. One major purpose of schooling was to produce readers proficient enough to read the Scriptures.

*Facsimile of a Horn Book from the Teaching Materials Center at Indiana State University, Terre Haute.*

Consequently, the content of the first primer to be widely disseminated in the United States was largely religious: The Lord's Prayer, the Creed, prayers, and hymns. This collection, *The New England Primer*, was first published circa 1690, and it continued to be published for one hundred and fifty years, totalling over three million copies. Throughout the eighteenth century a major purpose for schooling remained the fostering of active participation in one's own salvation through involvement in church liturgy and Bible reading.

The schoolroom use of books other than the Bible received impetus from the publication of the McGuffey Readers in 1835. According to a number of textbook researchers, McGuffey Readers constituted something of a phenomenon in textbook use and influence, perhaps exceeded only by the Bible and Webster's Dictionary (Bohning, 1986; Commager, 1962; Grancy, 1977; Mosier, 1947; Sullivan, 1927). More than half of the school children of America from 1836 to 1920 learned to read from the McGuffey Readers; during that period, over 122 million copies were sold (Livengood, 1947; Sullivan 1927). They served as the main reading materials, confirmed moral values and truths, and shaped the literary tastes of American children.

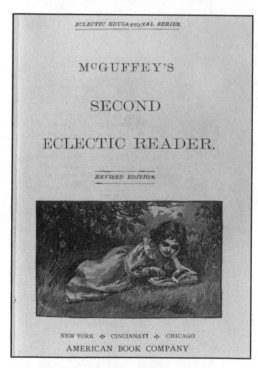

*Title page of* McGuffy's Second Eclectic Reader *(1879). Cincinnati: Van Antwerp, Bragg & Co.*

The McGuffey Readers appeared just as the free public school, or common school, movement was spreading across the country. A system of public, tax-supported common schools was destined to lead the way in accelerating the process of Americanization of millions of immigrants who were flocking into the United States by the 1830s. As educational leaders like Horace Mann, Henry Barnard, Cyrus Pierce, and Caleb Mills were establishing a system of common graded schools, graded textbooks that spoke to immigrant children of the values and ideals of American society became necessary, and McGuffey supplied the need. The focus of the textbook by the middle of the nineteenth century moved from a strictly religious orientation to a slightly broader stance permeated with ideals of democracy, hard work, and Protestant Christian moral values.

In 1835, almost concurrent with the publication of the McGuffey Readers, Francis Wayland, then president of Brown University, published the first edition of one of the most influential moral philosophy texts of the nineteenth century, *The Elements of*

Teaching Kids to Care

*Moral Science*. According to Hogan (1990), Wayland's book became a "scholastic tableau of Victorian moral culture that portray[ed] the intellectual history and politics of moral authority in America at a crucial moment in the making of modern American education." (p. 95) Wayland believed that with sound moral instruction, individuals were capable of fulfilling the obligations imposed by the moral law. The foundations of "habitual self-government" were laid as much in the home and *in the school* as in the church. (p. 110, emphasis added) "In the school" shows that this influential moral thinker, whose work permeated educational philosophy at the beginning of the era we are studying, had high expectations of the school climate.

Although we cannot recreate with historical accuracy the values teaching that occurred in classrooms of a hundred to a hundred and fifty years ago, we have records of a part of that teaching in the form of old textbooks that were used and some accounts of teaching. (Thompson, 1855; Thomas, 1880; Eggleston, 1915) On the basis of a fragmentary picture of the values education in the past, we can trace historical trends and make suggestions for the future of values education, acknowledging this caveat from historian Louis Gottchalk (1956):

> **. . . only a part of what was observed in the past was remembered by those who observed it; only a part of what was remembered was recorded; only a part of what was recorded has survived; only a part of what has survived has come to the historians' attention; only a part of what has come to their attention is credible; only a part of what is credible has been grasped; and only a part of what has been grasped can be expounded or narrated by the historian.** (p.45)

Through my research on old textbooks, I have attempted to specify which values were taught, especially in readers. I charted the distribution and frequency of values-laden vocabulary and values-laden selections in the textbooks. I also plotted the relationship between the values portrayed in the textbooks and the eras of American history.

Because the primary researcher and two of the four assistants were reading teachers familiar with the reading materials and pedagogy in today's schools, we were at first struck by the obvious religiosity of the subject matter in the old texts. Particularly in the 1700s and 1800s, entire Psalms from the Old Testament, chapters from New Testament books, and a number of Bible verses appear which were taught and memorized for their own sake or used as support for teaching particular lessons or morals in other selections. Not surprisingly, the pedagogical suggestions in the textbooks paralleled Biblical teaching. Parables, allegories, exhortations, rules, commandments of Bible teaching were very similar to other genres of imparting moral content and lessons in the old readers: fables, recitation, rules, homilies, adages, and so forth. We no longer see Bible passages in today's texts; the effect of Supreme Court rulings and

A.C.L.U. vigilance has been to expel the sacred texts of the Judeo-Christian tradition from the school books. Texts from other religious worldviews are permitted, not as religious texts per se but as expressive of the "multicultural" perspective. Content appearing as overt attempts at moralizing; shaping patriotic views; or holding up religious, political, and military leaders as figures to be emulated, is rarely seen in the school texts of today.

*"Evening Hymn" from McGuffy's* Second Eclectic Reader (1879). *Cincinnati: Van Antwerp, Bragg & Co.*

I was interested in the content as a reflection of the history of the phenomenon of values teaching. What inferences could be drawn from the story content that would illuminate various aspects of the culture and cultural change? With that question in mind, the content data in this study of the old textbooks was analyzed in conjunction with independent indices, namely cultural eras or norms. I correlated the eras of education as identified and described by Walker (1976) and others with the content of textbooks published during those eras, attaching to each are some actual stories and references. The eras of education as characterized by Walker, are "Education for Salvation," "Education for Democracy," "Education for Patriotism," "Education for the American Way," "Education for Survival," and "Education for Defense." (p.1) The time frames of these eras overlap. The texts reveal a general adherence to the political and philosophical themes of the times.

## Education for Salvation: Direct Teaching of Religious Tenets (1620–1850)

The earliest and longest-lived of the eras began with the arrival of the Jamestown and New England colonists in the 1600s and continued for two hundred years. We see a great deal of the "education for salvation" theme throughout this period, though it was gradually transformed into religion for secular gain and a good life. Walker (1976) wrote about this era:

> **The New England colonial school, with great emphasis on religion in their "reading and writing" schools, used the Psalter, containing the**

**Psalms, the Proverbs, the Sermon on the Mount, and the Nicene Creed. The New Testament and the Bible were used with more advanced students. The first book, available to each student, was the Hornbook, which usually contained the alphabet and the Lord's Prayer.** *The New England Primer*, **highly religious in nature, appeared in the late-seventeenth century.** ( p. 1)

One of the oldest books in the Floyd Collection is Dickinson's *Columbian Reader*, published in 1815. It contains many religious stories and references. Webster's 1829 speller, also in the collection, teaches a good deal more than spelling. One finds not only Biblical references and stories that teach moral values but also an actual "moral catechism," similar in format to catechisms of religious denominations. A series of questions and answers on humility, peace making, purity, and so forth exhort the students to follow the teachings of Christ. The first three questions below, taken from this speller, set the tone for what follows in the catechism:

> *Question: WHAT is moral virtue? [caps in original]*
> **Answer: It is an honest upright conduct in all our dealings with men.**
>
> *Q. What rules have we to direct us in our moral conduct?*
> **A. GOD's word, contained in the bible, has furnished all necessary rules to direct our conduct.**
>
> *Q. In what part of the bible are these rules to be found?*
> **A. In almost every part; but the most important duties between men are summed up in the beginning of Matthew, in CHRIST's Sermon on the Mount.** (p.156)

This and a number of samples from other readers of this era and those following show that religion was actively promulgated in the early days of textbooks, gradually decreased in importance, but did not disappear entirely even in the mid-twentieth century. For example, Town's *The Progressive Third Reader for Public and Private Schools* (1857) contains Bible references and the vocabulary of religion and morals. Osgood's *Progressive Fifth Reader* (1858) contains many quotations from the Bible related to obedience to parents, going to church, praying, and the fleeting joy of riches. The well-known chapter on love, I Corinthians, chapter 13, from the New Testament, is quoted in its entirety. The vocabulary of the Reader is very much that of the New Testament: love, forgiveness, justice, honor, hope, virtue, peace, charity.

Parker's *National Fifth Reader* (1864) contains the second and fifth commandments from Exodus 20 in the Old Testament. The stories reflect human dependence on God. For example, Parker's reader contains the story of a man who risks his life to save another and is rewarded by the Tsar of Russia. The man acknowledges that he was able to succeed only with God's help. Other stories emphasize the importance of home life, the duty of keeping one's word, and the sacredness and blessing of work. The vocabulary, as usual, is that of religious and moral education.

Parker's *National First Reader* (1869) includes the Golden Rule from the New Testament, "Do unto others as ye would have them do unto you." Sanders' *New School Reader* (1872) parallels other readers of this period in its liberal use of Bible passages as reading materials and its emphasis on democratic values: liberty, independence, freedom, justice, and law. Parker's *National Third Reader* (1875) stresses perseverance, obedience, mercy, brotherly love, usefulness, and spiritual values over material desires.

In Watson's *Independent Fourth Reader* (1876), the evils of idleness and procrastination are railed against. Specific morals, such as "God's ways are not our ways," "prayer can be answered," "self-sacrifice brings happiness," and "use your God-given abilities to help others," are included. Randall's *Reading and Elocution* (1880) contains many Bible passages and a section from the Declaration of Independence.

In Alexander's *Child Classics: The First Reader* (1909), the twenty-third Psalm from the Old Testament is "to be read by the teacher to the class with their books open." (p. 25) Further exploration of this series of readers, which is well represented in the Floyd Collection, reveals an emphasis on homilies, morals, and fables. Stories seem constructed to teach lessons in character building. In these stories, qualities of persistence, obedience, courage, and so forth are exemplified and rewarded.

From the dates of the readers cited above and others below, one can see that references to religion and Biblical characters continued to abound towards the end of the nineteenth century and at the beginning of the twentieth, but the religious teachings are less direct, and the focus is on human *exemplars* of values and character traits, rather than on a relationship with the divine.

Other textbook research (see chapter six) and my own study of the Floyd Collection suggest that only four percent of readers published between 1921 and 1940 make reference to morals and religion. Below I cite a few texts that are somewhat unusual in terms of their inclusion of religious materials. Numerous Biblical references appear in Searson's *Studies in Reading* (1923), but the movement is toward secular stories with a moral emphasizing social values. This reader, published after World War I, begins with a poem, "The American Boy." It is a dialogue between a father and son about patriotism. According to the author of this reader, the influence of the story "The Poor Little Match Girl" "founded many an orphan home and organized hundreds of societies for relief of the worthy poor," which indicates an emphasis on philanthropy and social work during the era of the Social Gospel. (p. 243)

Walker's *The Study Readers* (1924) include mention of the Bible and make reference to Bible stories and characters. The values of goal setting, saving, and pursuing one's dreams are set forth as worthy of consideration. Thrift, generosity, kindheartedness, and thoughtfulness are inculcated by the stories. In this series, we see one of the first references to reading itself as a value.

By 1929, as evidenced by Pennell's *The Children's Own Readers, Book Two*, there is much less direct quoting from the Bible. Although God is still mentioned and emphasized in connection with prayer and church, the stories in the readers of this era are moving towards fables and stories with morals, and away from direct reference to God as the source of human life. Stories like "The Shoemaker and the Elves," "The Hare and the Tortoise," and "King Midas" emphasize the rewards of doing good, patience, perseverance, and unselfishness. Pennell's series of readers is evidence that reference to things religious had not entirely disappeared in school books even as late as the 1930s, but religion in textbooks was no longer the mainstream of values instruction.

## Education for Democracy: Duty, Virtue, Bravery (1775–1800)

When America was launched as an independent nation in the late 1700s, Thomas Jefferson, Noah Webster, and other early literacy leaders envisioned a more educated populace that could contribute to the success and endurance of the newly founded republic. Webster wrote a number of textbooks for this new age of democracy: *A Grammatical Institute of the English Language, Part I* (spelling) in 1783; *A Grammatical Institute of the English Language, Part II* (grammar) in 1784; and *A Grammatical Institute of the English Language, Part III* (reader) in 1785. The Floyd Collection contains an excellent example of a Webster text from 1807, *A Philosophical & Practical Grammar of the English Language*, and quite a good selection of the Webster spellers, dating from 1795. A clear example of the era's exhortation to duty and virtue is found in the 1795 Webster speller:

> **A good boy is dutiful to his father and mother, obedient to his master, and loving to all his play fellows. He is diligent in learning his book, and takes pleasure in improving himself in every thing that is worthy of praise. He rises early in the morning, makes himself clean and decent, and says his prayers. If he has done a fault, he confesses it, and is sorry for it; and scorns to tell a lie, though he might by that means conceal it. He loves to hear good advice, is thankful to those that give it him, and always follows it. He never swears, nor calls names, not uses any ill words to his companions. He is never peevish and fretful, but always cheerful and good-humored. He scorns to**

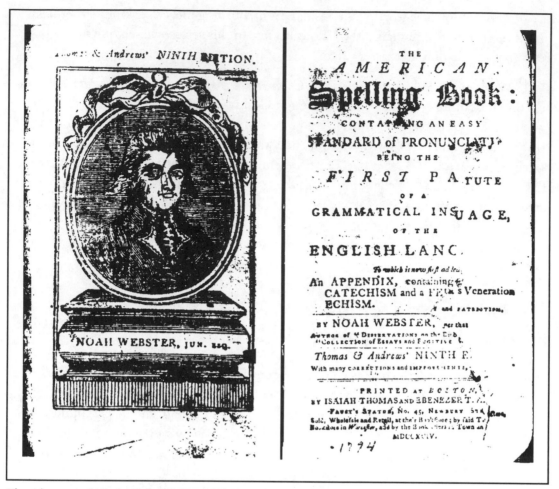

The title page of Noah Webster's (1795) The American Spelling
Book. *Boston: Isia Thomas & Ebenezer Andrews.*

**steal or pilfer anything from his play fellows; and would rather suffer
wrong than do wrong to any of them. He is always ready to answer
when he is asked a question, to do what he is bid, and to mind what is
said to him. He is not a wrangler nor quarrelsome but keeps himself
out of all kinds of mischief, which other boys run into. By this means
he becomes, as he grows up, a man of sense and virtue. . . .** (p. 105)

According to Walker (1976), Webster's books were not widely accepted, but the
results of his efforts to promote democratic ideals, as evidenced in the following
preface to his *Grammatical Institute of the English Language, Part III* (1785), lived on for
decades in the American public schools:

**In America, it will be useful to furnish schools with additional essays,
containing the history, geography, and transactions of the United**

States. Information on these subjects is necessary to youth, both in forming their habits and improving their minds. A love of our country, and an acquaintance with its true state, are indispensable. They should be acquired in early life.

Textbooks of this era were designed to make education truly American in nature—largely by publishing them on American soil and promoting American authors. The content of those books suggests that a good deal of what it meant to be "American" was supposed to be bound up with character traits of duty, virtue, cheer, reverence, bravery, piety, and faith. The next era of education would add a new dimension to the word "American": allegiance to a new home among millions of immigrants.

## Education for Patriotism: A New Allegiance (1820–1865)

From the 1820s until the start of the Civil War was an era of rapid and intense immigration into the United States, especially by northern and western Europeans and, early in the period, by enslaved Africans. As millions of immigrants poured into major cities, it became evident that the melting pot needed Americanizing on a grand scale. Common schools were conceived and established by Caleb Mills, Horace Mann, and others. As these large schools developed, and the children were organized into classes by age, the need for graded textbooks arose. The most successful series of textbooks ever published rolled from presses in this era: the McGuffey Readers. Developed by a Presbyterian minister, these texts inculcated the values of patriotism, morality, and religious fervor. The following stories from the 1879 edition demonstrate direct teaching of moral values common in the readers of the eighteenth and nineteenth centuries.

### LESSON XV.

| lĕast | thaw | slĭd′ing | plŭnġed | nāt′ured ly |
| bāde | scăt′ter | pre tĕnd′ | ex plŏr′ing | dĭs o bē′di ent |

HARRY AND ANNIE.

1. Harry and Annie lived a mile from town, but they went there to school every day. It was a pleasant walk down the lane, and through the meadow by the pond.

2. I hardly know whether they liked it better in summer or in winter. They used to pretend that they were travelers exploring a new country, and would scatter leaves on

the road that they might find their way back again.

3. When the ice was thick and firm, they went across the pond. But their mother did not like to have them do this unless some one was with them.

4. "Don't go across the pond to-day, children," she said, as she kissed them and bade them good-by one morning; "it is beginning to thaw."

5. "All right, mother," said Harry, not very good-naturedly, for he was very fond of running and sliding on the ice. When they came to the pond, the ice looked hard and safe.

6. "There," said he to his sister, "I knew it had n't thawed any. Mother is always afraid we shall be drowned. Come along, we will have a good time sliding. The school bell will not ring for an hour at least."

7. "But you promised mother," said Annie.

8. "No, I did n't. I only said 'All right,' and it *is* all right."

9. "I did n't say anything; so I can do as I like," said Annie.

10. So they stepped on the ice, and started to go across the pond. They had not gone

far before the ice gave way, and they fell into the water.

11. A man who was at work near the shore, heard the screams of the children, and plunged into the water to save them. Harry managed to get to the shore without any help, but poor Annie was nearly drowned before the man could reach her.

12. Harry went home almost frozen, and told his mother how disobedient he had been. He remembered the lesson learned that day as long as he lived.

### LESSON XVI.

| wife | ġreet | béard | wŏrm§ | prāyer§ |
| fāith | grōve | crŭsts | chûrch | fûr′nished |

BIRD FRIENDS.

1. I once knew a man who was rich in his love for birds, and in their love for him. He lived in the midst of a grove full of all kinds of trees. He had no wife or children in his home.

2. He was an old man with gray beard, blue and kind eyes, and a voice that the

*"Harry and Annie" (Obedience) McGuffey's (1879)* Third Eclectic Reader.

# McGUFFEY'S
# SECOND READER.

### LESSON I.

| | | | | |
|---|---|---|---|---|
| news'pā per | eōld | ôr'der | sēem | through |
| stŏck'ings | chăt | stō'ry | līght | Hăr'ry |
| brănch'es | kĭss | bûrns | Mrs. | e vĕnts' |
| an ŏth'er | Mr. | stōōl | lămp | mĕnds |

### EVENING AT HOME.

1. It is winter. The cold wind whistles through the branches of the trees.

(11)

2. Mr. Brown has done his day's work, and his children, Harry and Kate, have come home from school. They learned their lessons well to-day, and both feel happy

3. Tea is over. Mrs. Brown has put the little sitting room in order. The fire burns brightly. One lamp gives light enough for all. On the stool is a basket of fine apples. They seem to say, "Won't you have one?"

4. Harry and Kate read a story in a new book. The father reads his newspaper, and the mother mends Harry's stockings.

5. By and by, they will tell one another what they have been reading about, and will have a chat over the events of the day.

6. Harry and Kate's bedtime will come first. I think I see them kiss their dear father and mother a sweet good night.

7. Do you not wish that every boy and girl could have a home like this?

*"Evening at Home" (Familial love) McGuffey's (1879) Second Eclectic Reader.*

9. One evening, just as it was growing dark, they heard a sound that frightened them greatly. It was the roar of a tiger.

10. The kitten pulled at the chain, and tried to break away. With a sharp cry, it answered the voice outside.

11. All at once, a large tigress bounded into the middle of the tent. She caught her kitten by the neck, and broke the chain which bound it.

12. Then turning to the door of the tent, she dashed away as suddenly as she had come.

### LESSON XXXIII.

| | | | | |
|---|---|---|---|---|
| thĕn | ū'şu al | eoŭş'in | fīre'sīde | sew'ing (sō-) |
| Kā'tie | bĕt'ter | erăc'kle | knĭt'ting | per hăps' |
| Jăne | rēa'şon | to-nīght' | hăp'pi er | in strŭet'ĭve |

### THE FIRESIDE.

1. One winter night, Mrs. Lord and her two little girls sat by a bright fire

9. One evening, just as it was growing dark, they heard a sound that frightened them greatly. It was the roar of a tiger.

10. The kitten pulled at the chain, and tried to break away. With a sharp cry, it answered the voice outside.

11. All at once, a large tigress bounded into the middle of the tent. She caught her kitten by the neck, and broke the chain which bound it.

12. Then turning to the door of the tent, she dashed away as suddenly as she had come.

### LESSON XXXIII.

thĕn   ū′şu al   eoŭş′in   fīre′sīde   sew′ing (sō-)
Kā′tie   bĕt′ter   erăc′kle   knīt′ting   per hăps′
Jāne   rĕa′şon   to-nīght′   hăp′pi er   in strŭet′ĭve

### THE FIRESIDE.

1. One winter night, Mrs. Lord and her two little girls sat by a bright fire

in their pleasant home. The girls were sewing, and their mother was busy at her knitting.

2. At last, Katie finished her work, and, looking up, said, "Mother, I think the fire is brighter than usual. How I love to hear it crackle!"

3. "And I was about to say," cried Mary, "that this is a better light than we had last night."

4. "My dears," said their mother, "it

must be that you feel happier than usual to-night. Perhaps that is the reason why you think the fire better, and the light brighter."

5. "But, mother," said Mary, "I do not see why we are happier now than we were then; for last night cousin Jane was here, and we played 'Puss in the corner' and 'Blind man' until we all were tired."

6. "I know! I know why!" said Katie. "It is because we have all been doing something useful to-night. We feel happy because we have been busy."

7. "You are right, my dear," said their mother. "I am glad you have both learned that there may be something more pleasant than play, and, at the same time, more instructive."

### LESSON XXXIV.

dew′drŏps   hŏp′ping   lā′zi est   bĕndş   sŭng
pā′tiençe   in stĕad′   där′ling   ôught   rĕst
slŭm′ber   my sĕlf′   re plŷ′   miss   lose

*"The Fireside" (Work Ethic) McGuffey's (1879)*
Second Eclectic Reader

Walker (1976) listed the factors that contributed to the success and popularity of the McGuffey Readers, as follows:

> **First of all, William McGuffey was knowledgeable of the subject of reading. His selection of materials, his use of short, simple sentences that possessed logical sequence, and his use of numerous illustrations and pictures, enhanced the interest and readability of the content. Secondly, the standards of social life advocated in the McGuffey Readers were accepted, idealistically, as standards to strive for attainment in those times. Thirdly, the term "eclectic" as applied to the Readers, and to other schoolbooks later, was captivating and enhanced the sale and use of them.** (p. 12)

In the twentieth century, McGuffey Readers declined in sales until the back-to-basics movement began, when, at the height of this movement, in a dramatic increase in sales in one year (1985), 217,000 copies were sold. (Bohning, 1986) The renewed popularity of McGuffey indicates both a sentimental longing for a simpler time and a new interest in teaching values at school. In the twentieth century, most of the schools that used McGuffey's were either in small, rural communities or private church schools. The priorities of these schools were reflected in the lesson content of the McGuffey Readers: God and nature, the value of work, standards of personal behavior, and standards of social conduct. The McGuffey Readers are well represented in the Floyd Collection.

A contrasting and less popular text of the era represented in the Floyd Collection is Butler's Reader. Butler's *Goodrich Sixth School Reader* (1857) contains fewer religious sentiments than do other readers of the period. Values such as valor, humanity, justice, courtesy, honor, courage, and kindness mark this text and place it closer to the texts of later generations.

Another reader, belonging actually to the beginning of the next period but topically fitting best with this one, is Webb's *Model Fourth Reader* (1876), in which there is a passage entitled, "The Noblest Courage Is the Courage to Do Right." In it, a young man is in danger of succumbing to peer pressure. His friends say, "Be a man, William. Come along with us, if you do not want to be called a coward as long as you live." William fears that the evil principle in his heart is stronger than the good. Finally, he answers, "I will not go without asking my mother; and I am no coward, either. I promised her I would not leave the house without permission, and I should be a base coward if I were to tell her a wicked lie." The narrator takes the opportunity to turn the story to patriotic use, and he enjoins young men to be worthy of their country:

> **Our country needs such stout brave hearts that can stand fast when the whirlwind of temptation gathers thick and strong around them . . . .**

**Would you, young friend, be a brave man, and a blessing to your country?—Be truthful, never tell a lie, or deceive in any manner, and then, if God spares your life, you will be a stout-hearted man, a strong and fearless champion of the truth.** (p. 32)

Textbook authors had enlisted to develop fearless champions of romantically patriotic virtues—truth, honor, the American way—not a new idea. Other selections in this reader encourage children to show perseverance, determination, industriousness, obedience, and kindness.

By the early 1900s, in the middle of the next era, God was often mentioned in connection with country. For example, in Elson's *Grammar School Reader*, Book I (1911) we read a quotation from a less-familiar verse of our national anthem:

**Praise the Power that made and preserved us a nation!**
**Then conquer we must, when our cause it is just.**
**And this be our motto, "In God is our trust."** (p. 18)

The continuing need to help immigrants understand American customs and history would develop fully in the next era of education.

# Education for the American Way: Reforming and Conforming (1870–1920)

In both the previous era and the era 1870–1920, political leaders were gradually replacing Biblical characters in school readers as figures to revere and follow: George Washington, Abraham Lincoln, and Andrew Jackson in place of David, Solomon, and the Good Samaritan, although the values and religious sentiments of those political leaders were emphasized.

One reason for inclusion of these new exemplars of values was the need to introduce immigrants to the essential American history and ideals. Immigration of peoples from many parts of the world, particularly from eastern and Mediterranean Europe, continued during this era. In order to Americanize the new populace and aid in the amalgamation of these eclectic populations into a more conforming and cohesive society, political and educational leaders used the schools as forums for reinforcing the dominant cultural agenda and counteracting the perceived cultural limitations of immigrant customs and culture. An editorial from Indiana in the *Gary Daily Tribune* of the early 1920s stated as follows:

**There is a particular need of kindergartens in Gary, . . . for here the large body of foreign people will gain their first instructions in the English language and in American customs.** (Cited in Cohen, 1990, p. 11.)

Evening schools for the adult parents of these immigrant children also sprang up around the country. It is likely that the same texts were used for adults as for the children in the Indiana schools of this era. Thus the Americanization of the immigrant, and transmission via textbooks of the cultural and moral values of the birthright American populace, were not restricted to children only.

The use of short biographies of American leaders concentrating on their moral standards helped to inculcate the values deemed necessary for introduction and maintenance of a truly American way of life. Several examples of this genre from the Floyd Collection follow:

Themes of great men and patriotism go hand in hand in Baldwin's *School Reading by Grades: Sixth and Seventh Years Combined* (1897). Stories about Abraham Lincoln and Christopher Columbus tie high moral standards, bravery, and duty to American allegiance. Citizenship and patriotism are encouraged by such passages as "The Flag of Our Country," in which the author says the following of the flag:

**Before all and above all other associations and memories,— whether of glorious men, or glorious deeds, or glorious places,— its voice is ever of Union and Liberty, of the Constitution and of the Laws.** (p. 174)

A short piece entitled "Duties of an American Citizen" helped to reinforce the value of patriotism and to provide the new immigrant with a sense of the responsibilities and rights of membership in the patchwork community of their adopted country.

In Allen's *Fifth Reader* (1889), a number of heroes of Anglo-Saxon heritage were presented as paragons of virtue to the impressionable young students. Henry Wadsworth Longfellow is described: "He had a pure, noble, and serene nature and a warm and tender heart." (p. 9) Alfred the Great was also held up as a man to be emulated: "Misfortune could not subdue him. He was hopeful in defeat, and generous in success. He loved justice, prudence, truth, and knowledge." (p. 24) Of Sir Walter Scott, the author wrote, "His nature was manly, open, tolerant, and kindly." (p. 75) So, too, Oliver Goldsmith, though "reckless" and "thriftless," was "gentle, generous, and full of love and pity." (p. 112) Other readers in this series of the same publishing year include Biblical references, fables, and additional stories about great leaders. Finally, the reader learns that Andrew Jackson loved and obeyed his mother. (p. 241) Davidson's *Fourth Reader* (1922) quotes Abraham Lincoln: "I do the very best I know how, the very best I can; and I mean to keep on doing so to the end." (p. 2)

Other texts of the era also showed that the lives of great military and political leaders embodied the upright and successful life for which children should strive. In Alexander's *Child Classics: The Fifth Reader* (1909), we see two such stories. "The Character of George Washington," as the title of the story implies, shows him to be an example of "greatness," "power," "prudence," and "honesty," among other virtues. A speech of Patrick Henry's, in which the orator cries, "Give me liberty or give me death!" is also included as a reading selection.

In Elson's *Grammar School Reader* (1911), George Washington is revered and held up as a man to emulate in this rousing statement: ". . . till the last drop of blood shall freeze in the last American heart, his name shall be a spell of power and of might." (pp. 23–24)

The exemplars of "Education for the American Way"—the political and military leaders—do not fade at the end of that era. We see references to them well into the 1940s, the World War II era, a time when political and military leadership was on everyone's mind. In fact, the political leaders almost take on the character of saints, as seen in this excerpt of a little, bad, and untruthful poem about George Washington:

> **. . . he never broke a rule**
> **Or history would tell us so,**
> **For everyone would like to know**
> **About the boy who came to be grand**
> **Great father of our native land.**

The unfolding social consciousness of the era is reflected in Parker's *National First Reader* (1869) which promotes principles of health, such as breathing fresh air and exercise. This is undoubtedly directed at the children of immigrants and factory workers who lived in squalid conditions in the large cities of the country. "Early to bed, early to rise," from Franklin's *Poor Richard's Almanac*, suggests that children had been groomed for a factory system in which hard work and punctuality were essential for the success of the burgeoning industrial society. The vocabulary of this later reader suggests a movement toward social consciousness and mutual dependence—working together for the common good—temperance, cooperation, avoiding waste, helping the poor.

# Education for Survival: Managing and Reforming Society (1921–1940)

By the end of World War I, the burgeoning immigrant population in the United States, particularly in the big cities, led to demands for social reforms of all kinds. This in turn led to demands for educational reform that would prepare students to survive in "modern" society. Schools began to move aggressively into a socializing and controlling mode, especially in the cities. The superintendent of Gary, Indiana public schools, William Wirt, exemplified the belief that schools had the right, obligation, and mandate to cure social ills. In speaking to a Rotary official in the early 1920s, Wirt said this:

> **What I have in mind is that in the average city most of the public spirited citizens are giving a great amount of time and backing to all sorts of institutions and movements that are alright [sic] in themselves but can never do the work that the schools can do.**
> (Cited in Cohen, 1990, p. 79)

Wirt encouraged the incorporation of the Boy Scouts into the school system, stressing the school-home-church axis, and arguing as follows:

> **. . . [until] better schools, better teachers, better parents, more aggressive church leadership tackles [sic] the problem of youth's training, America cannot be builded [sic] upon a safe foundation. All other agencies but scratch the surface and really get nowhere.**
> (Cited in Cohen, 1990, p. 79)

Wirt was instrumental in the establishment of "platoon" schools which were conceived of as schools with "work-study-play" plans of organization. The organization was divided into two categories: fundamentals, such as reading, arithmetic, writing, spelling, and history; and special subjects, such as art, music, physical education, library, and manual arts. The students moved from activity to activity. (Cohen, p. 80) It was natural that Gary, a factory town, should spawn such a system, a factory model of education, but there was a great deal of opposition to it. According to Cohen, opposition was led by the Chicago Teachers' Federation. A spokesperson for that organization complained about the industrialization of education:

> **. . . to a nation that is fed on machines, eats, drinks, and sleeps by their assistance, the evils of this mechanicalized system of education, the platoon schools, are too subtle to be seen and understood . . . . They fail to recognize what the educator sees—the factory system carried into the public school, which needs only the closing time whistle to make complete its identification with the great industrial plants.** (p. 83)

The factory model of schooling has persisted in some degree throughout subsequent eras of education in the United States, and it still exists in public schools today. The factory model and progressive education that brought field trips, laboratory experiences, and individualization of the curriculum as thousands of immigrants poured into the cities, also resulted in the de-emphasizing of the textbook as the central fund of knowledge, whether for students or for teachers. In fact, the increasingly diverse cultural mix required that teachers seek out more diverse materials for inclusion in the curriculum. Students in American schools would never again be a homogeneous grouping of young people with northern and western European heritage. A new reality was exemplified in the following story told by a newspaperman about William Wirt:

> **He had thousands of kids in his schools, divided among fifty or sixty nationalities and all races, colors, and creeds. Those nice school ma'ams descended on his office and wanted to know what the dickens they were going to do about their Easter school programs. Couldn't tell those Mohamedan [sic] boys and gals about the great Biblical story. Couldn't have those Chinese and Japanese youngsters taking part in things their folks wouldn't approve. Russian and Greek Easter a week or so later. It was all mixed up, this business of making Easter programs.**
>
> **Never stumped Billy Wirt though. Just called all the teachers together and this is what he told 'em—Easter means lots more than all of us think. Resurrection—that's what it means in every sense of the word. The old earth's awakening at this time of the year. All those flowers and trees and everything on the face of this planet are springing into new life. Man's hopes spring up anew. People are better for the riddance of depressing winter. Just tell the boys and girls that and you'll have an Easter merrymaking that'll make every body [sic] happy.—Well, I saw one of those school pageants and sat between a swarthy Oriental woman and a high-cheeked Russian mother. And when their little boys came out on the stage and sang their songs, those mothers both looked so doggone happy that I wondered why the whole world doesn't adopt Billy Wirt's philosophy.**
> (Cited in Cohen, 1990, p. 120)

Although this story paints a rosy picture, it foretells the coming dilemma of trying to teach the values and standards of a northern-European Christian heritage to the heterogeneous population of immigrant Americans who would forever change the face of American schooling and society. The parallel change in American textbooks in regard to the teaching of moral values represents not so much an abandonment of values by textbook authors and publishers as a lack of either a clear direction or a view of humanity that was broad enough and charitable enough to encompass the diversity of thought on how humans ought to live their lives. Consequently, we see a gradual movement away from the religious teaching of previous eras towards generic, humanistic values.

Flinders (1986) discussed two influential men of this turbulent period. He related that Walter Lippman concluded after a decade of study that "the only viable option is to commit modern society to the foundations of humanism." (p. 4) Flinders had a good deal more to say about Daniel Kulp II, a prominent sociologist at Columbia Teachers College in 1932. Kulp introduced one of the earliest courses in Educational Sociology for America's prospective teachers. In his textbook, he defined and defended the need for American educators to give up the "supernatural" [religious] viewpoint and accept the ground rules of a scientifically based humanism. He believed that the educator with the "scientific" (non-religious) mind would always remember the relativity of social values to the three P's—period, place, and people. He taught his students that there were many foundations for moral behavior, not a single declaration from Mt. Sinai.

Flinders concluded that Kulp was introducing American teachers to a new standard for school textbooks regarding right and wrong. While we are unable to determine how pervasive Kulp's influence was, similar attitudes in others became widespread social theory that has since pervaded American textbooks. Even prior to Kulp and the generation of the social theorists who joined him, textbooks reflected a gradual turning away from the "supernatural," as Kulp classified religion.

Readers reflected the new social theory by at least the turn of the century. Clark's *Fourth Reader* (1899) indicated a movement toward secular treatment of values—stories that emphasized bravery, honor, kindness, and truth outside of a religious context. Cobb's *A Second Reader* (1911) continued to de-emphasize religion with an increase in the number of stories focused on values that are moral but divorced from religious content—"heed the deep low voice of conscience." (p. 126) Words like independence, liberty, justice and patriotism characterize the vocabulary.

We see an increasingly strong emphasis on social values in Davidson's *Fifth Reader* (1923). Stories about Camp Fire Girls and Scouts are records of the virtues of cooperation, obedience to law, trustworthiness, loyalty, helpfulness, and friendliness. Gender roles received further treatment and definition also. Though women had recently won the right to vote, and gender roles were changing, the text's author sought to maintain particular values in regard to women. Two stories in this reader enjoined women to be pure, loving, obedient, patient, kind, and to give service.

As the United States became increasingly industrialized, overcrowding, poverty, and illiteracy were rampant in the northern cities. The publishers of textbooks endeavored to do their part in advocating the goals of cooperation and contentment with the status quo for the young readers who were future workers in factories and other industrial workplaces. In Alexander's *Child Classics: The Fifth Reader* (1909), the story, "The Foundations of a Wonderful City," describes the social structure of a bee colony and its suggested advantages for human society:

> **It would almost seem that an essential law of the hive was that every worker should take a pride in its work, and all the work should be done in common, and so to speak, unanimously, in order that the fraternal spirit should not be disturbed by a sense of jealousy.** (p. 196)

Although there is nothing inherently wrong with advocacy of harmonious working conditions, it must be remembered that at the period in which this was written, the gap between the workers and the owners was widening. Conditions in factories, labor laws, and general living conditions were such that the admonition to be content with one's lot sounds calculated to keep workers in their sorry state so that an orderly society might survive and factory owners might increase their wealth.

Authors of later editions of the *Child Classics* series, such as the series published in 1918, continued to advocate thrift, tidiness, the work ethic. At this date, a few Biblical references remained; Psalm 100 and a discussion of "God as love" appears in the third reader of this series.

*The Elson Readers Book 6* (1927), appearing just prior to the Great Depression which began in 1929, was a promotion of the values of good citizenship. In a short selection by Woodrow Wilson entitled "Go Forth to Serve," young people were exhorted to improve communities and the world:

> **By doing what you can to make happier the people of your own neighborhood, your state, your country and also the people of other lands, you will make yourselves happier.** (p. 204)

The Camp Fire Girls and the Boy Scout oaths—inclusive of faith in God—appear in this reader. The patterns of values and the emphases in the textbooks of this era are consonant with the social mores of the times. Cohen (1990) wrote of an effort by educators to take a more socially minded tack to economic equity through education:

> **As the depression deepened, many educators, led by a group at Teacher's College, sought to transform society through a reconstruction of the school curriculum. Suspicious of untrammeled capitalism, they preached cooperation and a planned economy. They were heartened by many of President Franklin Roosevelt's New Deal programs, although they had hoped for even more radical efforts to bring about an equitable society.** (p. 122)

Teaching Kids to Care

By the end of the 1930s, Indiana and the nation, having survived the Depression, were ready for a new start when World War II pulled America out of the economic slump. Many social and educational theorists grasped for a social agenda and way to view values that would encompass the incredible diversity of the society. Many new stakeholders laid their claims to control of the schools during this period. National political forces, labor unions, minority interests, and business organizations promoted varying and divergent agendas for the schools: 1) Through newly formed unions, teachers gained unity and power; collective bargaining rights made them a force to be reckoned with in school politics and economics. 2) Business leaders, having weathered the Depression, began to question school taxes. 3) Race relations in the increasingly segregated cities fomented additional points of friction for the schools. 4) Friction occurred, as well, between academic and practical curricula, especially in the working-class schools. These issues and divisions would become more visible in the following decade. (For further discussion of this era, see Cohen, 1990.)

By the 1930s, "skill" words begin to appear in teachers' manuals, a few of which are contained in the Floyd Collection. In reference to students' reading abilities, terminology was evolving. For example, in Gray's *Teacher's Guidebook for the Elson Basic Readers* (1932), teachers are enjoined to work with the objectives of "initiative, "accuracy," and "classification" in order to promote "achievement" and "progress." The Dolch *Teaching Manual for the Extension-Reading Work-Book* (1934) had as its major aim the teaching of good citizenship.

## Post-1940

By the 1950s, fun, manners, helping, cooperation, entertainment, and family "togetherness" were beginning to replace other moral values in stories. In the "Preface" to *School Friends*, in a series called "Democracy Readers" by Lois Nemec (1940), the author emphasized that teachers should stress, and that her book focused on, love and respect, the rights of the minority, justice, freedom, and respect for religion. The message in the stories distills down to working together, playing together, sharing, being mannerly, and being on time. The values that make for an orderly, frictionless, and yet democratic, society are emphasized. The illustrations show White, middle-class children in segregated schools, but the stated purposes of the series sounded democratic. Nemec wrote in the "Preface:"

> **It is important in the long view of educational statesmanship that we take care to emphasize with children in constructive fashion the characteristics of democracy which belong to our heritage and which, if not emphasized, may be accepted with indifference and treated**

**with negligence. This indifference and ignorance will make our children easy victims of minority groups who assail the realistic weaknesses of our democratic institutions and exalt the idealistic virtues of other ways of life which are glamorous because they are distant [Nemec was referring to socialism, Nazism and other "minority" political parties].**

**It is essential in such a view that we teach our children to love and respect the democratic rights which our forebears have won. . . .**

This table of contents from Nemec's primary reader shows how democratic ideals were translated for children:

---

### TABLE OF CONTENTS

vii

---

The following story from the same reader shows "fundamental social virtues:"

### We Think of Others

"Mother, Mother! We want
to ask you something.
We want to know something.
We want to know
if we may do something.
Mother, Mother! Will you tell
us?"

63

"What is it, children?"
Mother asked.
"What is it you want to know?"
"It is this, Mother,"
said Sally Ann.
"There is a little girl at school.
She does not know the children.
May I have her come to supper?"

64

"Mother, Mother!" said Danny.
"There is a little boy at school.
He does not know the children.
May I have him come too?"
"Yes, children," said Mother.
"You may have the little girl
come to supper.
You may have the little boy
come to supper too."

"Thank you, Mother,"
said Sally Ann and Danny.

"It will be fun to have
the children come to supper."

"I will help you, Mother,"
said Sally Ann.

"I will help you too, Mother,"
said Danny.

"We will help you get supper."

66

"You are good children
to help me," said Mother.

"You are growing up, too.

You want to make the little girl
happy.

You want to make the little boy
happy.

You want to help me get supper
ready.

You are growing up."

"What do children do when they
are growing up?" asked Danny.

"They get bigger and bigger!"
said Sally Ann.

Mother laughed and said:

"Yes, Sally Ann, you are right.

Children get bigger when they
are growing up.

But they do some other things
too.

They do their work on time.

They want to make others
happy.

They want to help others.

So you see, children,
you are growing up."

68

"You think of others too.

You want to help others.

And in this way you are
growing up," said Mother.

Danny laughed.

"In another way too,
Sally Ann," he said.

"We grow bigger and bigger
every day!"

69

Teaching Kids to Care

These readers are an interesting combination of the controlled vocabulary and restricted sentence structure of readers of the '40s and '50s and of the "virtues" more apparent in readers in an earlier era. More typical of the postwar era, William Gray's *Fun with Dick and Jane* (1956) concentrated on family fun and manners in content (also with typical emphasis on restricted vocabulary and sentence structure), as this table of contents illustrates:

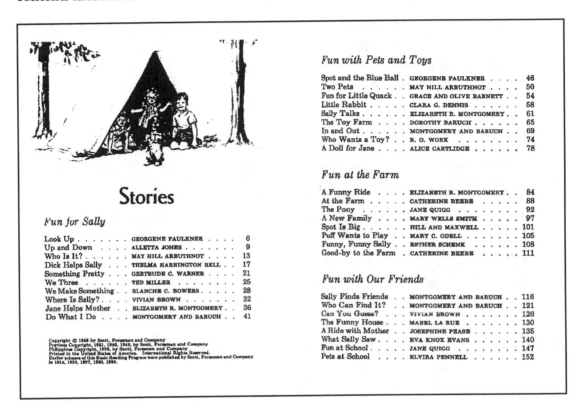

## Stories

Readers of the '60s and '70s increasingly emphasized training children in the skills of reading. The primary focus was teaching children *how* to read, with relatively little concern for the values contained in the readers. Some researchers of school texts from the '70s and '80s found an almost ludicrous decline of any type of values teaching in textbooks, due in part to the values clarification movement of the '60s and '70s. (See Sidney Simon, Leland Howe & Howard Kirschenbaum [1978]. *Values Clarification*. Hart Publishing Co.) The values clarification movement in education in the '60s and '70s was predicated on the belief that values are totally relative to culture and personal preference. That being the case, no set of values could be taught or promoted without offending someone. Textbooks of that era were systematically stripped of references to church, God, marriage, and the role of religion in history or current events. (For further discussion, see Apple & Christian-Smith [1991], Flinders [1986], Lystad [1980], Schmidt [1983], Tyson-Bernstein [1988].)

One hundred years of publishing readers for students had resulted in vast changes in the content of those texts. The substance, messages, and quality of the two passages below is obviously different. Because these passages are representative of their time and culture, they provide an example of the distance that values in textbooks had travelled over this hundred-year period. Contrast this typical passage from McGuffey's *First Eclectic Reader* (1879) (Christian School Edition) to the story that follows:

**When the stars at set of sun**
**Watch you from on high,**
**When the morning has begun,**
**Think the Lord is nigh.**

**All you do and all you say,**
**He can see and hear:**
**When you work and when you play,**
**Think the Lord is near.**

**All your joys and griefs he knows,**
**Counts each falling tear,**
**When to him you tell your woes,**
**Know the Lord will hear.** (p. 83)

"Can You Guess?" from William Gray's first-grade reader, *Fun with Dick and Jane* (1956) :

**"Guess what I am," Sally said.**
**"I am yellow, but I am not a chicken.**
**I have a tail, and I say quack, quack.**
**Can you guess what I am?"**
**Jack said, "I can guess.**
**A duck can say quack, quack.**
**So Sally is a duck.**
**She is Little Quack."**

**"Guess what I am," said Tom.**
**"I am not Sally's little duck, but I am a pet.**
**I am white, and I have a tail.**
**I have a little white house.**
**In I go! Hop, hop, hop!"**

**And the children laughed and said,**
**"We can guess what Tom is.**
**He is a rabbit." (pp. 126–127)**

Both selections are typical of their eras. The passage of eighty years between the publishing of the *McGuffey Reader* and the Gray reader shows the change in values teaching in readers. The purposes of reading textbooks had changed during this time period. McGuffey expected that the home, school, and church would provide a solid triad for producing readers with moral values. Gray was interested in teaching children how to read, period, with little interest in literary refinement or style, and the book was a values vacuum just as it was a literary wasteland. Gray's note to teachers confirms his purpose:

> The new *Fun with Dick and Jane* has a total vocabulary of 158 words. Of these, 100 words are new in this book; the remaining 58 were introduced in the Pre-Primers and are again carefully reintroduced and maintained in the Primer. No page introduces more than one new word. The first five uses of each word, both old and new, are bunched for easy mastery; there is no gap of more than five pages between any two of these five uses. Thereafter, at spaced intervals at least seven more uses of each word occur. Thus, each word is used a minimum of twelve times in the new *Fun with Dick and Jane*. (p. 158)

The word "fun" is actually used 24 times, confirming textbook researcher claims that over time, religious and moral values were exchanged for secular values of enjoyment and amusement. (See Lystad [1980] and de Charms & Moeller [1962].)

# 5 Statistical Study of Textbooks

## Vocabulary: References to Religion and Religious Concepts

Vocabulary use can give some clues to the beliefs and emphases of authors of textbooks and to the prevailing sentiments in the culture. Frequency-counts of vocabulary provide a simple statistical level of analysis regarding the values teaching in textbooks. Because of the more technical nature of the sciences and mathematics texts, the selections in these books were not generally focused on religious, moral, or values issues. For that reason, we have not included vocabulary data from those texts. A few religious references do occur in the early science texts, however, that are not seen in later texts. In the period 1860–1880, reference is made to "God" and "an all-wise Creator." In the period 1881–1900, reference is made to "God," "the Creator's handiwork," and to God as the "heavenly Father" and "Preserver" of the universe. Two examples from this period provide the context for the vocabulary. The end of Tenney's (1887) science text, *Young Folks Pictures and Animals*, contains the following note:

> **Dear Children, we have now come nearly to the end of [this book]. I hope that you have enjoyed reading these little stories, and that you now wish to know more about the many and wonderful animals which our Heavenly Father has made to live on this beautiful earth, and which He constantly watches over and cares for, forgetting neither the beasts of the field, nor the birds of the air, nor the fishes of the sea.** (p. 149)

Buckelew's (1888) biology textbook, *Practical Work in the School Room*, contains this passage:

> **. . . we speak of the goodness of God who made our wonderful bodies, made our hearts beat, and keeps them beating every day without our help; of His great wisdom in giving us hearts which go on beating, sometimes for a hundred years, without stopping to rest. These thoughts of God, as our Creator and Preserver, are naturally suggested and not soon forgotten by the interested listeners.** (p. 7)

By the period 1921–1940 and thereafter, there is no reference to God or a supreme being in the science texts of the Floyd Collection; by this period, texts are more likely to credit "nature" with the development of the universe and our bodies. For example, Emerson's (1928) *Physiology and Hygiene Book Two* asks, "Do you not think that since nature has given us such wonderful bodies we should treat them well?" (p. 216) I observe that, although there are a few excellent examples of science texts, they are not well represented in the collection. It may be that references to God or a supreme being occurred in other science textbooks of the period.

No references to God or religion occur in any of the mathematics textbooks of the Floyd Collection, except three references to "Christmas," and these are in the context of holidays rather than religious teaching.

Literature texts, grammar texts (including spelling), histories, and readers are well represented in the Floyd Collection. I assume, therefore, that the values-laden vocabulary in these books is representative of the values contained generally in the textbooks used during the eras analyzed.

In the following vocabulary analysis, shown in Fig. 5.1, we have separated vocabulary with religious references from vocabulary that has values or moral connotation only. The following table presents a frequency count of the vocabulary with religious references contained in these four prominent categories of textbooks. The numbers (n/n) represent number of religious references per number of textbooks analyzed.

## Fig. 5.1 *Vocabulary with Religious Reference*

| | History | Literature | Reading | Grammar |
|---|---|---|---|---|
| **1840–1860** | 2/6 | 0/3 | 13/7 | 24/14 |
| **1861–1880** | 5/8 | 5/2 | 44/10 | 66/29 |
| **1881–1900** | 30/19 | 15/12 | 11/12 | 46/30 |
| **1901–1920** | 33/27 | 35/27 | 9/18 | 51/33 |
| **1921–1940** | 18/12 | 16/9 | 3/30 | 12/19 |
| **Post–1941 (through 1956)** | 1/4 | 0/1 | 6/10 | 2/7 |

Examples of religious reference: *Christ, God, Deity, Church, Lord, Providence, Gospel, Bible, Prayer*

In the period 1840–1860, at least one or two religious references per textbook occur. This trend holds in the textbooks of the 1861–1880 era. By 1920, the reader textbooks are showing only one religious reference for every two textbooks. In the post-1940s era collection, there is only approximately one religious reference for every three textbooks. The trends observed in the work of previous researchers (de Charms, 1962; Lystad, 1980)—that is, a steady decline in religious reference in reading textbooks—are also evident in this data.

## Vocabulary: References to Values and Morals

Though the references to religion per se in the early science and mathematics texts are few, the prefaces to a number of early texts do reveal strong values in regard to the profession of teaching. Moreover, the texts' authors aimed to inculcate values in the teacher as well as the pupils. Thomson (1849), in *Elements of Algebra*, wrote in his preface, as follows:

> To mould the youthful mind *right* is an *arduous* and *responsible* task; sufficient to crush the jaded spirit and shattered nerves of a poorly paid teacher. Nevertheless it is a *high* and *noble* as well as indispensable work. Every conscientious teacher therefore . . . entrusted with this responsible charge, will cheerfully devote his energies to the work, whatever may be the sacrifice, or resign his trust to more faithful and able hands. (p. vi)

Contentment with their lot was an obvious message to teachers in this preface; for many, teaching was on par with missionary work and the calling to the ministry. Sacrifice and commitment were expected.

The grammar texts, which are the best represented in the Floyd Collection, contain nonreligious but values-laden vocabulary. In the texts of the eras prior to 1920, we found an interesting mix of both religious sentiments and secular values. Brown's (1846) *The Institutes of English Grammar, Methodically Arranged with Examples for Parsing, Questions* . . . is full of aphorisms, homilies, and the flowery poetry of the age, which were meant to provide values education as well as "examples for parsing." For example:

> Come, calm Content, serene and sweet!
> O, gently guide my pilgrim feet
> To find thy hermit cell;
> Where, in some pure and equal sky
> Beneath thy soft indulgent eye,
> The modest virtues dwell. (p. 45)

Values in regard to the reformation of personal morals are in obvious evidence, but not much in the way of civil-rights activism would proceed from the following homilies: "The pious cheerfully submit to their lots." (Brown, 1846, p. 180) "Be not forward in the presence of your superiors." (Harvey, 1869, p. 48) Reform of personal habits, such as the drinking of alcohol, was openly advocated, as in Clark's (1875) *The Normal Grammar Analytic and Synthetic*:

**The habit of intemperance produces much lasting misery . . . (p. 54)**
**Temperance and frugality promote health and secure happiness. (p. 171)**

The value of hard work is also extolled throughout the textbooks of the nineteenth century and well into the twentieth. Typical of these authors, Elson (1909), in his *Grammar School Fourth Reader for the Eighth Grade*, quoted Benjamin Franklin's *Poor Richard's Almanac*: "Industry need not wish, and he that lives upon hopes will die fasting." (p. 347) Sidwell (1928) wrote, "All true work is sacred; in all true work, were it to be hand-labor, there is something of divineness." (p. 129)

An analysis of the most frequently used values-laden vocabulary grammar and reading textbooks in the various eras of the collection is presented in Fig. 5.2:

## Fig. 5.2 *Most Frequently Used Values-Laden Vocabulary in Reading and Grammar Textbooks in Descending Order of Frequency of Occurrence*

|  | Reading | Grammar |
|---|---|---|
| **Pre-1840** | Faith | Wisdom |
|  | Honesty | Virtue |
|  | Virtue | Hope |
|  | Usefulness | Faith |
|  |  | Diligence |
|  |  | Justice |
|  |  | Piety |
|  |  | Bravery |
|  |  | Modesty |
|  |  | Charity |

|  | **Reading** | **Grammar** |
|---|---|---|
| **1840–1860** | Honor | Wisdom |
|  | Faith | Virtue |
|  | Kindness | Honesty |
|  | Courage | Industry |
|  | Honesty | Diligence |
|  | Virtue | Kindness |
|  | Gratitude | Piety |
|  | Benevolence | Truth |
|  | Nobleness | Faith |
|  | Humility | Honor |

"Family," "friendship," and "politeness" are mentioned only once each in the combined totals for readers of this period. These terms become much more popular in the decades following.

|  | | |
|---|---|---|
| **1861–1880** | Kindness | Wisdom |
|  | Faith | Honesty |
|  | Prayer | Virtue |
|  | Honesty | Industry |
|  | Humility | Faith |
|  | Bravery | Kindness |
|  | Usefulness | Honor |
|  | Honor | Obedience |
|  | Forgiveness | Patience |
|  | Virtue | Prudence |

|  | | |
|---|---|---|
| **1881–1900** | Kindness | Wisdom |
|  | Courage | Bravery |
|  | Virtue | Nobleness |
|  | Honor | Honesty |
|  | Obedience | Purity |
|  | Patience | Virtue |
|  | Nobleness | Honor |
|  | Wisdom | Obedience |
|  | Usefulness | Industriousness |
|  | Purity | Kindness |

| **1901–1920** | Kindness | Kindness |
| --- | --- | --- |
| | Nobleness | Honesty |
| | Wisdom | Nobleness |
| | Humility | Wisdom |
| | Thankfulness | Obedience |
| | Courage | Generosity |
| | Beauty | Bravery |
| | Happiness | Patience |
| | Friendliness | Honor |
| | Gentleness | Usefulness |

| **1921–1940** | Kindness | Courtesy |
| --- | --- | --- |
| | Courtesy (Thank you) | Friendliness |
| | Helpfulness | Honesty |
| | Friendliness | Courage |
| | Bravery | Kindness |
| | Family | Bravery |
| | Beauty | Health |
| | Christmas | Obedience |
| | Faith | Skillfulness |
| | Patience | Patience |

In the last era studied, "Romance" and "Santa Claus" are two examples of new vocabulary. The term "wisdom," which was deemed so important by the authors of texts in the 1800s and early 1900s, all but disappears after 1940. "Wisdom" was found a total of only two times in the readers of this periods and five times in the grammars.

| **Post-1940** | Friendliness | Courtesy |
| --- | --- | --- |
| **(through 1956)** | Family | Courage |
| | Courtesy (Thank you) | Wisdom |
| | Helpfulness | Strength |
| | | Honesty |
| | | Thoughtfulness |
| | | Helpfulness |
| | | Pleasantness |

In this period "wise" and "kind" are down to two uses each in the readers.

Fig. 5.3 shows values-laden vocabulary other than religious reference; this chart does not represent an analysis of content. These are merely words that were used regularly in the textbooks, and they are only an indicator of values expressed by the authors of these textbooks.

Figs. 5.3 and 5.4 show dramatic shifts in the use of vocabulary. In Fig. 5.3, "wisdom," "diligence," "virtue," and "faith" were high-use, values-laden vocabulary words for over one hundred years. They all began dropping in use after 1860. "Wisdom" is the only term of the four that survived as a high-use term after 1880. "Wisdom," however, increased again in use after 1940. This was due largely to the inclusion of folk and fairy tales in the literature selections after 1940 and in current readers. Folk tales commonly refer to "wisdom" and to characters who are "wise."

"Courtesy" is not a high-frequency term before 1900; however, its use dramatically increased, and it is ranked first of all values-laden vocabulary, by the 1920s. "Courtesy" maintains its position of highest ranking in the post-1940 textbooks of the collection (through about 1955—the latest publication date of textbooks in the Floyd Collection). The vocabulary of traditional values in general lessens in frequency over time. Powerful words such as "virtue," "diligence," and "wisdom" are replaced in the textbooks of the '40s and '50s by words such as "nice," "polite," "friendly," and "fun."

## Fig. 5.3 *High Frequency Values-Laden Vocabulary over Time in Grammar Textbooks*

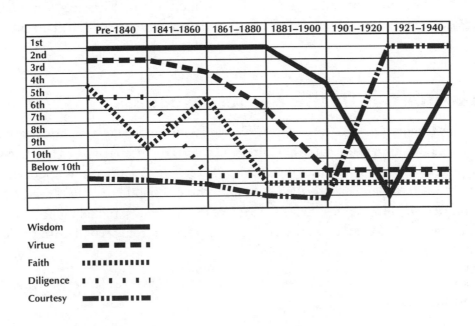

|  | Pre-1840 | 1841–1860 | 1861–1880 | 1881–1900 | 1901–1920 | 1921–1940 |
|---|---|---|---|---|---|---|
| 1st |  |  |  |  |  |  |
| 2nd |  |  |  |  |  |  |
| 3rd |  |  |  |  |  |  |
| 4th |  |  |  |  |  |  |
| 5th |  |  |  |  |  |  |
| 6th |  |  |  |  |  |  |
| 7th |  |  |  |  |  |  |
| 8th |  |  |  |  |  |  |
| 9th |  |  |  |  |  |  |
| 10th |  |  |  |  |  |  |
| Below 10th |  |  |  |  |  |  |

Wisdom ▬▬▬▬

Virtue ▬ ▬ ▬ ▬

Faith ▪▪▪▪▪▪▪▪▪▪▪

Diligence ▪ ▪ ▪ ▪ ▪ ▪

Courtesy ▬▪▪▬▬▪▪▬

Fig. 5.4 is focused on the values-laden vocabulary of history textbooks over time.

## Fig. 5.4 *High Frequency Values-Laden Vocabulary over Time in History and Social Studies Textbooks*

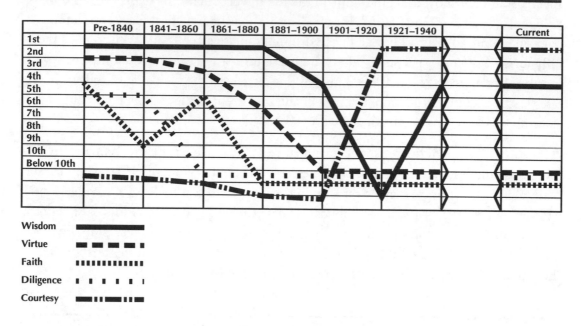

"Bravery/courage" made steady gains among the top values-laden vocabulary throughout America's history, and "bravery/courage" is today the number-one value in basal readers. "Honor" did not continue its high rank into the post-Vietnam-War era. It ranks close to the bottom in usage of the values-laden vocabulary of the current readers.

# Data Analysis of the Modern Readers

The values teaching in readers of the 1990s was less didactic and straightforward than those of one hundred years ago; therefore, an analysis of vocabulary was less likely to yield a picture of values-teaching than in the old readers. A more careful perusal of the selections was in order. As described in chapter three, a number of raters read selections and recorded the values thrust for each of the selections, including poems, but excluding language-skills lessons in three or four readers from second–fifth grades in each of the series.

Fig. 5.5 shows the data on values for individual current basal reader series by publishing company and series.

## Fig. 5.5 *Report Card on Values in Basal Readers*

### Open Court Publishing Company

**Total number of selections: 280**
**Total number of selections with traditional values: 90**

| Values Content in Rank Order | Percentages |
| --- | --- |
| Entertainment, humor, content areas | 68 |
| Appreciation of differences | 4 |
| Bravery | 4 |
| Work ethic | 3 |
| Conservation of nature | 2 |
| Consequences of doing wrong/right | 2 |
| Maintaining friendship | 2 |
| Familial love/home | 2 |
| Gender equity/equality | 1 |
| Self-sacrifice | 1 |
| Other (various) | 11 |

### Silver-Burdett, Ginn Publishers

**Total number of selections: 155**
**Total number of selections with values: 58**

| Values Content in Rank Order | Percentages |
| --- | --- |
| Entertainment, humor, content areas | 63 |
| Self-concept/identity | 4 |
| Love/familial love/home | 4 |
| Appreciating differences | 3 |
| Conservation of nature | 3 |
| Bravery | 3 |
| Value of reading/writing | 3 |
| Initiative/self-reliance | 3 |
| Work ethic | 3 |
| Cooperation/teamwork | 2 |
| Kindness | 2 |
| Perseverance | 2 |
| Other (various) | 5 |

### Riverside Publishing Company

**Total number of selections: 165**
**Total number of selections with values: 53**

| Values Content in Rank Order | Percentages |
| --- | --- |
| Entertainment, humor, content areas | 68 |
| Bravery | 4 |
| Appreciation of differences | 2 |
| Teamwork/cooperation | 2 |
| Familial love | 2 |
| Kindness | 2 |
| Perseverance | 2 |
| Gender equity/equality | 2 |
| Compassion | 2 |
| Value of reading/writing | 2 |
| Work ethic | 2 |
| Wisdom | 2 |
| Other (various) | 8 |

### Harcourt Brace Jovanovich, Inc.

**Total number of selections: 158**
**Total number of selections with values: 62**

| Values Content in Rank Order | Percentages |
| --- | --- |
| Entertainment, humor, content areas | 61 |
| Value of reading/writing/schooling | 10 |
| Appreciation of differences | 4 |
| Self-concept/identity | 4 |
| Bravery | 3 |
| Gender equity/equality | 3 |
| Conservation of nature | 1 |
| Freedom | 1 |
| Initiative/self-reliance | 1 |
| Teamwork/cooperation | 1 |
| Justice | 1 |
| Forgiveness | 1 |
| Consequences of doing wrong/right | 1 |
| Other (various) | 8 |

### Heath Publishers

**Total number of selections: 166**
**Total number of selections with values: 63**

| Values Content in Rank Order | Percentages |
| --- | --- |
| Entertainment, humor, content areas | 62 |
| Bravery | 5 |
| Appreciation of differences | 4 |
| Conservation of nature | 4 |
| Work ethic | 4 |
| Perseverance | 4 |
| Familial love | 4 |
| Self-concept/identity | 2 |
| Compassion | 2 |
| Value of reading/writing | 2 |
| Self-sacrifice | 2 |
| Gender equity/equality | 2 |
| Consumer awareness | 2 |
| Other (various) | 1 |

### Macmillan Publishing Company

**Total number of selections: 154**
**Total number of selections with values: 63**

| Values Content in Rank Order | Percentages |
| --- | --- |
| Entertainment, humor, content areas | 59.1 |
| Values of reading/writing/schooling | 7.8 |
| Appreciation of differences | 4.5 |
| Bravery | .5 |
| Conservation of nature/animals | 3.2 |
| Work ethic | 3.2 |
| Self-concept | 2.5 |
| Initiative | 2.5 |
| Familial love | 1.9 |
| Consequences of doing wrong/right | 1.9 |
| Perseverance | 1.9 |
| Gender equity | 1.9 |
| Honesty | 1.2 |
| Appreciation of beauty/art | 1.2 |
| Other (various) | 2.7 |

### Holt, Rinehart, Winston

**Total number of selections: 137**
**Total number of selections with values: 39**

| Values Content in Rank Order | Percentages |
| --- | --- |
| Entertainment, humor, content areas | 71.6 |
| Appreciation of differences | 2.9 |
| Bravery | 2.9 |
| Self-concept/individuality | 2.1 |
| Work ethic | 2.1 |
| Familial love | 2.1 |
| Self-sacrifice | 2.1 |
| Courtesy | 2.1 |
| Wisdom | 2.1 |
| Honesty | 1.4 |
| Help/cooperation | 1.4 |
| Justice | 1.4 |
| Patriotism | 1.4 |
| Other (various) | 4.4 |

### Houghton-Mifflin Publishing

**Total number of selections: 118**
**Total number of selections with values: 39**

| Values Content in Rank Order | Percentages |
| --- | --- |
| Entertainment, humor, content areas | 67.0 |
| Appreciation of differences | 6.7 |
| Perseverance | 3.3 |
| Bravery | 3.3 |
| Achievement | 2.5 |
| Familial love | 1.7 |
| Consequences of doing wrong/right | 1.7 |
| Work ethic | 1.7 |
| Sharing/cooperation | 1.7 |
| Conservation of nature/animals | 1.7 |
| Other (various) | 8.7 |

The total number of selections read in all series was 1,432, of which 502 selections were considered to contain some particular values thrust. Fig. 5.6 shows that the average percentage across all current series (state-adopted in Indiana for years 1989–1995) of selections teaching values was 35%. Approximately 65% of the selections across all readers pertained to entertainment, humor, and the reinforcement of, and coordination with, other school content areas such as social studies and science.

## Fig. 5.6 *Values Content in Current Basal Readers (Top 25 Values)*

| Values Content | Number of Selections | Percentage of Total |
|---|---|---|
| Entertainment, content areas | 930 | 65.0 |
| 1. Bravery | 50 | 3.5 |
| 2. Appreciation of differences | 49 | 3.4 |
| 3. Work ethic | 32 | 2.2 |
| 4. Value of reading and writing | 30 | 2.1 |
| 5. Self-concept | 29 | 2.0 |
| 6. Familial love | 29 | 2.0 |
| 7. Conservation of nature/animals | 25 | 1.7 |
| 8. Perseverance | 24 | 1.7 |
| 9. Gender role equity | 19 | 1.3 |
| 10. Consequences of doing wrong/right | 17 | 1.2 |
| 11. Initiative/self-reliance | 16 | 1.1 |
| 12. Cooperation/teamwork | 14 | 1.0 |
| 13. Self-sacrifice | 12 | 0.9 |
| 14. Kindness | 11 | 0.8 |
| 15. Wisdom | 10 | 0.7 |
| 16. Forgiveness | 9 | 0.6 |
| 17. Justice | 9 | 0.6 |
| 18. Compassion | 8 | 0.5 |
| 19. Freedom/patriotism | 8 | 0.5 |
| 20. Honesty | 8 | 0.5 |
| 21. Courtesy/manners | 6 | 0.4 |
| 22. Generosity/altruism | 5 | 0.3 |
| 23. Ingenuity/achievement | 4 | 0.3 |
| 24. Service ethic/social action | 3 | 0.2 |
| 25. Humility | 3 | 0.2 |
| Other values | 72 | 5.0 |
| **Total number** | **1,432** | **100.0** |

The 72 selections (or 5% of the total) in the "Other" category represent a broad spectrum of values teaching: patience, loyalty, political action, love, hope, unselfishness, peace, contentment, trust—a traditional, values-rich collection, but each representing only a fraction of a percentage point of the total. It is fair to say that the values content in today's readers is significantly different from those of a hundred years ago, and the values teaching is significantly less traditional.

A brief comparison between the percentages and types of values taught in past and present readers demonstrates the contrast. A content analysis of a sampling of readers from different periods shows that in *The Columbian Reader* (1815), 82% of selections taught traditional values. In the Webb *Model Readers* (1876), 66% of the selections in the readers taught traditional values. In Searson's *Studies in Reading* (1923), 80% of selections taught traditional values. Current basals, on average and by contrast, contain only 35% traditional values.

Most of the traditional values in these readers still appear in today's readers, although with a few exceptions, like "humility"—they rarely appear as the major thrust of a selection in today's readers. Stories that embrace this quality were also hard to find for the bibliography of current trade books, as reported in chapter nine below.

McGuffey Readers are well represented in the Floyd Collection, which enabled us to read whole series for a particular year, as we also did with the current readers. Because the McGuffeys were used widely and over a long period of time—more than half of American children between 1840 and 1920 learned to read from McGuffey Readers— their influence by far outweighed the influence of other readers during those eighty years. We therefore thouroughly read and ranked the selections in the McGuffey Readers. Our data based on the McGuffey Readers from grades two through five published halfway through that eighty-year period (1879), shows that 66% of the selections were attempts to teach traditional ethical values. Even in those readers, there was some emphasis on amusement and informational selections. Fig. 5.7 shows a detailed breakdown.

## Fig. 5.7 Top 25 Values in the McGuffey Readers

| Value Content Ranked | Percentage of selections teaching values: | |
| --- | --- | --- |
| | Selections | Percentage* |
| Amusement, Information | 127 | 34.0 |
| 1. Trust in God's presence and power | 23 | 6.1 |
| 2. Value of home/family/family love | 21 | 5.5 |
| 3. Work ethic | 18 | 4.7 |
| 4. Consequences of right/wrong doing | 18 | 4.7 |

| | | |
|---|---|---|
| 5. Bravery/courage | 13 | 3.4 |
| 6. Honesty | 10 | 2.6 |
| 7. Obedience | 9 | 2.3 |
| 8. Patience | 9 | 2.3 |
| 9. Kindness | 9 | 2.3 |
| 10. Generosity/charity | 9 | 2.3 |
| 11. Value of reading/writing/thinking | 8 | 2.1 |
| 12. Temperance | 7 | 1.9 |
| 13. Honor/respect for parents | 7 | 1.9 |
| 14. Gratitude | 7 | 1.9 |
| 15. Perseverance | 6 | 1.6 |
| 16. Gentleness | 5 | 1.3 |
| 17. Humility | 5 | 1.3 |
| 18. Futility of war | 5 | 1.3 |
| 19. Compassion | 4 | 1.1 |
| 20. Unselfishness | 3 | 0.8 |
| 21. Initiative | 3 | 0.8 |
| 22. Self-sacrifice | 3 | 0.8 |
| 23. Justice | 3 | 0.8 |
| 24. Teamwork | 2 | 0.3 |
| 25. Forgiveness | 2 | 0.3 |
| Other values | 40 | 11.6 |

*"Rounding up" of percentages causes total percentage to be more than 100%

**Total number of selections (grades 2–5):** **376**
**Total number of selections with values:** **249**
**Percentage of selections with values:** **66 %**

---

The McGuffey Readers were designed to support the school/home/church triad. It is not surprising, therefore, that the number-one value in the selections of the McGuffeys was "trust in God's presence and power." Also not surprisingly, the value of "home and family" was a fairly close second.

Thirty years later, just before World War I, the Howe Readers (1909) show similar rankings in the values present in stories, but the percentage of selections containing traditional values is smaller than the McGuffeys. In fact, the percentages of selections containing traditional values as opposed to entertainment and information is mid-way between the McGuffey Readers and the percentages in the modern readers. Fig. 5.8 shows the data on values from the *Howe Readers*.

## Fig. 5.8 Values in the *Howe Readers* (1909)

| Value Content Ranked | Percentage of selections teaching values: | |
| --- | --- | --- |
| | Selections | Percentage* |
| Entertainment, Information | 202 | 55.0 |
| Trust in God's presence and power | 29 | 7.8 |
| Patriotism | 21 | 5.7 |
| Bravery | 19 | 5.1 |
| Work ethic | 17 | 4.6 |
| Perseverance | 10 | 2.7 |
| Consequences of right/wrong | 8 | 2.1 |
| Altruism/generosity | 6 | 1.6 |
| Wisdom | 6 | 1.6 |
| Kindness | 5 | 1.3 |
| Values of reading/writing/knowledge | 5 | 1.3 |
| Honesty | 4 | 1.0 |
| Justice | 3 | 0.8 |
| Obedience | 3 | 0.8 |
| Duty | 3 | 0.8 |
| Humility | 2 | 0.5 |
| Gratitude | 2 | 0.5 |
| Sharing | 2 | 0.5 |
| Faithfulness | 2 | 0.5 |
| Conservation of animals | 2 | 0.5 |
| Peacemaking | 2 | 0.5 |
| Other values | 20 | 5.6 |

*"Rounding up" of percentages causes total percentage to be more than 100%.

| | |
| --- | --- |
| **Total number of selections (grades 2–5):** | **368** |
| **Total number of selections with values:** | **166** |
| **Percentage of selections with values:** | **45 %** |

In contrast to the basal readers of a hundred or more years ago, today's readers show considerably fewer selections that teach traditional values, and those that do teach values reflect today's cultural and relationship standards, just as the school books of a century ago reflected the values of Protestant Christian and frontier America. Our data from the readers of the late 1800s show that approximately 65 percent of the selections contained ethical or traditional values content as contrasted with 35 percent in current basals of the late 1900s. There is also a qualitative difference in the values being taught. In the late 1800s, the values of *wisdom, honesty, virtue, obedience,* and *bravery* were taught directly through selections that focused on Biblical precepts, moral tales and fables, or the hallowed lives of great political and military leaders.

The textbooks of yesterday provided almost the entire content of curriculum. Although those books contained many values messages, including those of patriotism and democracy, the methods of teaching were didactic, with a preference for memorization and rote learning, rather than for stimulating opportunities for the students' own voices to be heard and choices to be made that could lead to a true understanding of democratic action and society. Curriculum guides were nonexistent outside of the textbook itself, which often was little more than a sequence of coursework based on the chronology of historical events or the difficulty level of the reading. This curriculum was largely past oriented; Biblical stories and characters or political and military heroes were cited as exemplars to teach values. The goal of schooling was instruction for salvation, survival, and Americanization, and the textbooks reflected that goal.

In today's curriculum, the great river of "time-on-task" flows on, carrying away with it all question and curiosity. The aching blandness of read, recite, regurgitate—still present as a model of instruction in many classrooms—dulls the thinking of all but the very best, most highly motivated students and those whose family backgrounds have insured their permanent membership among the literate elite. Little is left in the text-driven curriculum to cause the mind of the average student to spring to life and ask "Why? Who? What? When? Where? and How does this affect real life— *my* life!" This assembly-line, factory model of education has mimicked big business, but education factories no longer serve us well. The goal of education today is a life measured by advanced education, economic success, and progressive consumerism, while factory jobs are disappearing fast. The factory mind-set that calls on workers and students to follow directions and do their jobs without question, without thought, must also disappear. Education conceived in the image of the factory is an intellectual dinosaur. The future pulls us away from being cogs in an education machine and forward into the information age.

In the late 1900s, the diversity of our society and our interpretation of civil and social equity has spawned a new generation of values. "Appreciating difference," "self-concept," and "conservation of nature" have appeared as values in our basal readers because they are perceived to be either the current or needed values approved by a controlling segment of our culture and because they are being pursued by politically correct opinion-setters. Additionally, an emphasis on "entertainment" and integration of subject areas with reading has generated a large category of selections that reflect humor, science, and social studies topics.

What does this say about today's basal readers? First, it is likely that censorship has led publishers of basals to provide selections that contain less direct and indirect teaching of traditional values aimed at improvement of character and socially approved behavior. A great deal of research and writing on censorship issues related to textbooks and library materials was done in the 80s. (See Jenkinson [1980], Kamhi [1981], Rodrigues [1981], Criscuolo [1982]. For more current discussions of the social and political influences on the textbooks, see Apple and Christian-Smith [1991] and Tyson-Bernstein [1988].)

Second, a variety of other influences on the field of education generally, including the integration of disciplines and the perceived need for humor and entertainment, has contributed to the decisions about which selections to include in basal reader series.

Third, the desire to please many groups and offend none has left publishers with a values dilemma: The very stories that teach values are often so close to the heart of particular cultures or religions, that by their very nature they seem to threaten the belief systems of parallel, but different cultures in the society.

What to do? If the answer is to then move away from textbooks and basal readers, as the major sources of information on a topic, then this will call for major changes in school book publishing and curriculum design. It will move us towards inquiry curriculum that brings together a variety of resources, restricted only by the negotiated values of the groups connected with particular classrooms. Textbooks hence become one among many sources of information; they no longer carry the dual burden and honor of being the primary "knowledge bearer" and "standard bearer."

In the information age now already dawned upon us, texts will no longer be the major source of information. Instead, textbooks will be compendia of local and global issues, with controversies and multiple viewpoints acknowledged. Our children's classrooms can no longer be intellectually and emotionally isolated from the issues of the day, moving casually through the surface waters of basal history, basal geography, basal literature, and basal science. Texts will become anthologies of possibility, problem centered and issue oriented. The topics and sequences of learning will be chosen, based on the needs and interests of the students, guided by the teachers, responsive to the parents, and fulfilling the purposes of the American nation to educate for democracy. These local learning communities will then follow their own leads in pursuit of knowledge. Curriculum will be future oriented, global in perspective, participant-initiated, and learner controlled. The values of understanding, respect, and tolerance will result in the emergence of education for the compassionate life—the quintessence of democracy.

Teaching Kids to Care

# Results of the Historical and Statistical Studies

## I. These data corroborate other studies of old textbooks.

Since the 1920s, scholars have been conducting studies of textbooks, and they have concluded that there is a shift away from religious and moral values towards information, skills, and entertainment, reflections of secular American cultural values in the twentieth century. For example, Lystad (1980) examined the children's books published between 1821 and 1976 and documented this shift. Fig. 6.1 below summarizes part of Lystad's data covering the hundred years from 1836 to 1935. The category "religious behavior" included exhortations to obey God, to follow the tenets of Judeo-Christian faith, and to attend worship services. The category "social behavior" included applications of the tenets of faith and moral tenets in general in daily life—honesty, purity, courage.

### Fig. 6.1 *Purpose of Books (Percentages)*

| Publication Date | Religious Behavior/ Social Behavior | *Instruction* | *Understanding* | *Amusement* |
|---|---|---|---|---|
| **1836–1855** | 77 | 49 | 0 | 7 |
| **1856–1875** | 68 | 56 | 0 | 17 |
| **1876–1895** | 41 | 37 | 1 | 33 |
| **1896–1915** | 17 | 37 | 4 | 42 |
| **1916–1935** | 2 | 11 | 22 | 58 |

The table suggests that the purpose of textbooks a hundred and fifty years ago was the promotion of religious and social behavior in the readers of those books. The impartation of knowledge to feed the intellect, and lighthearted fare for mere amusement, were not particularly valued. Not surprisingly, the two eras (1836–1875) that reflect the highest percentages of religious and social behavior were two eras in which the McGuffey Reader was widely distributed. McGuffey emphasized the home/school/church triad and traditional moral values.

The results of my study of the nineteenth-century readers parallels Lystad's findings: The data reflect increasing emphasis on information and pleasure, parallel to Lystad's "understanding" and "amusement" categories. My historical data in chapter four also parallel Lystad's conclusion that values content and emphases in textbooks have changed over time. The data in chapter five show substantially the same trend.

In another examination of over 1,200 readers used in schools between 1776 and 1920, Perkins (1921) noted a sharp decline over time in the percentage of stories containing religious and moral content. Given the similarity of my findings, I seem to have used criteria for judging moral content that were very similar to his, although Perkins's work did not influence my study. Fig. 6.2 shows a simple comparison between the sets of data and the similarities between the sets of data. Note that Perkins's last *two* time periods encompass my *five* time periods, though our percentages vary insignificantly.

## Fig. 6.2 *Selections Containing Religious and Moral Content*

| Perkins Data | | Andrews Data | |
|---|---|---|---|
| **Period** | **Percentage** | **Period** | **Percentage** |
| 1776–1786 | 100 | | |
| 1787–1825 | 50 | | |
| 1826–1880 | 21 | 1840–1860 | 20 |
| | | 1861–1880 | 20 |
| | | 1881–1900 | 18 |
| 1916–1920 | 3 | 1901–1920 | 7 |
| | | 1921–1940 | 4 |

Like Perkins, I found an increasing percentage of selections devoid of religious and traditional moral content in readers of the twentieth century in contradistinction to the readers of the nineteenth century. The percentages in this table for both studies are based on samples of stories within several basal reading textbooks from each era.

In another representative textbook study, de Charms and Moeller (1962) conducted a content analysis of fourth-grade readers used between 1800 and 1950. The basic results are similar to my more detailed analysis of the Floyd Collection. They reported that in 1810, 16 of 25 randomly selected pages in readers contained moral content. By 1910, only four pages in 25 of the basal reading textbooks reflected moral instruction. By 1950, the percentage of pages containing moral instruction was reduced to .06 of a page per 25 pages.

Martha A. Hoover, whose unpublished doctoral dissertation study is cited in Flinders (1986), studied reading and history textbooks published by four companies that had been in the textbook business for over one hundred years. Like my chronological categorizations of the Floyd Collection, Hoover analyzed text samples at twenty-year intervals beginning in 1880 (I began in 1840) for content according to patriotic values and moral values, personal belief statements and others' belief statements. These categories are similar to my "religious," "moral," "patriotic," and "exemplar" categories related to the eras of educational focus (see chapter four). Hoover concluded that there had been a general shift in content in reading textbooks since about 1920; references to God, morals, or religion are almost nonexistent in readers since World War I. My sample of 1,432 selections from 32 textbooks agrees with Hoover's conclusions. I found that less than 1/2 of 1% of the stories contained religious references.

Results of other studies of old textbooks confirmed my conclusion that textbook content emphasizing traditional moral values has dramatically decreased over the past one hundred and fifty years. It may well be that the teaching of traditional moral values is less important to the average parent or teacher today than it was a hundred and fifty years ago. It is certain that there is more diversity of opinion now than there was a hundred and fifty years ago on what values should be taught, how they should be taught, and who should teach them.

## II. These data corroborate other studies of new textbooks.

Although researchers argue that textbooks have been reduced to a minor role compared to their status in the eighteenth century (*The New England Primer*) or the nineteenth century (McGuffey Readers), the textbook industry in the United States is still a billion-dollar enterprise that strives to make its products acceptable to the large groups of buyers in the most populous states. For this reason, research on textbooks is being conducted as never before, and there are some telling studies of today's textbooks in light of values.

For example, Vitz (1986) examined 90 current social-studies textbooks and readers from 11 publishers. He determined that this group of texts was used to instruct more than 80 percent of American school children. He was interested in determining what treatment was given to religion and family values, both in the actual text and in the illustrations in those textbooks. Flinders (1986) reported that the results of Vitz's study were "sobering."

> **None of the 40 social studies texts has a single reference to a primary religious activity occurring in contemporary American life. In these books, which averaged two images per page, no book had more than one . . . religious image per 200 pages. The direct references to American religion are all related to the early colonial period. . . .**

> [W]hen one corrects for the number of pages of coverage for each
> century and notes the references to religion in America in either text
> or image in all of these books combined, the results are instructive.
> In the few pages referring to the 1600s, slightly over 50% made some
> reference to religion. During the 1700s, this figure diminishes to less
> than 10%. It is 3.4% for the 1800s and 1.2% during the 1900s.
>
> In the 22 basals for grades 3 and 6, religion was for all intents and
> purposes excluded. There were scores of articles on animals, archae-
> ology, fossils, or magic, but nowhere [sic] on religion. . . (p. 9)

My data corroborate Vitz's figures on the frequency of references to religion in texts
from the 1700s to the 1900s. Vitz (1986) also searched for family values in textbooks.
Flinders described Vitz's study:

> In the social-studies texts for grades 1–4, there is not one text refer-
> ence to marriage as the foundation of the family. Indeed, not even the
> word "marriage" or "wedding" occurs once in the forty books [in an
> American context]! . . .[N]either the word "husband" nor the word
> "wife" occurs once in any of these books. . . . Not one of the many
> families described in these books features a homemaker—that is, a
> wife and mother—as a model. There is not one citation indicating
> that the occupation of mother or housewife represents an important
> job, one with integrity, one that provides real satisfactions. (p. 7)

I also found that few of the selections in the current basals (1989–1995) deal with
family themes. One of the few family selections in Holt, Rinehart, & Winston's *Patterns* is set in the American West in 1817, and it ends with a statement containing
several of the very few values-laden terms in the entire book: *We were working hard, but
our work was filled with hope and a lot of love. We were making a new life for our family, and
our feelings for our new home grew stronger and stronger.* (p. 54) Though this is a reference
both to family and to values, neither modern nor contemporary family life and values
are stressed anywhere in this textbook. Scattered selections on home and family do
occur in other basals and some with specific focus. Silver, Burdett, Ginn's basal for
fifth-grade readers, *Dream Chasers* (1989), contains a unit comprising several selections
with the theme of "home" or "family." Despite these and some other selections focused on the values of home and family, in only 2% of the selections in our sample was
the main focus of the story familial love.

People for the American Way, a lobby group based in Washington, D.C., commis-
sioned a study, published in 1986, of contemporary U.S. History textbooks. The

examining panel was struck to find that "religion is simply not treated as a significant element in American life—it is not portrayed as an integrated part of the American value system or as something that is important to individual Americans." (Flinders, 1986, p. 3)

Schmidt (1983) studied 34 basal readers from eight major publishing companies to ascertain their educational content, the functional or applied knowledge content, and their "ethos (ethics or virtue) component." He wrote of ethos, " [It] explains or demonstrates what people ought to do in order to live rightly; it presents the ethical knowledge of ordinary life with its time-tested virtues." (p. 6) My data corroborate what Schmidt found, that the ethos component was present especially in folk and fairy tales from a variety of cultures, but that, nevertheless, of the selections read within the 34 basals, totalling almost 2,000 individual pieces, 87.7% had no ethos content. Fig. 6.3 shows Schmidt's total data on the ethos component (see p. 13).

## Fig. 6.3 *Frequency of Content Categories on the Ethos Dimension*

| Ethos Content | Number of Selections | Percentage of Total |
|---|---|---|
| No ethos content | 1,719 | 87.7 |
| Humility | 20 | 1.0 |
| Patience/Forbearance | 18 | .9 |
| Courage | 77 | 3.9 |
| Kindness/Generosity | 91 | 4.6 |
| Hope | 6 | .3 |
| Other | 12 | .6 |
| Totals | **1,959** | **100.0** |

Although my analysis of the modern readers corroborates these findings, my findings differed from Schmidt's in the *types* of values found in the texts: A much broader array of values that fits Schmidt's "ethos dimension" was evident in the readers from the 1990s. (See the "top twenty-five values" in the modern readers in chapter five above.) My study demonstrates further that changes in values teaching reflect a new set of values emerging from new events, conflicts, and insights in our culture, a new set of values that nonetheless fits Schmidt's "ethos dimension." It is possible that in 1983, when Schmidt's study was done, few textbooks included selections that taught "appreciation of difference," "conservation of nature," or "good self-concept." It is also possible that Schmidt and associates did not perceive these to be values as such—any researcher of values, ourselves included, can be blind to manifestations of values current in the researcher's culture, too close to be seen. As researchers and teachers operating in school cultures a decade later than Schmidt's, we have a slightly broader view of values—one that includes our current culture with its new emphasis on multiculturalism in the broadest sense.

My analyses of the basal readers in use in the 1980s and early 1990s reveal a further phenomenon, also corroborating one of Schmidt's findings: The references to God, church, and morality occur almost exclusively in stories that would be considered either multicultural or legends.

## III. The core of mainstream values has been perpetual for over one hundred and fifty years.

The publishers of textbooks have in recent years responded to criticisms both from the right and the left, that what remains in the way of values-oriented materials and selections is offered as safe for all and inoffensive to anyone. A core of traditional mainstream values remains, however, amounting to about 35% of the selections.

Curriculum always reflects someone's world view. Textbook publishers select from a wide spectrum of knowledges and many versions of social reality. The controversies over "official knowledge" that usually center around what is included in, and excluded from, textbooks signify the presence of more diverse political, economic, and cultural relations and histories in the society that pays for those textbooks (Apple, 1991). According to Fleming (1987), in order for all parties, from author to school textbook committee and every stakeholder in between, to agree to approve a particular textbook, it must be "bland." Parker (1987) concluded that over the past one hundred years, public-school textbooks have been revised to reflect various public criticisms, and this has resulted in changes in the treatment of history, literature, and religions in the classroom. One researcher stated that ". . . the nature of the process by which knowledge is cut, pared, peeled, diced, sorted, and re-arranged to satisfy the political system before it can be served to public school students, is a national scandal." (Arons, 1983) The result, as shown in the tables in chapter five, has been a reduction in the traditional values-oriented selections that have survived the process of editing. Selections in readers still embody a core of mainstream values, but much reduced in quantity.

## IV. Recent readers teach a new set of values.

I can only speculate on the sources of the new values appearing in the most recent basal readers. By far, the largest values category in the study after "bravery," a value which has endured throughout all decades of our history, is a new value, "appreciating differences." This value is reflected in stories about understanding different races, cultures, and disabling conditions. Civil-rights legislation, the Regular Education Initiative (REI) at the national level, and other factors have contributed to a growing awareness of humane and equitable treatment of all groups in society.

The third-most-common category was "work ethic"—safe, familiar, and undisputed as a cultural value. A number of selections demonstrating this value could be found in every series. For example, in Open Court's second-grade reader, *Slide Down the Sky*, several stories demonstrate the work ethic: e.g. the fables, "The Ant and the Grasshopper" and "The Shoemaker and the Elves," and a new selection, "Friday Night is Papa Night" ("Everyone had a job to do on Friday night").

The fourth-largest category of new values related to "valuing reading and writing," but this value is not entirely new. Throughout the history of textbook publishing, there has been some mention of the value of books and of education. The new emphasis on high quality in children's literature in the basal texts and the focus on "author studies"—both of these emphases have come about through the influence of Whole Language, according to the basal-reader publishers' representatives whom I interviewed—have spawned a "mini-genre" of selections that promote authors and, therefore, promote reading, writing, and authorship. Most of these selections are short biographies or interviews with the authors about their books. One of the most effective examples, lengthier than most, is from The HBJ Reading Program (fifth grade) *Skylines*. Children's author Patricia Reilly Giff wrote, in "Painting Pictures with Words," about one of her favorite children's author's, Laura Ingalls Wilder. Before recounting for her fifth-grade audience Wilder's experiences that led her to write the "Little House" series, Giff wrote:

> **The *Little House* books were part of my childhood, a wonderful part. I wasn't sure then that there really was a Laura. I thought perhaps that someone had made her up.**
>
> **Laura, the person, became a love for me as I wrote about Laura, the writer. I spent long evenings writing and rewriting. I wanted to make this book one she'd approve.**
>
> **It became important to me to tell children how difficult some of the times in her life really were . . . times she accepted and wrote about so matter-of-factly. Most of all, I wanted to tell about the qualities of love and courage that are so apparent to us in Laura's stories.** (p. 6)

More typical of this mini-genre is Macmillan's "Meet the Author" component. Here is an example from the second-grade reader, *Friends Aloft*:

## Lucille Clifton

**Children and family are very important in Lucille Clifton's life and work. She was one of four children growing up near Buffalo, New York. "We didn't have much money," Clifton recalls, "but we had a lot of love." Now she is a successful writer with over twenty books of fiction and poetry for children and adults. And she has six children of her own.**

**"I write in spurts," says Clifton. "I never do all the things I'm supposed to do, like write at a set time. And I can't write if it's quiet." Clifton may break many of the rules of writing, but in books like *My Friend Jacob* she has given us people to remember.**

Stories and poems about valuing and accepting oneself constituted the next most evident category of values. From what does this emphasis spring? The pervasive influence of psychology as witnessed in the proliferation of "self-help" and "self-concept" books on the market, widely available in the 1970s and 1980s, has filtered into the public pedagogy. Most of the examples of "self-concept" selections occur in second- and third-grade readers, where that topic tends to surface in social studies, science, health, and various other school-based mental-health programs for students. In McGraw-Hill's (1989) second-grade reader, *Wake the Sun*, several selections focus on self-concept: "Just Me," "The Caterpillar and the Polliwog," and "Impossible Possum." In Silver Burdett Ginn's (1989) third-grade reader, *On the Horizon*, "Just Me" also appears, along with "The Big Orange Splot," "Ali Baba Bernstein," and "People Are All the Same."

The sixth-most-common value was familial love or the value of home, representing 2% of the total number of selections in all reading textbook samples. The seventh-most-common category, the environment, is not surprising in view of the current emphasis on preserving the planet. Stories about conservation of plants; natural habitats; and protection of, and kindness to, animals occurred in at least one story in about half of the basal readers in our sample. They are so common in the trade-book market and so familiar as a topic of study in many classrooms as not to require an example here.

Generally, I found that the majority of selections in the modern basals treated subjects such as neighbors, friendship and cooperation, fun, and science and social studies topics. Treatments were factual or humorous rather than didactic in the sense that readers of a hundred years ago were. Most of the few selections in which the authors presented moralistic content or situations requiring values-oriented decision making were in the context of folk or fairy tales that somewhat remove the possibility of applications to character formation from young readers' real lives.

Though there were few stories that promoted gender role equity (1.3% of the total), some outstanding selections on historical figures showcase women's achievements. For example, in *Dream Chasers* (fifth grade) from Silver Burdett Ginn (1989), "The Brooklyn Bridge: Emily's Triumph," set in the late 1800s, relates that "every day [the central woman character] made critical decisions" in a time in which women made few decisions in the workplace, especially in the building of bridges. Similarly, in the same series, in a selection entitled "A Paying Job," the central male character wants to babysit, and when his mother implies that babysitting is the province of girls, he chides her, "Mom, that's sexist."

There were very few stories that demonstrated political or social action, and even fewer that mentioned church or religion. One story that mentioned both was found in Open Court's third-grade reader, *Time for Dreams*—"Father Hidalgo," a story of Mexico's fight for freedom from Spain. Also, very few readers contained any Bible stories, and those that did often excluded mention of God. For example, in Open Court's fourth-grade reader, *Over the Moon*, the story "Joseph and his Brothers" is recounted with the focus being forgiveness rather than God's guidance, as would have been the focus a hundred years earlier.

## V. A new balance between conformity and uniqueness is presented in today's readers.

The distribution of reading textbooks—indeed, all mass-produced reading material—has always encouraged conformity and assimilation into mainstream institutions rather than critical thinking and uniqueness. The historical analysis above in chapter four shows that textbooks have reflected the perceived needs of America in society: "Salvation" in the 1700s and early 1800s, "Democracy" in the late 1700s, "Patriotism" in the mid-1800s, the "American Way" in the late 1800s and early 1900s, and "Survival" in the early and mid-1900s. Although people have acted individually to form their belief systems, to choose their learning communities, and to develop their identities, they have done so within the framework of cultural, political, and economic constraints, hence the school-based effort at persuasion to conform to prevalent social and cultural norms.

Although most textbooks introduced in schools have traditionally supported mainstream culture and values, publishers today are responding to various interest groups who are demanding inclusion. Sales representatives, editors, authors, and the president of a major basal-reader publisher made this concern quite clear to me when I interviewed them about the values in their readers. My initial question to those interviewed was this: *How are selections chosen for inclusion in your basal-reader series?* Their responses are ranked in order in the following list from most frequently mentioned to least frequently mentioned. Stories, they replied, must be characterized by the following:

- **Balanced: multicultural, gender-inclusive, ethnically and racially sensitive, responsive to handicaps**
- **Stories/authors are award winners**
- **Field approved by children and teachers**
- **Chosen by an editorial staff**
- **Recommended by librarians and classroom teachers**
- **Chosen by grade-level editors (mostly women)**
- **Chosen by children's-literature experts**
- **Models for writing and strategic reading**
- **Classics—best known, best loved**
- **Recommended by sales representatives**

*Everyone* who was interviewed stated that stories must reflect "balance": multicultural awareness, gender-inclusiveness, and handicap awareness. This criterion for choosing stories was viewed as a market constraint by some of those interviewed. One editor stated, "It's more difficult now to publish basal readers. There are many market constraints. Districts look at the stories for multicultural fairness, gender equity, and so forth." Others viewed this criterion as a progressive development. One sales rep stated: "Inherent in today's basal [reader] is a valuing of the individual's perspective. We are coming to value each person's uniqueness, perspective, and contributions."

The second interview question concerned values: *What are the most important values taught in your basal reader series?* Again, responses are listed in order from the most frequently mentioned to the least frequently mentioned:

- **Tolerance/appreciation of difference**
- **Honesty/ethical values**
- **Individual self-worth**
- **Conservation/appreciation of nature**
- **Loyalty**
- **Caring/kindness/love**
- **Helpfulness**
- **Work ethic**
- **Justice**

- **Family life**
- **Good over evil**

The interviews of editors and publishers show that the understanding of qualities that embody "values" seems to differ little from the definition of values reflected in most studies of textbook values (old or new), and it differs little from the definition of values assumed for purposes of the research reported in this book. In other words, the values mentioned appear to be past and present moral values. These interviews showed further that views diverged concerning the role that the textbook plays in the teaching of values. One sales rep said, "The attempt in the series is not to push values, but to show the contributions of various groups." An editor concurred, saying this:

> **We did not pick the stories based on values, but I would say that we are interested in stories which show good over evil, kindness, and family life. However, some stories are just for enjoyment. I think the values are embedded in the literature. But we are very interested in diversity; children need to know about the differences between themselves and others, and to see where we are the same. Multiculturism is not a value, but appreciation of difference is.**

I understand this editor to be saying that although stories were not chosen based on values *per se*, they were chosen based on their multicultural emphasis, which in turn supports the value, "appreciation of difference."

A third interviewee, also an editor, stated her position on the teaching of values in readers in even stronger terms:

> **We do not take the responsibility of teaching the message. That's not our job. We teach the children to read. However, we include nothing that reflects bad values. Certainly, some values are reflected in universal themes of literature and so would be included in the series— things like loyalty, trust, honesty, appreciation of diversity and getting along with others.**

In contrast to the three publishers' agents above, one publisher saw the teaching of values *per se* as a major mission. M. Blouke Carus, president of Open Court Publishing Company, when asked about the values in their basal readers, said: "That's our reason for existing. When we did our first set of readers in the 1960s, we went back to the old readers in the University of Chicago collection for ideas and stories with values." Carus mentioned values such as honesty, work ethic (industry), loyalty, and justice as examples of values taught in their basal-reader series. He also included appreciation of science, nature, music, and art as values. However, a review of Open Court's sales materials that describe the series suggests a distinction between "content" units and "values" units (a distinction that I made also in my review of the old readers in this study). The preliminary draft copy of promotional materials forwarded to me by Carus states as follows:

> The learning units in Open Court include content and values-oriented materials. The content units focus on coherent usable knowledge, with units on Social Studies (The American West, The Civil War, Colonial Life, and Ancient Civilizations) and units on Science (Wildlife in the City, Astronomy, Technology, and Medicine). The values-oriented units focus on empowering concepts that can help students make sense of their worlds. Examples are Friendship, Surviving, and Responsibility. All of the selections revolve around concepts that are worth thinking and learning about.

In another Open Court flyer, called "The Basic Principles of Open Court Reading and Writing," one reads the following:

> Open Court believes that some things are more important for children to read than others; in the early grades, this includes, in particular, fables, folk tales, myths, Bible stories, and both traditional and contemporary children's literature. This belief in cultural literacy is reflected not only in the choice of literature selections but also affects the kind of non-fiction selections that are chosen. Non-fiction selections are chosen, therefore, not only for their intrinsic values and interest but also to ensure that children are exposed to facts and ideas basic to our civilization.

An editor from another company also made the "content/value" distinction:

> As far as values teaching goes, "good things" are implied in most of the stories. Values teaching can be done with any piece of literature. Good literature can be chosen to reflect particular values. *Charlotte's Web* can be about friendship or loyalty. The grade level may affect the values you chose to emphasize. Of course, if you are reading a non-fiction piece about snakes, there isn't much in the way of values teaching.

What do the views of basal publishers add to the discussion of values in textbooks? Although these interviews were in no way a "scientific" sampling, and the selected comments cited here do not represent all basal authors, editors, and sales representatives, they do give a sense that the term "values" has some common meaning and that there is some diversity of opinion among those involved in publishing the basals as to whether the *role* of textbooks is to teach values directly or merely to reflect "good values" as a function of the literature chosen to be included in the series. One hundred years ago the degree of consensus on the role of textbooks in teaching values would have been greater.

These interviews also highlight an emphasis on balance in today's readers: balance among groups in society, balance between conformity and uniqueness as represented by values of "appreciation of difference," and "self-image." This new emphasis finds some previous discussion in a fascinating study by David McClelland (1975). He set out to show that periods of war and peace in England and in America could be predicted by the cultural emphasis on themes of "achievement," "affiliation," and "power" found in ballads, plays, children's literature, popular literature, and hymns. He wrote:

> **Coding historical documents for motivational variables provided a method of estimating the strength of various motivational forces at critical periods in history, thus enabling historians to better explain subsequent events.** (p. 395)

The "achievement" motivation was defined as the drive instilled in a person to live up to ideals. The "affiliation" motivation was defined as concern over establishing, maintaining, or restoring a positive affective relationship with another person. The "power" motivation was defined as the need to control or dominate.

McClelland's basic unit of measurement was the number of times "power," "affiliation," or "achievement" thoughts or images occurred for each sample of a hundred lines of text. He found that in the children's reading textbooks, whenever "power" motivation was high in a given decade, the "affiliation" motivation tended to be low, and vice versa. His overall findings indicated that high "power" motivation combined with low "affiliation" was associated in modern nations with dictatorships, suppression of liberty, and domestic and international violence. The inverse—high "affiliation" and low "power"—preceded eras of peace and prosperity.

High "achievement" motivation was usually associated with economic cycles. When the gap between aspiration and opportunity in a society was large, violence ensued. When there was little or no gap, a period of economic growth followed. McClelland's historical analysis showed that the achievement stage in a society is preceded by a stage in which strict moral codes demand behavioral conformity of the individual; thus he could predict the emphasis on moral teaching early in the history of the United States. A gradual movement toward "achievement" motivation in the late nineteenth and early twentieth centuries, in which individuals began to set their own standards for success, coincided with the decline in strict moral teaching.

At the time of the writing of his book in 1975, McClelland lamented that historical researchers had not used his method in the fifteen-year time span since the publishing of his first work on this topic. I am intrigued to attempt a sort of comparison of my data with McClelland's themes. Although I have not used his data collection or analysis methods, I have used similar source material, and I find it interesting that I have arrived at some similar conclusions. If we take his themes as predictors of periods of peace and prosperity, on the one hand, or of war and political violence, on the other, and assign to those themes the major values constructs that appeared in the modern readers in my study, we can make an extremely tentative prediction about the next decade in this country. For example, the "power" motivation could have "bravery" as a parallel values construct.

In Fig. 6.4, I present the graph from chapter five of the frequency of the appearance of the word "bravery" as reflected in textbooks over a one-hundred-year period. Fig. 6.5 is McClelland's table showing "power motifs" in children's readers, hymns, and popular fiction over the same period.

## Fig. 6.4 *Frequency of Occurrance of Word "Bravery" in Textbooks*

|  | Pre-1840 | 1841–1860 | 1861–1880 | 1881–1900 | 1901–1920 | 1921–1940 |
|---|---|---|---|---|---|---|
| 1st |  |  |  |  |  |  |
| 2nd |  |  |  |  |  |  |
| 3rd |  |  |  |  |  |  |
| 4th |  |  |  |  |  |  |
| 5th |  |  |  |  |  |  |
| 6th |  |  |  |  |  |  |
| 7th |  |  |  |  |  |  |
| 8th |  |  |  |  |  |  |
| 9th |  |  |  |  |  |  |
| 10th |  |  |  |  |  |  |
| Below 10th |  |  |  |  |  |  |

## Fig. 6.5 *Levels of Concern for "Power" in Popular Literature*

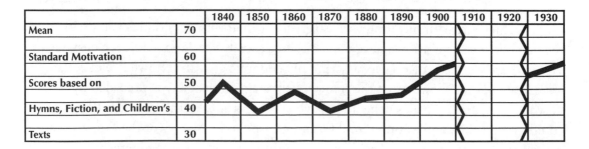

|  |  | 1840 | 1850 | 1860 | 1870 | 1880 | 1890 | 1900 | 1910 | 1920 | 1930 |
|---|---|---|---|---|---|---|---|---|---|---|---|
| Mean | 70 |  |  |  |  |  |  |  |  |  |  |
| Standard Motivation | 60 |  |  |  |  |  |  |  |  |  |  |
| Scores based on | 50 |  |  |  |  |  |  |  |  |  |  |
| Hymns, Fiction, and Children's | 40 |  |  |  |  |  |  |  |  |  |  |
| Texts | 30 |  |  |  |  |  |  |  |  |  |  |

Note the similarities between the frequency rankings of the vocabulary in my graph and the frequency of units of data referring to "power" in McClelland's graph. Since McClelland has a gap in his data from 1905 to 1920, I removed this section from my chart also, so that the reader can more readily compare the charts.

If McClelland's theses hold true, viz., 1) that themes of high "power" and low "affiliation" lead to war and political violence, and 2) that themes of high "affiliation" and low "power" lead to times of peace and prosperity, and if my study of values in children's readers can be used as a parallel predictor, then it appears that we are entering a period of balance between "power" and "affiliation." The rankings of most commonly found values in the readers of the early 1990s indicate that "bravery" (a value parallel to McClelland's "power" theme) and "appreciation of differences" or tolerance (a value parallel to McClelland's "affiliation" theme) are the top two values. "Achievement" parallels such as "work ethic," "self-concept," and "perseverance" are also high. McClelland's analysis shows that when both "power" and "achievement" were high, and "affiliation" low, then periods of war and unrest ensued.

Although there seems to be a balance between the themes in the current basals, McClelland issued a caveat based on his conclusions. He found, as he traced the historical trends of these themes, that if the "power" and "achievement" motivation themes were high, but the economic climate of the country was such that there was no outlet for citizens to realize their ambitions in a productive and peaceful way, then these motivations led to political violence, unrest, and war. Were the current economic climate in the United States to remain sluggish, unemployment high, and the anxiety caused by free-trade policies and corporate downsizing to continue, one might speculate that "achievement" motivations in U.S. citizens could well be thwarted over the next decade. My entirely tentative conclusion is that the "affiliation" motivation current in society is strong enough to balance the "power" and "achievement" motivations, if our politicians can find meaningful ways to stimulate the economy such that we can productively employ our citizens.

# 7 Implications of the Historical and Statistical Studies in Light of the Current Context for Values Teaching

Results of the historical and statistical studies thus far presented may be summarized as follows:

1. Since the 1920s, scholars have been conducting studies of textbooks and have concluded the shift is away from religious and moral values towards information, skills, and entertainment. My study corroborates earlier studies, showing that approximately 66% of the selections in McGuffey readers contained traditional moral values, as compared to 35% in today's readers. It may well be that the teaching of traditional moral values is less important to the average parent or teacher today than it was a hundred and fifty years ago, or it may be that publishers feel that the market today demands humor and information more than it does traditional values teaching or else they are fearful of offending this or that sensitivity over values in today's climate of "political correctness."

2. In the past ten years, a new emphasis in basal readers has been focused on multiculturalism, self-concept, and conservation of the natural environment. "Appreciation of difference," "self-concept," and "conservation of nature" are three of the top ten values in today's readers. These "new" values reflect the current diversity of our society, an emphasis on development and understanding of the "self," and a concern for environment as reflected in the many contemporary conservation and ecology movements.

3. Although the publishers of textbooks have responded in recent years to criticisms both from the right and the left, such that what remains in the way of values-oriented materials and selections is offered as safe for all and inoffensive to anyone, there remains a core of traditional mainstream moral values: Approximately 35% of the total selections in my study contained traditional values.

4. Though most textbooks introduced in schools have traditionally supported mainstream culture and values, publishers today try to respond to various interest groups who are demanding inclusion.

**Top publishers of basal readers indicated in interviews that their goal is "balance"—inclusion of selections that treat all groups fairly.**

The results of these textbooks studies are neither complex nor unexpected, but in order to appreciate their implications, I want to reframe them in an historical context.

# Textbooks: Restrictions, Resources, Redundancy?

In many classrooms today, textbooks are still the major source of content. Teachers rely on them for pre-selected goals and content. The textbooks are answer centered—teachers tell students: "Read the chapter (or story) and answer the questions." A hierarchical sequence of coursework, based on the school's curriculum guides or the scope-and-sequence chart in the teacher's manual that goes with the textbook, controls the students' largely passive learning. The pursuit of knowledge is hardly possible, let alone interesting, even when the hot issues are given a paragraph in the text. (A second-grade teacher told me that her students wanted to do a thorough study of endangered species; they were not satisfied with the two pages allotted this subject in the science text.)

Textbooks represent the political, cultural, ideological and economic values current in the country in which they are published. The authors who communicate their ideas and values through textbooks, nevertheless, must walk a tightrope between defending and challenging the status quo. Because today's textbooks are conceived, developed, written, and published in an atmosphere of squabble over cultural diversity, social trade-offs, and prohibitions and affirmations of "political correctness," presentation of balanced treatments of various groups within society seems impossible. Authors, publishers, and marketing personnel all have their agendas, and they confront one another over the role, content, and use of the textbook—how the textbook will present the world and what will be transmitted to the young. The diverse consumers of textbooks also have their own agendas, and they are becoming ever more vocal in their criticisms.

Textbooks are a controversial subject, so there are diametrically opposed points of view. Apple (1991) believed that authoring of textbooks is controlled by a set of political and economic dynamics that has contributed to, rather than diminished, class, gender, and racial discrimination; that those who have been excluded from power have been denied this forum for relating their history, culture, and labor. At the other end of the political spectrum, the Council for Basic Education expressed the opinion that textbooks can make youth into anarchists and anti-education activists; that many textbooks are communistic, socialistic, anti-American, unpatriotic, anti-free enterprise, anti-capitalistic, and anti-business. (Down, 1988)

The general unrest spawned by current criticism of our educational system has given rise to several movements that are attempting to influence textbook content, among them the minimum-competency testing movement, the back-to-basics movement, and several "values" movements. All of these movements have in common the wish to turn the attention of their devotees to a simpler time in the history of American education. Many of the advocates of these movements would point us to the era of the *McGuffey Eclectic Reader* and the values of a hundred years ago. What did the old textbooks offer children in the way of values teaching? What attracts so many parents and educators to them today? (Sales of reprints of the old McGuffey Readers peaked at 217,000 in 1985.) Certainly, most citizens would not dispute the necessity of teaching justice, loyalty, honesty, virtue, bravery, and the whole list of values that were at the fore in generations past, but neither would the average citizen dispute the need for teaching tolerance, respect, appreciation of differences, social equality, and healthy self-concept which are part of our current cultural atmosphere.

All materials used in the classroom need to be discussed and critiqued by students, teachers, parents, and other community members, but not with the intent of removing those materials. Children and parents need not fear the written word if they are given the opportunity openly to discuss and critique the foundations and sources of the knowledges and values being promoted. We need to discern the orientation of any written material used in school. Does it seek to make readers conform to a particular political and social agenda? Does it seek to reform particular segments of society? Does it seek transformation, critique, and renewal of old structures and ways of thinking? Richardson (1986) offered a useful suggestion:

> **When we consider a book, we mustn't ask ourselves what it says but what it means. We need to produce materials which embody this point—which equip pupils with skills to subject books to enquiry . . . . We need lots of exercises such as these, carefully structured and focused to equip pupils with skills in analyzing the schoolbooks in use in their own, and in other, classrooms. Amongst other things, such exercises should quote from schoolbooks produced in other countries, and from schoolbooks of earlier generations.** (p. 39)

Richardson's ideas would help protect us and our children from either inappropriate values teaching or lack of it through increased critical thinking, open discussion, and thoughtful communication. Others' opinions agree with Richardson's, and his argument can be extended to include information from all forms of media. For example, Neil Postman (1985) suggested that we are in a race between education and disaster because of television. He argued that if we do not find ways to help our children critique and understand the effects of media—the printed word, television, and all other electronic media—on their lives, culture, and thinking, that we are doomed to a society in which people no longer know how to think:

> **[T]here has been no worthwhile discussion, let alone widespread public understanding, of what information is and how it gives direction to a culture. . . . What is information? . . . What are its various forms? What conceptions of intelligence, wisdom and learning does each form insist upon? What conceptions does each form neglect or mock? What are the main psychic effects of each form? What is the relation between information and reason? What is the kind of information that best facilitates thinking? Is there a moral bias to each information form? . . . Does television, for example, give new meaning to "piety," to "patriotism," to "privacy?"** (p. 160)

Richardson's and Postman's arguments add additional fuel to the fires already raging about the teaching of values in the schools, but at the same time they call for a rational and critical approach to the valuing of information as presented in any medium. The message to students is this: Don't stop thinking for yourself, being cognizant of the influences on you, and the goals of those promoting particular points of view. Analytical thinking about media and values can be accomplished in schools; according to many it *must* be accomplished in schools. George Wood, coordinator of the Institute for Democracy in Education at Ohio University, Athens, said "schools cannot be value-neutral" and he supported that claim by providing guidance and opportunity for teachers to experiment with curriculum and styles of teaching that help students to make choices and to think for themselves. (Wood, 1988)

Textbooks will continue to play a role in the classroom or media center, but in our information era of disposable facts and quickly outdated materials, textbooks of the near future will best serve as softbound/data-disk volumes that are compendia of thoughtfully juxtaposed issues, *anthologies of possibility*, that take advantage of the power of television and video as ready-made "teachers" of positive and negative values. These future, paperless textbooks ought not to be thought of so much as inculcators of values, but as presenters of issues.

Textbooks will become, and probably should be no more than, one of a number of resources for the formulation of attitudes, opinions, and values. In the context of schooling, teachers, peers, guest speakers, magazines, newspapers, information networks, and other sources will be increasingly more viable resources for information and values formation. It is likely that the schools not only will supply the textbooks and information for the formulation of values, but also will be called upon to provide ever more compassionate and caring environments for the practice of those values—environments like the two classrooms described in the first two chapters of this book.

Textbooks and the school environment must meet the challenge of an ever more harsh cultural climate for children outside the schoolroom.

## The Broader Context for Values Education

A brief look at the demographic trends in the status of children today (U.S. Bureau of the Census, 1988) shows that in 1987 there were over two million reported cases of maltreatment of children, and the trend was upward; 20% of children were living below the poverty level, and the trend was upward; in 1987, it was predicted that 50% of children would experience divorce in the family by age eighteen, and the trend was upward. Poverty, family instability, and violence against children are increasing such that schools will need to take on the additional responsibilities of providing not only the education, counseling, and nutrition programs now available in some schools but also of fostering environments of care and nurture that become havens for the development of positive values away from an increasingly chaotic world.

Even for those families that do not suffer from violence, poverty, and instability, social factors mitigate against the development of a lived and consciously demonstrated positive values structure in the home. For example, trends in social factors (U.S. Department of Labor, 1987) indicated that the average American reads only one book in his/her lifetime after formal schooling, whereas the average American family has the television on seven hours a day, and the most-read publication is *T.V. Guide*.

Even though families are working more, watching more television, and spending less "quality" time in which positive values could be taught, parents apparently do want straightforward values teaching to occur at school. A 1992 Gallup poll for Phi Delta Kappa showed that "developing standards of what is *right* and *wrong* " was second only to the number-one goal of "developing the ability to speak and write correctly" in a list of twenty-five educational goals ranked by parents. (Elam, et al., 1992) In the 1993 poll (Elam, et al., 1993), the Kappan/Gallup pollsters asked more direct questions related to attitudes about values teaching in public schools. In answer to those questions, over 90% of those polled said that *honesty, democracy, acceptance of people of different race or ethnic backgrounds, patriotism and love of country, care for friends and family members*, and *moral courage* should be taught in public schools. (p. 145)

Schools around the country are attempting to meet the challenge by direct teaching. According to an article in the *Wall Street Journal*, the schools in Clovis, California are committed to "an unrelenting drive to create people who know the difference between right and wrong." (Nazario, 1992) Studies at schools where values education is in full swing report successes:

> **Major disciplinary problems have dropped 25% in some Los Angeles schools, for instance, after one year of using the Jefferson Center for**

Character Education's 10-minute daily values lessons. Another study, by Jacques S. Benninga, an education professor at California State University, Fresno, tracked the effects of Clovis's efforts over four elementary school years; children registered significant improvements in helpfulness and cooperation, and ranked higher in these areas than control groups. (Nazario, 1992, p. B6)

Because of the current interest in teaching values in schools, we seem to have come full circle over the years of our country's history: from the direct teaching of Victorian values in the 1800s to the increasingly values-neutral stance of the mid-1900s to the current belief at the end of the twentieth century that values must be *taught* to secure the stability of society. We cannot merely return to where we were one hundred and fifty years ago. The context of values has changed too drastically.

Fig. 7.1 shows the evolving context for values education, past, present, and future. An extrapolation of my conclusions about the teaching of values, the chart suggests an interpretation of the data, the literature, and the current studies of values teaching. The word "context" in the title frames the various facets of culture and education that impact on the teaching of values. "Past," "present," and "future" are general terms that encompass roughly a two-hundred-year span, 1800–2000.

## Fig. 7.1 *The Evolving Context for Values Education*

| Past (nineteenth Century) | Present (twentieth Century) | Future (twenty-first Century) |
|---|---|---|
| **Culture** | | |
| 1. Monocultural | 1. Monocultural/ Multicultural | 1. Multicultural/ Metacultural |
| **Economics** | | |
| 2. Agrarian era/ Pre-industrial | 2. Industrial era/ Information era | 2. Information era |
| **Guiding principle** | | |
| 3. Religion/ Americanization | 3. First Amendment/ The American Way | 3. First Amendment/ Global Responsibility |
| **Broad Goal of Education** | | |
| 4. Education for Americanization | 4. Education for cooperation | 4. Education for compassion |

# Context: A Call for Metaculturalism

"Culture," the first subhead in Figure 7.1, relates to the ethnic and racial make-up of the United States. The data—the historical and statistical studies described in chapters four and five and the literature cited—indicate that we have moved from a relatively simple bi-cultural society (Northern European and Native American) to our present-day complex multicultural diversity. Based on our current emphasis on "appreciation of difference," I predict that we will move toward a **metaculturalism** by the end of this century, i.e., a perspective that embraces the appreciation of one's own culture as well as the cultural uniqueness of other groups, and involves one in active learning and exchange. *Tolerance*, as a preferred mind set, has served us as a necessary step in the movement toward a just and compassionate society, but not well enough to prepare for the demands of the future. Tolerance implies a grudging, arms-length acceptance of those who do not fit our preconceived notions of the "right" class, ethnicity, gender, or other differentiating characteristics. Even *acceptance* leaves much moral ground uncovered and room for the kind of connected learning required in our shrinking global village. We will move beyond parallel cultures to a metaculturalism—an open-minded, open-eyed, open-hearted perspective in which we strive for an all-embracing regard for one's brother and sister human beings as essentially politically and socially equal in all respects that matter. We will come to view "differences" as an opportunity to learn, to outgrow outmoded thinking that is not useful to the goals of a compassionate and democratic society.

Multiculturalism is a stress on the differences in the manifestations of belief, of behavioral mores, of culture. Metaculturalism is an emphasis on the essential unity of our common humanity—it transcends multiculturalism. An act of coming to respect and learn from another's belief system is an adaptive metacultural event that need not threaten, but does enlighten. Thoughtfully adapting one's belief system to others against a backdrop of a values that lead to a compassionate, just, and democratic society, will bring America to a more thorough sense of democracy than we have had for the past two hundred years.

## Economics: The Information Age

The second subheading in Figure 7.1 is *Economics*. The United States was founded in a pre-industrial, agrarian era in which a slower pace of life and a family structure bounded by the economic interdependence of family members dominated. The industrial era of the 1800s and early 1900s witnessed the disintegration of farm life and a movement to "Americanize" the burgeoning immigrant population. The historical study in chapter four bears witness to the impact of the changing economic scene on the values taught in textbooks. Now, at the end of the twentieth century, we are moving into an even faster-paced information era, in which the role of textbooks as arbiters and inculcators of values may be waning, even as the influence of the nuclear family has declined.

## The Guiding Principle for Values Education

The founders of America established our laws and form of government on English common law, which in turn was influenced partly by the moral and ethical principles of Judeo-Christian religious tradition. The third subheading in Figure 7.1 shows the guiding principles of past, present, and future American culture. In most of the examples from textbooks from the late 1700s and early 1800s, the "American Way" was synonymous with the moral values taught in Judaism and Christianity as understood by Protestants from the British Isles. As the culture of the country became more diverse, we looked to the First Amendment of the Constitution as a guiding principle to mediate among conflicting religious ideologies. The text authors of the 1800s and early 1900s turned from Biblical precepts to the lives of military and political heroes for the teaching of values. As authors of textbooks and other instructional materials now turn to Hollywood and television as sources of values and concerns in an age of global responsibility, a great deal of work in values consensus and inquiry curriculum will have to be done.

The time is right for this pursuit. *Newsweek* magazine of June 8, 1992 reported that all around the country, schools were again in the business of teaching values: Morris Dees of the Southern Povery Law Center directs a project that instructs teachers on how to promote racial harmony among school children; "Educators for Social Responsibility" in Cambridge, Massachusetts, promotes community service as a prerequisite for high-school graduation; in Atlanta, students must perform seventy-five hours of service at places like hospitals and shelters before they graduate; schools in Brookline, Massachusetts have a program called "Facing History and Ourselves" which helps students to examine racism, prejudice, and anti-semitism in the twentieth century; the Institute of Global Ethics in Camden, Maine, has recently produced a videotape for use in high schools: *Personal Ethics and the Future of the World*; "Just Community" experiments in public schools, and inquiry curriculum are additional examples of this change in values orientation in school materials and requirements.

## The Broad Goal of Education

In view of our metacultural environment and our renewed sense for the value of values orientation, what is the purpose of education? The fourth subheading of Figure 7.1 shows the change in the goals of education throughout our country's history. In order to establish the United States as a separate entity in the global family of nations, education for Americanization became a necessary goal. The textbooks on our early history reflect that emphasis. As our country has become more ethnically and culturally diverse, however, we have seen the evidence that textbooks have been written to embody values that lead to "cooperation," "teamwork," "friendliness," and "courtesy"—the desire for cultural values that promote a frictionless society.

Critics of our educational system have been warning us for years that the primary function of literacy in capitalist societies is to increase the number of consumers and the quantity of consumption. (Freire, 1970; Illich, 1971; Giroux, 1991) Our history bears witness to this interpretation of our education goals. In the nineteenth century, as we moved from an agrarian to an industrial era, mass production and marketing spawned an age of increasingly mindless consumerism. Early in the twentieth century, a factory model of schooling—hierarchical, technocratic, and piecemeal—followed suit. Now, late in the century, the same wealth and technical expertise that has brought about the information age and given us a cultural and economic instant replay, whereby we can export the effects of our consumerism and our standard of living to the rest of the planet, will give us another new approach to education. Values education in light of this rapidly changing social and economic environment must be an ever more accessible conversation about individual and global responsibility.

The goals of education in the broadest sense must evolve in order to keep pace with moral and social challenges. If inquiry curriculum as described and reported above in chapters one and two are an indication of future goals of education (and I hope they are), one of the goals of future education will be "education for compassion." Education for compassion is neither a passive religiosity nor a bleeding-heart political liberalism, but rather a compassionate willingness to strive for global understanding; work for equality of gender, culture, and race; and to use one's individuality for the common good.

We are no longer battling, as we did two hundred years ago, for survival as a nation. Our goal in this century has become "the good life." That quest for the good life among the industrialized and high-tech nations has led to environmental, economic, and social problems in other parts of the world. Pressing social, economic, and environmental needs will demand a future in which all humanity must aspire to "the responsible life." In this country, need dictates a democracy predicated on equal parts freedom and responsibility. Whatever becomes of home life —"family units" are reconstructed year by year and many children are left homeless—or happens to the organized religion—formal worship is very important to many citizens but meaningless to others—the schools will survive as the places where we study and practice our highest sense of right-doing, right-dealing, respect, and discipline.

Teachers and students in classrooms around the country are embarking on a curricular adventure that will usher in a new era of values teaching. The living classroom provides a more comprehensive unit of analysis for research on values teaching than does the inactive textbook. Chapters one and two are varieties of a learning process that has been described in many ways: "inquiry approach," "process approach to reading and writing," "issues approach," "theme cycling," "projects approach," and the "Foxfire approach." The essence of this style of education is that the student's own voices are heard, their choices honored, their collaborative partnerships encouraged, their interests pursued and not the teachers' or the parents' only. This perspective is a curricular statement that educators care about the people being educated.

## The Classroom as a Context for Values Teaching

*How are we to bring children to the spirit of democracy and humanity which is postulated by democratic societies? By the actual practice of democracy at school. It is unbelievable that at a time when democratic ideas enter into every phase of life, they should have been so little utilized as instruments of education.*

Jean Piaget (1965): 366.

*To the degree that classroom learning requires of children that they conform to what others say is important, learn it in ways that others say is the way to learn, and separate this learning from all other contexts of experience and learning that children bring to school, the school then is remarkably and predictably effective in getting children to regard the classroom as an uninteresting place. . . . It does not produce citizens who desire to continue individual growth.*

Seymour Sarason (1991): 88.

The classroom described by Sarason's remarks is not only an uninteresting place, but also it violates all of the underlying principles of democracy. That classroom lacks the choice, engagement, and reciprocal teaching/learning relationships that make Piaget's ideal classroom fertile ground for the development of moral values. Unfortunately, most of our classrooms look much as they did 100 years ago. (See Cuban [1984, 1986] and Mayher and Brause [1986].) Not only do the materials, methods, and the sense of isolation from the rest of the world continue to separate what goes on in schools from meaningful learning, but also the materials and methods we use often deprive students of valuable learning. Education is more than going through the motions of sorting and deciphering the small fraction of all possible facts and perspectives that fill our textbooks. Neither traditional values teaching nor in-depth studies are functions of today's textbooks. What are some alternatives to teaching values in the classroom today?

## Approaches to Teaching Values

Across the spectrum of values, from traditional to futuristic, and the methods used to teach them, from incidental discussion to packaged programs, we can organize the typical instructional approaches under two headings: the "process" and the "product" approaches to values education. The results from the historical and statistical study suggest that traditional moral values were taught in the textbooks one hundred years ago and that the home and place of worship reinforced those values: a didactic, product approach. Today, because the teaching of traditional moral values has declined to a smaller percentage of the selections in students' readers, and is accomplished in more subtle ways, efforts are afoot to return to the more didactic teaching of moral values through product approaches, e. g., the recent popularity of the McGuffey readers. The product is the outcome, namely, the inculcation or learning of particular values.

### A Product Approach: Core Values through Direct Teaching

Some researchers and theorists in moral education refer to the specific products or outcomes of values education as "fixed" values, "core" values, or "moral basics." They believe that a consensus prevails about central values, such as "respect" and "responsibility" "that can be conveyed to children without hesitation." (Pritchard, 1988) Goble & Brooks (1983) site group such as the American Institute for Character Education, that developed the *Character Education Curriculum* based on values gleaned from a worldwide study of values systems. In this study, fifteen basic values were identified as shared by all major cultures and world religions: **courage, conviction, generosity, kindness, helpfulness, honesty, honor, justice, tolerance, sound use of time and talents, freedom of choice, freedom of speech, good citizenship, the right to be an individual, and the right of equal opportunity.** (p. 88) This collection hardly seems "international" when one considers that few countries in the world have operating democracies that promote values such as "tolerance" and "freedom of speech." *Amnesty International* might report quite the opposite opinion about the widespread acceptance of these democratic values in the numerous repressive societies which it monitors. The "right to be an individual" is directly contrary to the cultural value of "tradition" in many parts of the world. International or not, these are American democratic values. This American Institute seems to have read these American democratic values into more cultures than one can objectively say they represent.

Goble and Brooks further cite twelve values embodied in a code of behavior developed by the Thomas Jefferson Research Center which "when properly defined, understood, and practiced, can lead to health, happiness, and success for the individual and society." (p. 89) Those values are **wisdom, integrity, love, freedom, justice, courage, humility, patience, industriousness, thriftiness, generosity, objectivity, cooperation, moderation, optimism.** (p. 90) With the exception of "objectivity," this list sounds much like the "top twenty-five" values found in basal readers of one hundred years ago.

The Association for Supervision and Curriculum Development (ASCD) convened a panel on moral education that submitted six major characteristics of the morally mature person, which, panel members believed, derive from universal moral principles. (ASCD Panel on Moral Education, 1988) A moral person would, according to ASCD, **respect human dignity, integrate individual interests and social responsibilities, demonstrate integrity, reflect on moral choices, and seek peaceful resolution of conflict.** (p. 5)

As compelling as the notion of teaching these virtues is to many individuals and groups, critics of character education find fault with lists of character traits like these, as did Lockwood (1991): "The major problem with lists is that they do not provide such clear guidelines for behavior as many character educators would lead us to believe." (p. 257) However, some school projects have at least moved from "lists" of virtues to open discussion of those virtues in classrooms. For example, Kuhmerker (1992) reported on the Heartwood Project developed for public-school elementary students in Pittsburgh. In this program, classic children's stories from around the world were categorized according to seven universal values: **courage, loyalty, justice, respect, hope, honesty,** and **love.** The program's activity cards developed for classroom use give suggestions for defining the virtues and "implementing" them. Many teachers and researchers, however, have been less than enthusiastic about this "prepackaged" approach to teaching values. They advocate, instead, a "process" approach.

## A Process Approach: The Classroom as a Context for Values Clarification

Opponents of moral education based on some set of fixed or core values are believers in the *process* of coming to know one's values—values clarification. Process educators believe that the fundamental error of traditional approaches to values education cited above is that it results in *indoctrination*; none of us, they argue, has the only "right" set of values to pass on to other people's children. The values clarification movement in education in the '60s and '70s was predicated on the belief that values were totally relative to culture and personal preference. That being the case, no set of values could be taught or promoted without offending someone. In this approach, therefore, the teacher was to promote growth, freedom, and ethical maturity, beginning with the recognition that there is no right or wrong answer to any question of values. Textbooks of that era were systematically stripped of references to church, God, marriage, and the role of religion in history or current events. (See Apple & Christian-Smith [1991], Flinders [1986], Lystad [1980], Schmidt [1983], and Tyson-Bernstein [1988].)

Kohlberg (1971), although he subscribed to a process approach, rejected the values-clarification approach as being too relativistic and unlikely to result in justice. He was interested in moral development that would result in justice for all people. He believed that human beings progress through stages of moral development, and that it is much more important to emphasize *how* children and adults understand and justify the values they hold, than it is to develop lists of values to inculcate. According to his research, Kohlberg concluded that all people progress through the following stages of moral development:

**Stage 1. Moral action is motivated by avoidance of punishment, and by "conscience" in a nonrational fear of punishment.**

**Stage 2. Moral action is motivated by desire for reward or benefit. Possible guilt reactions are ignored, and punishment is viewed in a pragmatic manner.**

**Stage 3. Moral action is motivated by anticipation of disapproval of others, actual or imagined or hypothetical.**

**Stage 4. Moral action is motivated by anticipation of dishonor, that is, institutionalized blame for failure of duty, and by guilt over concrete harm done to others.**

**Stage 5. Moral action is motivated by concern about maintaining respect of equals and of the community (assuming their respect is based on reason rather than emotions).**

**Stage 6. Moral action is motivated by concern about self-condemnation for violating one's own principles.** (Kohlberg, 1971)

Kohlberg believed that children cannot develop moral insight if they are not given choices and opportunities for dialogue on issues that are meaningful and difficult. He demonstrated that the progression through the stages of development can be supported by classroom processes for stimulating moral judgment in children, in combination with the more direct character-education approach. (Kohlberg, 1976)

I interpret Kohlberg to have meant that without choices in the classroom and the opportunity to discuss the dilemmas inherent in any problem-solving approach to controversy, children cannot connect first-hand experience with the *meaning* of trust, the *purpose* of honor, the *usefulness* of loyalty; hence, the values remain only "passed-down," second-hand, whether from parents, peers, larger society, or the teacher.

## An Integrated Approach: The Classroom as a Moral Community

The classroom can become a moral community, one in which children in their moral development can be sustained and facilitated through an integrated approach to values enquiry. The classroom process itself can embody elements both of core values teaching (product) and moral development (process). Aspects of both approaches are essential for education in a democratic society.

If we accept prepackaged programs aimed at transmitting lists of moral basics, we then are in danger of a narrow parochialism. If we accept the sociological definition of values and a values-clarification approach, then values are nothing more than the customs of particular groups, and there is no core of consistent and worthy values to be transmitted. What approach to values education, what instructional method, is consistent with the principles of an ideally just and democratic society? What curriculum and method are appropriate for purposes of educating students to take their place among a just and compassionate citizenry?

Even despite hearty and heartfelt disagreement over the idea of teaching "core values," can any thinking person believe that there are no core values inherent in human beings? We share common moral ground by virtue of the very fact that we are human: whatever is good for humans is a human good; therefore, it is moral. Rushworth Kidder (1993), President of the Institute for Global Ethics was, at the time of this writing, developing a book on global ethics. On his research for this book, he reported:

> **[A]gain and again is this century, America and the world have stumbled over ethical relativism. All ethics, we have been told, is merely situational. All moral values are culturally determined, constantly up for grabs, and wholly subjective. So (it has been asserted) ethics is a mere plaything for the cultural elite, a luxury with no bearing on the "real" world. Teachable? Not at all, says this view: After all, whose values would you dare to teach, since each person has his or her own?**

> **Put that question to wise people around the world—ask them whether moral values are merely relative—and you nearly get laughed out of town. *Of course*, they say, there is a handful of moral precepts we all share—not because we're born into this or that culture, or hold this or that political view, but because we're human.** (p. 3)

Kidder put this question to "ethical thinkers and actors" (as judged by their peers) around the world: *If there could be a global code of ethics for the twenty-first century, what would be on it?* He asked Muslims, Buddhists, and Christians, men and women, liberals and conservatives. Of these interviews, he wrote as follows:

> **From the scores of moral values mentioned in these interviews, eight of them came up so consistently that they surely belong on anyone's list of global core values:**

> - **love (caring or compassion)**
> - **truth (honesty or integrity)**

- **freedom (liberty)**
- **fairness (justice or equity)**
- **unity (a sense of community or wholeness)**
- **tolerance (respect for diversity)**
- **responsibility (accountability)**
- **respect for life (avoidance of killing)** (p. 3)

Even if one cannot concur with this list in every detail, e. g., Muslim societies may have some difficulty with respect for diversity, I proceed, nevertheless, with the following assumption: *There is a near-core of values worthy of investigation and pragmatic adoption by the young, those values that can be interpreted as leading to a just, democratic, and caring society.*

If, then, there is a near-core of human values worthy to be taught to students, what instructional methodology best promotes context or strategies for this moral instruction? Many researchers and educational theorists have responded to this question. John Dewey (1966) believed that America could not survive simply by perpetuating its institutions, but that democracy is a moral ideal that depends on particular values and specific modes of education. He was critical of teachers who equipped students with mental crutches that kept them from having to think for themselves or to form critical judgments. (p. 339) Jean Piaget (1965) also believed that blind obedience to the authority and will of the teacher stultified intellectual and moral development, and that peer relations, more than teacher intervention, fostered mutual respect and rule-governed behavior. Both Dewey and Piaget saw students—even young ones—as collaborators in their own moral development. Collaboration implies a change in teaching methods from mere transmission of information to joint research and exploration in the classroom.

Specific values are best taught not in the abstract or apart from a demonstration of values, but by following a method that enhances content through posing moral dilemmas, matters of import, hot issues, and controversies. The instructional successes enjoyed by the sixth-grade class and the third-grade class described in chapters one and two, were due largely to the implementation of these collaborative measures. Methodology must embody choice, decision making, and reflection. Students cannot develop morally and be prepared for active democratic citizenship through authoritarian and undemocratic methods.

One might ask, how did the undemocratic teaching practices of the eighteenth and nineteenth centuries produce a democratic America? I concede that those teaching practices have delivered a version of democracy that served frontier America with its ever-expanding borders and seemingly endless land and dreams of wealth for all. Values of the free-enterprise market place—discipline, order, punctuality, obedience—

have, similarly, undergirded our notions of democracy; however, the values that have little to do with either the frontier or the free market—justice, compassion, fair play, and equality—will be needed to ensure a future society worth living in. The authoritarian teaching mode that supported earlier values must make way for parallel and alternative teaching modes that support even more democratic values. The student as collaborative learner, critical thinker, and decision maker is the future citizen who needs practice in newer ideals of democratic society—a manifest destiny of justice and compassion. I agree with Lickona (1991), who believed that schools should offer a setting for this decision-making:

> **Children will need lots of practice at being moral persons: many opportunities to solve problems, act upon their best moral reasoning, be in social roles that give them real social responsibilities, and otherwise participate in a moral community. . . . The character development goals**
> **. . . may be pursued through four classroom processes:**
>
> 1. **Building self-worth and moral community**
> 2. **Cooperative learning**
> 3. **Moral reflection**
> 4. **Participatory decision making** (p. 68)

I would add a further component, mentioned by Nel Noddings (1992): essential to the concept of the classroom as a moral comunity is **caring**. The integrated approach to values teaching that provides processes and discussion of desired values and caring was demonstrated in chapters one and two. How to build a curriculum that incorporates an integrated approach is outlined below.

# The Values-Centered Classroom: Building the Curriculum

I agree with Seymour Sarason (1991) that "we need an extremely well trained capacity for inquiry." Because of the need to learn about, and deal with, the complex issues facing our world, goals of the issues/choice-centered curriculum are different from the traditional one. The differences in goals are reflected in the components of the approaches. In the following comparison chart, I briefly outline the major differences.

**Traditional Curriculum**

1. Answer centered
2. Assessment by tests
3. Past/present oriented

**Inquiry/Issues Curriculum**

1. Problem centered
2. Assessment through projects
3. Present/future oriented

| 4. Product oriented | 4. Process oriented |
| 5. Textbook focus | 5. Multiple resources/many foci |
| 6. Preselected content/goals | 6. Participant-developed goals |
| 7. Mono/multicultural | 7. Multi/metacultural |

These comparisons do not require much explanation, but the structure of inquiry curriculum does. *I define inquiry curriculum as a discovery and research process engendered by a group of students and a teacher in a specifically caring relation to each other for purposes of understanding themselves, their roles, and their responsibilities towards other human beings and the planet.* Inquiry curriculum is not a set of steps to be followed; it is a moral enterprise to be worked through by using dialogue and a problem-posing pursuit of real questions to define what the learners want to find out about. These questions may be undetermined at the beginning of the process and span many subject areas of the traditional curriculum.

The subjects we now call science, reading, art, history, math, and social studies need to be viewed as perspectives on the world of information to be used for the development of issues in an inquiry project. For example, to ask the question, "What was the Civil War like for families as portrayed in fictional novels?" is to take an across-the-curriculum sociological and literary perspective on an historical event, in contrast to traditional curricular segregation according to which students read a chapter in social-studies class on the Civil War, then read a novel in reading class, but no one ever poses the question that would help make useful connections. Even if the novel is related to the social-studies unit, a bridge between the two learning experiences is typically never built except perhaps in the minds of a few exceptionally bright students.

A number of educational theorists and practitioners have reported highly effective interdisciplinary inquiry projects with students, but most of them fail to make the connection of this method to the teaching of values. When I began to study the values in old and new textbooks, I realized that a gaping hole exists in the traditional curriculum that separates the teaching of values from the content of the curriculum. Inquiry projects can fill this need. In today's traditional classrooms, where textbooks are almost the only curriculum, very little in the way of values will be taught except for the values that are embedded in the textbooks. Undoubtedly, many good teachers demonstrate their personal values by way of example: honesty, care, and compassion in their dealings with students; thereby, good teachers promote a sound moral atmosphere in the classroom. Moreover, students and teachers sometimes allow themselves to get off the prescribed topics long enough to hold an interesting conversation. The issues, controversies, and life-problems that would be the meat of a concerted, collaborative, reflective analysis of right and wrong in an inquiry curriculum, however, find no proper forum in most classrooms. The following chart shows the relationship of inquiry curriculum to values.

## Fig. 7.2 *Values and Inquiry Curriculum*

| Phases in Inquiry Curriculum | Processes | Values Demonstrated |
|---|---|---|
| Generation of Topic<br>*What shall we do?* | Brainstorming/group processes/dialogue | Group problem solving<br>Teamwork |
| Semantic Web (schema)<br>*What do we already know?* | Brainstorming/group processes/dialogue | Consideration/Turn taking<br>Teamwork |
| Research Questions/Controversies<br>*What do we want to know?*<br>*What are the possibilities we could know?* | Operationalizing curiosity | Understanding, respect of group & self interests, independence, individuality |
| Methodology/Resources<br>*Where dowe search, whom do we ask?*<br>*How do we search for new knowledge?* | Group Inquiry<br>Individual Inquiry | Mutual support, compromise, shared decision making, interpersonal reasoning |
| Organization<br>*How do we make sense of new knowledge*<br>*which we have discovered, constructed?* | Process Reading/Writing<br>Problem Solving<br>Critical Thinking | Mutual support, compromise shared decision making, interpersonal reasoning, perseverance |
| Demonstration<br>*How do we share new knowledge*<br>*(skills, affect)?* | Critical Thinking | Courage, respect, understanding, initiative achievement |
| Evaluation (self, peer, teacher)<br>*How do I know **that** I know & **what** I know?* | Critical Thinking | Compassion, honesty reasoning, tolerance, respect |
| Application and Transfer<br>*How do we apply what we have learned to*<br>*our lives, our community, the world?* | Social/Civic Action | Compassion, unselfishness justice, initiative, work ethic, empathy, peacemaking, relationality |

The processes of an inquiry curriculum structure a context in which values can be explored, demonstrated, discovered, and lived. Obviously, not all possible values are listed in Fig. 7.2; however, the "AIDS Project" with sixth graders in chapter one and the "Homelessness Study" with third graders in chapter two, make us realize that many unpredicted values surface as a result of the process and are reinforced through the process. "Gratitude" as a quality of thought in the third graders was unscheduled but nonetheless stimulated through their study of homelessness. Appreciation of their homes and families was highlighted. "Compassion" as a quality of thought in the sixth graders was stimulated through their study of AIDS. Understanding of the plight of victims was evident in their work.

Children and their teachers, more than theorists and ideologues, have led me to my current beliefs about the classroom contexts necessary for the teaching of values in today's schools. The following scenario gives an additional glimpse into a context of caring:

The fifth graders in a small rural school in southern Indiana decided to study handicapping conditions. Each team of children in the class focused on a specific condition: deafness, blindness, conditions that confine people to wheelchairs, retardation, and others. One team of five boys who studied physical handicaps was interviewed shortly after the study was completed.

*Interviewer: What did you learn during your theme cycle on handicaps?*
*Andy: We learned that all buildings have to be handicap accessible. We learned that handicapped people can do many things we can do. We learned that all public swimming pools being built now have to have ramps or lifts. We built up our courage to call [State Senator] Frank McCloskey. That's how we learned about the building codes.*
*Jason: Then we got a wheelchair from the school nurse and tried to get around the school in it. We found out how hard it is to get around this school. Out of the five boys' bathrooms in the school, only one is accessible—the one by the principal's office. In the first-grade hall, the sinks are only 24" tall, but they have to be 36" high to accommodate a wheelchair. We made a video of us trying to come in the front door without help. You know, a lot of handicapped people want to get around by themselves. Coming in the door in the wheelchair is really hard. There's a bump there and you get stuck. Also, the ramp coming in is steep and if you put on the brakes, the chair spins.*

*Interviewer: Where did you get all of your information?*
*John: We got most of our information about the school by taking the wheelchair all over the school and making the videotape ourselves. The librarian was real helpful. We learned to use the CD ROM, and also they FAXed us stuff from the main library where my mom works.*

*Interviewer: Did you learn anything from your teacher?*
*Andy: Well, not really. Well, she did tell us where to go to find the information, but she didn't know a lot of this information. We learned it from experts we called, from the books in the library, and from doing projects ourselves, like taking the wheelchair around the school. We also learned a lot from the school nurse.*

*Interviewer: Did you learn anything about what it's like to be handicapped?*

*Andy: I learned it's a lot harder than people think to get around in a wheelchair. I thought before, "Oh, this will be a piece of cake," but it's not. It's hard.*
*Jason: See, my dad's a contractor. And so is Andy's. And John's dad is a plumber. We know this guy who had an accident on a tractor and lost both legs. John's dad*

*fixed all the plumbing in their house so it was accessible to a wheelchair. My dad fixed all the counter tops. Now he's really independent. He can do more for himself.*
**Andy:** *We called about the new pool they are putting in here in town. They told us they were putting in a walkway and a handicap ramp. But our school nurse went out there and she said there's no handicapped parking and she didn't see any ramp or walkway. So we don't know if they're just telling us a story. We're going to check again.*

Doug and Randy in this same fifth-grade class learned about coping with deafness. I asked them what they learned personally from studying about this topic.

**Randy:** *I learned that you should think more about handicapped people. I used to not think about them at all. As a matter of fact, I used to make fun of them. Now I don't do anything like that any more.*
**Doug:** *I used to think deaf people were kind of stupid . . . .*
**Randy:** *I did too.*
**Doug:** *[B]ut when we did this theme cycle, I learned that they aren't stupid, they're just deaf.*
**Randy:** *I think deaf people can make real good friends, too. When Matt [deaf visitor who with his interpreter demonstrated American Sign Language] showed us how to use his language, it was great. We could hear him making noises as he signed to us . . . . I have a deaf uncle. I used to think he was a nut. I used to think he was real weird because he makes these real weird sounds. Now I know what he's doing. One time at Thanksgiving we were all sitting around the table, just sitting there. He signed to my aunt and answered a question that one of us asked. He read our lips.*

As the interviewer of this group of children, I was moved by their concern, their serious attitude, their commitment to their learning, and their maturity in pursuing information, synthesizing, and organizing it. These children and many others have helped me recognize the power of choice, interest, and the investigation of meaningful social issues for the negotiating of positive social and personal values. The reactions of teachers and children to an inquiry-curriculum format/project, as demonstrated in chapters one and two and glimpsed in this scenario, have touched me more than any teaching/learning setting I have ever experienced. There is a connection—a personal, caring connection—among those who work together in these projects that calls forth ethical feelings of compassion for others, which one can describe only as humanly moral.

This fifth-grade scenario shows a successful working partnership among all the major stakeholders in values education: a State Senator responded to the children's questions about laws related to their topic of study. The teacher set up a limited school democracy in her classroom so that children could pursue their own questions, make decisions, and build their knowledge base. (Her effort to give the students ownership of the curriculum was so successful that in response to the question, "Did you learn anything from your teacher?" They answered, "No, not really. She told us where to find the information and we found it ourselves.") Parents contributed to helping their children find information, and they demonstrated their own concern and compassion for the handicapped. The relationships among these stakeholders—the State, the teacher, the parents, and the students—are sometimes uneven. Finding balance and maintaining joint ownership of the educational enterprise deserves more time and effort than we have given it.

# 8 Stakeholders in Values Teaching

The various stakeholders in values teaching in schools are all legally bound to participate in some way in the common educational enterprise: the state, teachers, parents, and students.

**THE STATE**
**(upholder of democratic principles)**

- Teacher Education
- Curriculum Guides
- Textbook Adoption Committees
- Staff Development Workshops

**THE TEACHER**
**(facilitator and guide)**

- Read-Alouds
- Basals
- Literature Circles
- Theme Cycles

**THE PARENT**
**(nurturer, educator, exemplar)**

- Book Sharing
- PTA Library Funding
- School Steering Committees
- Mediator of Values Sources

**THE CHILD**
**(active constructor of values)**

- Self-selected Reading Material
- Individualized Reading
- Internalized and applied values

## The State: Upholder of Democratic Principles

> **And when the harvests from the fields, and the cattle from the hills, and the ores from the earth shall have been weighed, counted, and valued, we will turn from them all to crown with the highest honor the State that has promoted education, virtue, justice, and patriotism among its people.** (Howe Readers, *Fifth Book*, 1909, p. 309)

Public officials have often looked to the schools for the promotion of morality. From a 1647 Massachusetts law promoting schooling and attesting that "evil feeds on ignorance," to the latest Supreme Court decision, the state has drawn an intimate connection between liberty and virtue. In *West Virginia State Board of Education v. Barnette* (1943), the Supreme Court ruled that public schools are allowed to teach particular values essential to an orderly school environment. In *Amback v. Norwick* (1979), the Court affirmed that schools have a role in promoting values necessary to a democratic political system. In 1982, in *Board of Education v. Pico*, the Court held that "there is legitimate and substantial community interest in promoting respect for authority and traditional values, be they social, moral, or political (cited in Born [1993]). The Supreme Court has affirmed the schools' rights and responsibilities to inculcate the values that uphold democracy.

State textbook adoptions committees, Departments of Education, and local school boards also play a role in determining the kinds of values taught through their choices of books to be used in schools and in curriculum goals and objectives to be followed. Teachers are expected to use those materials and guidelines to impart values that further the democratic system in which we operate, and children are expected to attend school and participate in a curriculum that imparts those state-supported democratic values.

Although the state has always expected teachers to impart democratic values, children to attend school and learn those values, and schools to promote morality, it has in general protected students from indoctrination into particular *religious* beliefs. The most basic protection is found in the First Amendment to the United States Constitution:

> **Congress shall make no law respecting an establishment of religion, or prohibiting the free exercise thereof; or abridging the freedom of speech, or of the press; or the right of the people peaceably to assemble, and to petition the government for a redress of grievances.**

After two hundred years, the basic fairness and balance of the First Amendment remains compelling. A great deal of case law has accumulated regarding children's First-Amendment rights, and it seems unlikely that an adherence to the principles of protection of children's intellectual rights will diminish. According to American law, school children are free to explore any idea, but they are protected from specific indoctrination other than that of the principles of democracy.

## Teachers: Facilitators and Guides

Teachers are agents of the state and, therefore, part of their role is to inculcate the values held to be worthy by the state: In America, this means upholding the democratic values that underlie notions of choice, freedom, responsibility, equality, and constitutional justice. Teachers' interpretations of this charge vary considerably; they have

Teaching Kids to Care

some latitude in their give-and-take with parents and local communities that allows them to interpret traditional values to students in the context of the school setting. Some teachers assume that they have discharged their duty to teach democratic processes when they have led a discussion of the social-studies textbook chapter on "American Government: Its Origins and Operation Today." Other teachers sense that their duty has not been discharged unless they "live" those processes in the classroom by maintaining an environment in which students make actual choices about classroom government, rules, processes, and topics of study. Teachers such as Jean and Shelli represent the latter view. Their classrooms, described in chapters one and two, are school settings in which the teachers value the experiencing of democratic processes at school.

Something of the human, moral, and spiritual nature of the human being is brought to bear upon the common, daily life of classrooms when students' individual knowledges, skills, and social attitudes ripen through work with a compassionate teacher. She sets a tone of respect, teaches strategies for reasonable communication, mediates conflict, and becomes a resource person for the investigation of issues that are important to the students and the community. This sense of limited school democracy allows for the emergence of other values. In order for the teacher to set this kind of curriculum in motion, there must be relationships of trust established with other stakeholders in the school setting.

I interviewed several parents whose children participated in the AIDS project described in chapter one. My first question to them was, "What was your reaction when you received Jean's letter saying that the children were doing a self-selected in-depth study on AIDS?" One mother said, "I trust Jean. I know her values. She's very loving and she cares about the kids." Other parents said essentially the same thing. They recognized the importance of the teacher's role, and they demonstrated in the interviews that their personal relationship with Jean and their knowledge of her relationship with their children was important in establishing safe ground for discussion of values and controversial social issues in the classroom.

The role of the teacher one hundred and fifty years ago was that of unquestioned *authority* for curriculum and instruction in the classroom. More recently, developments in prepackaged curriculum and scripted basals have changed the role of the teacher to that of *manager* of curriculum and instruction. Curriculum revision alone, however, cannot be an adequate response to the social challenges facing schools today, and neither can more efficient academic instruction. Authoritative or expertly managed instruction based on a new or revised curriculum is not the teacher's only task or even the main task; it is one task among many. Noddings (1992) reasoned that, "We cannot ignore our children—their purposes, anxieties and relationships—in the service of making them more competent in academic skills." (p. 10) She asserted that most of our educational movements today are more technology and method than personal and social.

> [They are] guided by an ideology of control and dominated by a search for method. The idea is to make the individual teacher, the individual student, their relationship irrelevant to the success of instruction, which is posited as the primary goal of schooling. Once objectives are chosen, they are not supposed to deviate from them. They are to seek means within a narrowly defined standard form to reach the objectives, and, further, the objectives now established are almost entirely cognitive. The purposes and objectives of the students are ignored (indeed denied as random behavior) unless they happen to coincide with those of the teacher. (p. 10)

The future will see the increased moral engagement of the teacher. Her role will more and more be that of *facilitator* and *guide*, *co-learner* and classroom *researcher*. The relationships established with parents and students lay the foundation for trust and dialogue on values issues, and they build a stronger sense of community. The moral engagement of those in community produce mediating influences of compassion and strength that flow back and forth between the community and the individual teacher for the good of school children. Unfortunately, this moral action for good often falls outside of the purview of our sense of professional responsibility as teachers. Noddings (1992) criticized this abdication of the teacher's moral responsibility to the parents and the community. Teachers owe more and better to "their"—the parents', the community's, *and* the teachers'—children:

> At the public school level, teachers are often unwilling even to talk with their students about moral matters. I have heard teachers say, "We're not trained for that. That's a job for psychologists" (or counselors, or parents, or pastors). Pressed, many will protest that they do not have a right to impose their values on students, but these same teachers enforce all sorts of rules—sensible and mindless equally—without questioning the values thus imposed. Surely intelligent adults can and should talk to the children in their care about honesty, compassion, open-mindedness, nonviolence, consideration, moderation, and a host of other qualities that most of us admire. This talk need not be indoctrination any more than mathematics teaching need be lecture and rote learning. (p. 39)

What better place is there to become a worthwhile, compassionate, informed human being than in the classroom with the help of an educated professional who cares about

Teaching Kids to Care

children and their whole lives as well as their intellectual learning. The stultifying notion that schools have only one main goal—intellectual development—has been panned by many educational theorists. (Gardner, 1983, 1987; Eisner, 1982; Noddings, 1992) Noddings wrote passionately on the issue:

> **I would take the risk [of impeding intellectual development] if I could produce people who would live nonviolently with each other, sensitively and in harmony with the natural environment, reflectively and serenely with themselves.** (p. 12)

Classroom teachers do not have all the answers to the questions and problems of their students' multifaceted developmental processes, and no one expects them to. Nor do curriculum developers, textbook publishers, college professors, or parents have all the answers. What we must expect and demand from teachers, and from all of the stakeholders in education, is engagement and caring. My experience with elementary school teachers, ninety percent of whom are women, is that this ethic of caring is alive and well. Noddings (1992), Comer (1988), and others also believe that teachers care, but that they are unable to make the connections that would complete caring relations with their students. Inquiry curriculum, however, as discussed in this book, can provide a context of give-and-take connections and caring in which teachers could appropriately enlarge their role. Changes in the teachers' role from manager of a static curriculum to co-researcher and guide will affect classroom environments and materials as well as the ways in which teachers interact with parents and students.

School teachers speak for a segment of society whose goals and aspirations include the daily care and nurturing of children. They also represent a group whose professional training and daily experiences with children provide them with a strong impetus for grappling with their own views on values and the teaching of values in schools. A brief and nonscientific survey reaffirmed my perception that teachers believe they should teach values in the classroom. At two workshops for teachers on using children's literature in the classroom, one given at the 1993 annual national conference of the International Reading Association, and the other at a state-wide Department of Education workshop in Indiana, about 60% of those attending these events responded to the following affirmations in a brief post-session survey:

1. *It is important to teach social values at school.*
2. *It is a teacher's responsibility to teach social values.*
3. *Parents expect schools to teach values.*
4. *I am comfortable helping children understand important social values.*
5. *I deal with important issues in my classroom by doing the following:* [the teachers wrote their individual statements]

Teachers attending a workshop on "social issues" and "critical thinking" and "children's literature" would likely have been predisposed toward values teaching in the classroom, and the workshop itself probably primed these teachers to agree with the idea of teaching values in the classroom. Nonetheless, 96% of those responding to the survey agreed that "it is important to teach social values at school"; 92% agreed that "it is the teacher's responsibility to teach social values"; 84% agreed that "parents expect schools to teach value"; and 100% of the respondents "felt comfortable helping children understand important social values." The teachers often cited literature and textbooks as means of teaching values and dealing with important social issues. They also indicated that they taught values "as they come up" in topics of discussion in social studies and literature, particularly. No teachers specifically cited formal programs for the teaching of values.

As teachers struggle with their role in the teaching of values to students, they are constantly aware of the role and rights of parents. Teachers who are committed to demonstrating democratic values and who are attempting to build classroom environments that allow for meaningful inquiry into social issues and values-based decision making, view parents as partners in the teaching enterprise. A view of parents as anything less than partners opens schools up to unnecessary controversy and mitigates against the trusting relationships that allow values consensus and/or tolerance to emerge.

## Parents: Nurturers, Educators, and Exemplars

Parents are their children's first and most influential teachers. Parents have the authentic and natural role of assuming the voice of the larger culture in conveying to their children the values, traditions, religious faith, family solidarity, and ethnic and class identities. Primitive societies did not even develop schools—families and the communities were the educators. In ancient cultures, the values, wisdom, and culture of the group were passed down to children largely unchanged from generation to generation, parent to child. The advent of formal schooling had a mediating influence on that unquestioned transmission of culture; in nontraditional cultures, professional educators teach the next generation the knowledge, skills, and beliefs that the family circle is too small to provide.

As early as 400 B.C., educators assumed a modifying position on parental influence. One of the first recorded inklings that educators, with their educational theories, were questioning the role and ability of parents to educate their children adequately appears in Plato's *Republic*.

**Do you not know then, that the beginning in every task is the chief thing, especially for any creature that is young and tender? For it is**

then that it is best molded and takes the impression that one wished to stamp upon it. Quite so. Shall we, then, thus lightly suffer our children to listen to any chance stories fashioned by any chance teachers. . . . By no manner of means will we allow it. We must begin, then, it seems by censorship over our storymakers, and what they do well we must pass, and what not, reject. And the stories on the accepted list we will induce nurses and mothers to tell to the children and so shape their souls by these stories far rather than their bodies by their hands. But most of the stories they now tell we must reject. (cited in Hamilton and Cairns [1971] p. 624.)

In the Greek model, education was controlled, and children were socialized to fit the needs of the city-state. Any benefit to individuals and families was secondary. Western education, including the models of public education in the United States, have largely followed this model. Schools were established in this country with the first settlers. The parents' roles in these early schools were limited, although in a sense, parents were de facto co-teachers because the goals of parents, of teachers, and of churches were identical: education for salvation and survival. Parents who read the Bible at home expected their children to learn to read the Bible at school. During the colonial period and after, parents were guided in educating their children by teachers like Benjamin Wadsworth, who wrote a parent-education book published in Boston and widely disseminated, *Composed for Help of Parents in Teaching their Children how to carry it in their Places during their Minority*. (See Rothman, D. & S. Rothman, 1972.)

In the 1800s, parents continued to look beyond the clergy for child-rearing advice to the increasing number of publications such as *Mother's Magazine* and *Parents' Magazine*. Parent groups began meeting in 1815 in Portland, Maine, and by 1897, interest in parent/teacher cooperation was sufficient such that the national Parent Teacher Association (PTA) was founded.

As prosperity and the industrial revolution changed the face of economics, it also changed the face of the family. The agrarian lifestyle, that had supported daily close family contact, gave way to a lifestyle according to which one or both parents worked away from home and children spent their days at school regularly. Parents gradually assumed an advisory role in schooling, and this secondary role has continued for over one hundred years. Parents have filled helping roles at school, such as volunteer readers, paper-graders, and field-trip sponsors. The link between parents and the schools has been the weakest link in the modern professional and formal models of public-school education in this country.

A movement is afoot today, however, to restore parents as more than passive advisors, to see them as more equal partners in the educational process of their children. As a result of initiatives such as Middle Grades Assessment Programs (MGAP), America 2000 grants, and other school-audit and restructuring efforts, a small but vocal core of parents is serving as members of steering committees and other real decision-making bodies within school districts. Parents, teachers, and children, as well as administrators, are learning together to understand and appreciate each other's values and goals, and to engage in genuine discussion when there are differences of opinion. Parent education and collaborative efforts between schools and parent groups will be the wave of the future.

What values do parents want taught to their children? Do parents agree that schools have a role in teaching values? What if the parents' values and the teacher's are different? Is the school a logical forum for debate over values?

In the spring of 1993, while I was working on this book, two articles in the local newspaper typified the hot issues that parents and teachers are now being asked to make decisions about. At one middle school, parents and other community members were invited to attend discussion sessions at the school about a sexual abstinence program for seventh and eighth graders. Sexually transmitted diseases, unwanted pregnancies and AIDS were among the topics to be discussed. ("Middle School to Discuss Sex Education," *The Herald-Times*, Bloomington, Indiana, April, 1993.)

At another middle school, some parents were seeking to halt a new reading program because they said it was teaching the wrong values. The books in the program dealt with issues of divorce, family structure, self-esteem, and integrity, but several parents said that "schools should just concentrate on teaching academics . . . values are better left to the families to discuss." The superintendent of the school district disagreed, however; he affirmed that values teaching is within the province of schools: "Values should be taught at home, but we're responsible for teaching values at school, too. When somebody gets in a fight, we tell them it's not right to fight. If they lie, we tell them it's wrong. We have a responsibility beyond reading, writing and arithmetic." And beyond fighting and lying, one might add.Teachers, too, defended the program, more on academic grounds. One teacher said, "We found that we did a good job teaching kids how to read [before this program], but not teaching them the joy of reading. Now they're reading 30 novels a year on their own because of *Reading for Real*." In class discussions, "their answers are becoming so insightful that it's exciting." That "insightfulness" in students is the very aim of teaching. Elementary school children will very often make good decisions and choices when the alternatives are presented. ("Some Parents Believe that Reading Program Teaches Wrong Values," *The Herald-Times*, Bloomington, Indiana, April 10, 1993, p. B3.)

The materials we use in schools to develop meaningful units of study and to challenge students to do their best thinking will continue to come under attack as long as parent groups are kept at arms length by the schools. By contrast, an inquiry process that encourages input from, and interaction with, parents in the classroom can stimulate a meaningful dialogue on shared values. Parents and teachers alike have as their primary goal the nurturing and education of children, so that those children will be ready to assume their places in society as informed, just, and compassionate citizens.

## Children: Their Role and Their Rights in Constructing the Knowledge Base for Values

From a hundred and fifty to two hundred years ago, children in schools were essentially passive recipients of knowledge. Memorization and recitation of lessons from the teacher and the textbook were the primary means by which they learned. A glance into many classrooms today would reveal that the standard mode of teaching and learning—reading, note-taking, recitation, and testing—is still essentially what it has ever been: Our classrooms, generally, do not show a significant difference in operation from classrooms of 100 years ago. (See Cuban, 1984, 1986; Mayer and Brause, 1986.) Schooling is, however, changing somewhat; student choice and decision-making is altering the role of the child from that of passive recipient of knowledge to active constructor of his or her own understandings of the world and relationships. Chapters one and two of this book, describing the inquiry method in third- and sixth-grade classrooms, give examples of children as active constructors of knowledge.

Ought children to learn how to support their opinions, listen to others, debate, and cite their sources? Undoubtedly. Ought they to acknowledge others' rights to their own opinions? Of course. Ought they to think humanely about the planet and the fellow creatures living on it? No question. Today we would get very few negative responses to these questions. We are beginning to recognize that compassionate understanding of others in our global community, growing smaller and smaller as its diverse population grows larger and larger, cannot wait for the dispassionate reasoning of politically correct adulthood.

Contrary to many theorists' opinions of children as self-centered beings who revolve in their own orbits, Piaget (1965) and others believed that young children quickly develop a sense of industry, care, and fairness. Kohlberg (1985) believed that children will develop these virtues when given the environment, practice in, and support for moral decision making. Are elementary-school children too young and immature to deal compassionately with serious issues? Many children deal daily and personally with abuse, neglect, divorce, and homelessness, and if they do not deal with these issues firsthand, they do witness violence and social conflict on television and know about it in the lives of their friends and classmates.

Although some very conservative parent groups want only "the basics" taught, I believe that it is naive to think that children should not be "exposed" to the serious issues of our time in school for, in fact, they have already been exposed if they are alive and aware. Because they have already been exposed to moral threat, the school's role becomes very much more important in teaching them to think as active, concerned citizens whose hearts, hands, and minds can actively engage in improving their own reality and the larger community's. This is, in fact, what parents ultimately want, and what the state requires.

Given the relatively defenseless nature of children and our responsibility for their welfare in school, how can we educate them to desired values while protecting them from indoctrination into political or religious beliefs which their parents and other community members might find objectionable? David Moshman (1989) argued that the only safeguard we have for continued protection against use of public schools for indoctrination is a principled commitment to children's First Amendment rights. His argument leaves the reader with two pressing questions: *What will become of us if we fail to transmit the knowledge, values, and principles that have brought us this far? And, conversely, What will become of us if, in our zeal to inculcate, we blindly cast a pall of orthodoxy over the future?* (p. 187) Stakeholders in schools may not agree on which textbooks and curriculum guides inculcate the best values or provide the most freedom of expression, but we, the parents, acting as we, the people, have, through the courts, insisted that schools may not indoctrinate students in a particular political or religious viewpoint. That insistence, however, does not leave us in a "values vacuum." The challenge before us as parents and educators is to avoid both a narrow parochialism that can lead to fear, bigotry, and isolationism and a relative values system in which values are nothing more than the customs of a particular group.

Schools can meet this challenge by opening to children a forum for thinking, growing, and becoming compassionate, responsible citizens. How? Through inquiry curriculum with a compassionate teacher, we can declare a forum for critical thinking in which students learn to ask, "How do past and present values, views, and decisions affect me, my neighbors, and the planet?" A reasoned and reasonable approach to First-Amendment freedoms in which all stakeholders collaborate on curriculum and school climate will provide a context for values teaching. The doing of democracy in schools is the composite meta-value that makes possible the exploration of all other values that the stakeholders in any particular school may hold dear.

# 9 Building a Classroom for Values Teaching

## Limited School Democracy: Beginning Strategies

A virtual turning over of the classroom to the students, allowing for choice of topic and ways of acquiring and presenting information, may seem like a tall order to many teachers. How can a teacher ease her classroom into a sustained limited school democracy?

This chapter is devoted to instructional strategies that support teachers and students in their desire to live and learn together in a classrooms where democratic processes make demonstrated values possible. These strategies include establishing general democratic practices, using literature to begin discussion of controversial topics, and reading children's trade books that embody democratic and traditional moral values. Lickona (1991) talked about a school-wide culture for values teaching, suggested some specific strategies for building a classroom climate for values teaching. I focus more specifically on children's literature as a springboard to values teaching.

The ways teachers structure their classroom can either hamper or enhance students' development as active thinkers and doers who value and respect themselves, others, and the planet we all inhabit. In America, we share some common assumptions about schools and democracy:

- The future of democracy rests on well-informed citizens who are willing to consider alternative choices and make responsible decisions.
- One purpose of tax-supported public schools is to develop literate, critical thinkers and to promote decision making in the minds of active, independent learners.
- Another purpose of public schools is to inculcate the principles and values of democracy.

In order, therefore, to develop a learning atmosphere in which democratic values can be promoted, teachers must themselves behave as decision makers in their own classrooms, developing curriculum along with their students in the give-and-take of the democratic process. If teachers behave as benevolent dictators, the school hardly functions as a school for democracy. I must acknowledge, however, that schooling contexts function as limited democracies, at best. The notion posited by critical theorists and socio-political reading theorists that a democratic understanding of society has, as a given, the equal participation of all members in all forms of social life, including the processes of teaching and learning in schools, is flawed. Teachers and administrators are not elected either by students or directly by students' parents. Children do not choose to go to school—they are required by law to attend (though many parents are opting for home schooling). Democracy touches the school indirectly and representationally through elected school board members who hire the teachers and administrators. Despite this arrangement, however, schools can still function to demonstrate and foster limited living democracies in which students participate in rule making and curriculum building, classroom activities, social behavior, and even their own academic assessment.

The qualities of thought, character, and interaction demanded by democracy include at least the following: mutual consideration, care for others, patience, risk taking, critical thinking skills, and positive attitudes towards, and respect for, peers. As we teachers think about what we value, and as we communicate with the parents of our students and learn what *they* value, we need to make a list. Just as James Madison and Thomas Jefferson published their lists, their manifestos of democracy in Declarations and Constitutions, so ought we to post our lists somewhere in our classrooms. By involving our students and their parents, and then publishing our ideal results, we all come to know what matters in the limited democracy of the classroom.

## Theoretical Memo: Choice is Healthful for the Mind

Teachers can operationalize the idea of democracy by encouraging students to participate responsibly in constructing the intellectual curriculum, the class rules, and the social arrangements within which they work. In so doing, the experience of power sharing, collaborative structuring, and a sense of community conditions a powerful sub-set of lived values. Do children, however, have total freedom? Are just *any* choices for study acceptable? No. These choices must be hammered out in the context of a compassionate and democratic learning community. Classroom rules that reflect emotional and physical safety, respect, tolerance, and justice help to develop a caring environment in which the local school curriculum, the wishes of parents, and the desires of the students for particular areas of study are negotiated. In America, inquiry is front-loaded in the educational system by the Constitution. The Supreme Court has consistently reiterated the public school teacher's responsibility to inculcate the 1st Amendment values of democracy, all of which can be summarized in the single term, inquiry.

Children of all ages need choices in the classroom for the same reason that muscles need exercise. A political hostage regained freedom after 48 months of captivity. The most difficult aspect of his new freedom was making decisions. For four years, the man had made no decisions for himself and no moves on his own—he had been fed, clothed, and ordered about at the command of his captors. Now, after his release, his life again demanded constant decision-making, but even the most mundane choices—what to eat or what to wear—caused him severe confusion and fatigue.

Children in classrooms similarly become deadened to independent intellectual thinking and doing when they are forced to go without opportunity for making choices. Making curriculum decisions based on personal interest or community needs is a healthful habit of the mind to form in the citizens of a democratic society. If children are not allowed to make real choices in school, then this habit of the mind is liable to atrophy, and the foundations of democratic society will erode.

Choice empowers students. To this end, Noddings (1992) argued for a future in which curriculum would be cooperatively constructed by teachers and students:

> *Teachers will have to predict what students may want to study. Some money will have to be set aside for midyear allocation to resources that could not be ordered ahead of time. Patterns of spending will shift from an emphasis on textbooks to one of paperbacks, kits, charts, tools, art implements, excursions, and museum minicourses. Issues of control and power arise here and must be resolved in favor of [student] empowerment.* (p. 176)

Teacher, think about your classroom! How many substantive decisions do your students make routinely in a day? If your answer is, "Not many," then ask yourself a second question: Can we continue to function as a democratic society if our citizens' education consists largely of pre-digested curriculum in which goals, objectives, and content are pre-selected and incrementally dished out? Expensive programs for teaching democratic processes are unnecessary. Materials now at hand in your classroom provide ample opportunity for choice and decision making. You can begin today with the children's literature in your classroom library and some hours devoted to building a democratic learning community.

In the following pages, I offer several instructional strategies and curriculum structures as a place to begin the development of values necessary to the formation of a caring and democratic citizenry.

# Instructional Strategies

## ■ Strategy: *Choose Your Learning*
## Value: Making Choices/Decision Making

### Objective

Students will learn to view decision making as a routine part of their educational experiences with the goal of becoming thoughtful lifelong decision-makers. They will learn to respect and appreciate the choices that others make.

### Procedures

Begin slowly with students who have not previously had the opportunity to make choices about their own schooling. Examples of choices that students can make include the following:

- choose books for free reading
- choose topics for writing
- choose from a variety of classroom centers
- choose topics for in-depth study from the social-studies and science curricula
- choose aspects of a topic for individual research and report
- choose method of presenting new information to the class
- take responsibility for a classroom display or bulletin board
- help plan the daily classroom schedule
- choose which learning goals are to be pursued individually and with classmates
- choose an individualized curriculum plan
- keep a "Choices/Consequences" log in which students keep a daily record of their choices and consequences over time

For each choice, help your students think and talk about why they made particular choices: *Why is it a good choice? What did you learn about making choices? What are your goals?*

### Results

Students will begin to take responsibility for their choices. They become more independent in their learning, and they develop critical-thinking skills. They become more reflective about their own preferences and talents. Analytical discussions of decision making scenarios from children's literature can spark reflective decision making in the classroom, as demonstrated in the following strategies. By focusing on decision-making of characters in literature, and recognizing the consequences of that decision making, students become more aware of the correlation between actions and their consequences—the concept of accountability.

---

### ■ Strategy: *Decision-Making Charts and Webs with Literature*
### Value: *Making Choices/Decision Making*

## Objective

Students will reflect on the bases upon which decisions are made; they will consider alternative decisions. Students will see the relationships between various characters and their decisions, and they will understand that an individual's decisions can effect others.

## Procedures

*Either . . .*

- Read a book that has a number of instances of characters making difficult decisions, such as *The Legend of the Bluebonnet*, retold by Tommie de Paola; *I'm Terrific*, by Marjorie Weiman Sharmat; or *Two Bad Ants*, by Chris Van Allsberg.

  In *The Legend of the Bluebonnet*, the people are starving because of a drought. The holy man of the tribe tells the people that there is a drought because the people have become selfish. After the shaman makes the announcement that the Great Spirit wants a sacrifice of the most valued possession of the tribe, several of the people refuse to give up their possessions. An orphaned girl who loves her people, sacrifices her only possession, a doll. In the place where the ashes of the doll were scattered, bluebonnets grew the next day. The drought ended, and to this day, as legend has it, bluebonnets grow in the hill country of Texas as a memorial to this girl's sacrifice.

- After reading the book, list all the characters in one column on a sheet of chart paper. In the column across from the character's name, list the decisions that the characters made.

  ### "The Legend of the Bluebonnet"

  | *Characters:* | *Actions based on decisions:* |
  | --- | --- |
  | The people | • take from the land (implied decision) |
  | The shaman | • seeks message from the Great Spirit |
  | The dancers | • do rain dance to end drought |
  | A woman of the tribe | • does not offer her blanket |
  | A warrior | • does not offer his bow |
  | She-Who-is-Alone | • offers her doll |

- Discuss each character's decision and what might have prompted that decision.
- Discuss the consequences of the decision and some possible alternatives.
- Discuss whether the decision was a good one, and why.

*Or . . .*

- Put the "problem" from the story at the center of the web. An interesting discussion (I've seen this done successfully even with first graders) about the *real* (as opposed to folkloric) problems of drought and starvation is likely to occur.
- A variety of additions to the web may follow: Who made decisions? What were those decisions? What factors influenced those decisions? What alternative decisions might have been made? What were the consequences? What might some alternative consequences have been?

## Results

Students will see that feelings and desires lie behind and motivate actions, that decisions bring consequences, and that reconsidering motives may affect our decisions. Students will recognize that actions are based on conscious or unconscious motives. Sometimes those motives are noble and selfless and are consonant with the good of the group. Sometimes motives are selfish and directed towards benefit to the individual only. Depending on the maturity of the class and the thoroughness of the discussion, the varying reasons for making decisions can be questioned, and additional possible motives can be assigned.

## Example

First-grade teacher, Carol Turner, decided that her students needed more choice and opportunity for making decisions in the classroom. She was already implementing a Whole Language curriculum in which her students chose their books and their writing topics, but she wanted to emphasize the idea of decision making, that actions have consequences, that we are responsible for our actions and decisions. As she reflected on some possible directions for meeting this goal, she realized that the part of the curriculum she and the children loved most—books—could provide the basis for study. She began to reread some of her favorites, noting the characters' decisions and the consequences. This seemed like a logical way to introduce the topic of decision making to the class. First, Carol brainstormed with the students to see what concepts of decision making they already held. Here is the semantic web they generated with Carol as the scribe.

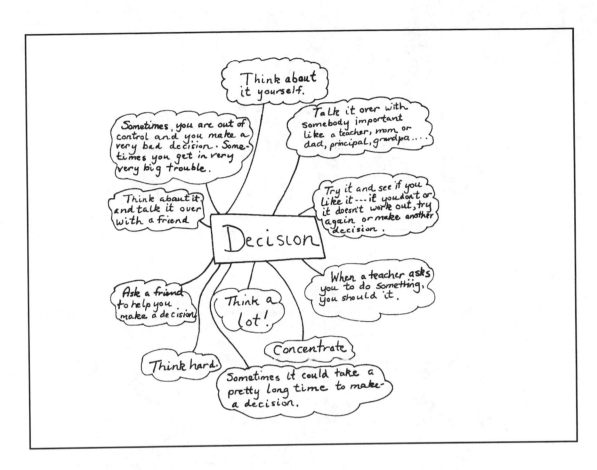

In the next few weeks, Carol shared a number of books with her students, including *New Blue Shoes* and *I'm Terrific*. She had the students respond in writing to the stories by recording the decisions that characters made and their feelings about those decisions. *New Blue Shoes* is a story about indecision and getting new shoes. The main character finally decides on a pair of blue ones. Here are some examples of the students' responses.

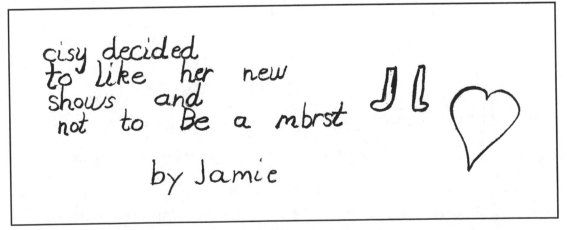

[Cissy decided to like her new shoes and not to be embarrassed.]

MIkki DecISIONdeCIded
I will TRYTOLOOKHaPeY
IN MY NEWSHEWS
I Fel Eoney
BUTI Like MYSHEWS

[Decision decided, I will try to look happy in my new shoes.
I feel funny but I like my new shoes."]

Voseph She decidid that she ditint riky Wat
the chos in thin She ditint.
She faht Haqqy.

[She decided that she didn't really want the shoes and then she *didn't* [sic: sc., *did*]. She felt happy.]

DecioN                        Tiffany
Mom haw Do You
LIc my Noow shoos
oh ta are fantastec
▦▦▯▦▯a ILIdmY noow
shoos ta filgOooh my fet

[Decision. Mom, how do you like my new shoes? Oh, they are fantastic! I like my new shoes. They feel good on my feet.]

Decision making soon became the theme for this first-grade classroom. The children's journals were full of decision-making that touched on school, playground, and home decision-making situations. Here are some examples from their journals:

[I decided to listen to the story. It was a good decision. I liked the story.]

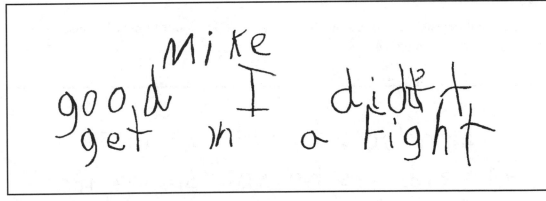

[Good (decision). I didn't get in a fight.]

[I made a decision to save electricity. I felt happy because I made a right decision.]

Kim
I Made A bad Desisan
to not eat my Bnana

Becas I was not hucree

Beac I dont have vary mach
energe

[I made a bad decision to not eat my banana because I was not hungry because [now] I don't have very much energy.]

when you do math you are
makidesis honsbecous you Are
deslidin   Whenyouarethinking
likethisone7+7=14   Josh

[When you do math you are making decisions because you are deciding when you are thinking. Like this one: 7 + 7 = 14.]

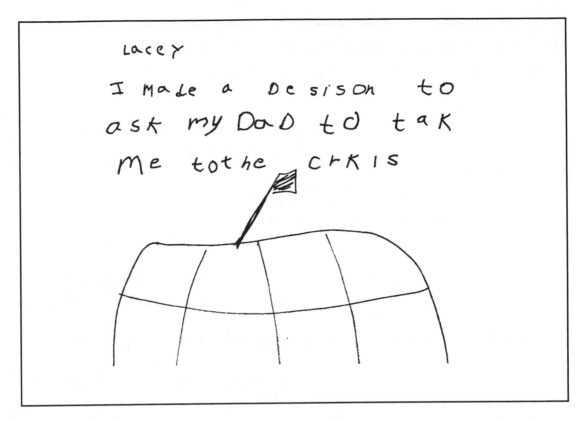

[I made a decision to ask my dad to take me to the circus.]

Carol often presented her own decision making dilemmas to the students. For example, early in the school year, she had agreed to make a presentation at a conference, not realizing that it occurred during her spring break. After much discussion, the first graders advised Carol against the making the presentation.

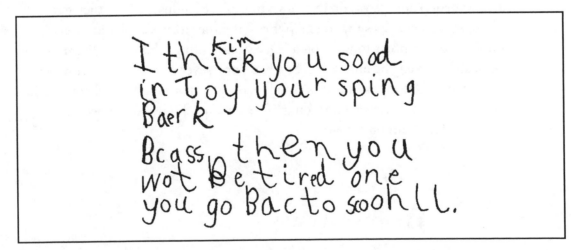

[I think you should enjoy your spring break because then you won't be tired when you go back to school.]

## ■ Strategy: *Decisions Made by Storybook Characters*
## Value: Making Choices/Decision Making

### Objective

Students will recognize the processes and motivations for decisions in children's literature and develop inferential thinking.

### Procedures

Collect a number of books that emphasize the decisions made by characters and consequences of those decisions. Suggestions: *Two Bad Ants*, by Chris Van Allsberg; *My Wicked Stepmother*, by Nancy Leach; *Pierre*, by Maurice Sendak.

- Begin with a discussion of decisions. As students volunteer decisions they have made, list them on chart paper. Invite them to categorize into good, bad, and neutral decisions.
- Read a story aloud, asking your students to listen for the decisions being made.
- Ask your students to volunteer to role-play the characters and tell about their decisions and why they made them.

### Results

Students will become more consciously aware of the constant decision making in which they engage every day. They will learn to make inferences about characters' intentions and motivations.

### Example

Carol read aloud *Two Bad Ants*, in which two ants decide to leave the safety of their group and go off on their own to explore a house, where they get into many dangerous situations. After reading the story, Carol asked her students to volunteer to write on a "Decision-Making Chart" and list all of the decisions that the ants made. She had hung several pieces of chart paper in the room so that her students could record decisions made by characters in the various books they were reading. The students discussed the decisions and recorded them on a chart:

Decisions

Two BAD ANTS Go home

Bad decisions
TA bST DETNTGNTAT RAS
They decided not to go with the other ants.

They wiNT To CHRABL . NAW THAT
WAS A VARE BAD Decision

to GT SM SrSM Kimn
To get some sugar.

to Go N the hoMe

On another day, the class read *I'm Terrific*, by Margaret Weiman Sharmat, about a perfectly clean, orderly, obedient, self-righteous little bear named Jason who decides to change himself in order to make some friends. The children dictated his "plan" and the decisions he made:

• get dirty
• be not nice
• dissatisfied with "terrific" Jason, he will become a new mean Jason
• stop eating spinach
• not clean his house
• tie his friend's fur in knots
• kick his other friends' nut piles

The children then discussed the results of Jason's plan and that his decisions failed to help him meet his goal of making friends. A passage from the book exemplifies the importance of decision making. When Jason's "plan" fails for changing himself from a super-righteous little bear with no friends to a very naughty little bear with friends, he talks with his mother, and his response signifies the change of heart and the lessons learned. The following passage illustrates the point that bears (and children) need many opportunities to think, to try out new ideas, to struggle until the problem is solved. Jason Bear and his mother talk things over:

> "Nobody likes the new me," he said, "and neither do I." Jason sat down beside his mother. "Now I don't know who I am."

> "I know who you are," said Mrs. Bear. "You are a good bear who is thinking things over."

"Well, that is a good thing to be," said Jason. "A thinking bear."

Jason spent the rest of the day thinking. "This is the first real thinking I have done in a long time. I am out of practice. I hope I don't make a mistake."

Jason went to bed thinking. The next morning he woke up and ran downstairs shouting, "Mother, I am what I am. I am Jason Everett Bear, and I'm glad of it."

Several weeks after the decision-making emphasis began in Carol's room, a tragic event heightened even more dramatically the role of decision making in everyone's lives. The instructional assistant in the classroom was arrested for murder in a local bar—eyewitness reports in the newspaper seemed to confirm his guilt. Many weeks of serious and tearful discussion followed this incident. The first graders wrote letters to their jailed friend, and they tried to understand how he could have made the decision to kill someone. They had many questions: How long would he be in jail? Could they visit him? Would he get the electric chair? Could they pay money and get him out? Would a jury decide? The children—graduate-level TV watchers—were, of course, amazingly well versed in the vocabulary and concepts of crime and punishment. The students all agreed that people should be punished for committing crimes, especially for killing someone, even though this man was their friend and he had made a very bad decision. On that issue, the first graders had no doubts.

Some parting advice from first grader, April, on decision making:

1. think
2. talk abot it
3. Nnow
4. Do it.
                                        April

[1. Think, 2. Talk about it, 3. Now, 4. Do it.]

On a more philosophical note, classmate Jason remarked:

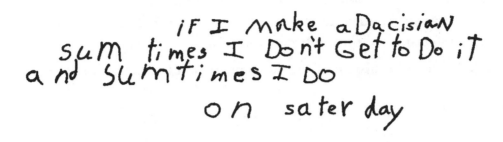

[If I make a decision, sometimes I don't get to do it and sometimes I do on Saturday.]

---

## ■ Strategy: *Telling Stories with a Moral*
## Value: Consequences of Right/Wrong Doing

### Objective

Students will reflect on their experiences, telling a moral story that enables them to assume and articulate responsibility for thoughts, feelings, and actions related to decision making.

### Procedures

Ideally, this strategy follows the reading aloud of a piece of children's literature (or perhaps the teacher's telling of her own moral story) in which characters make difficult choices. This strategy is most appropriate for upper-elementary and middle-school children. A supportive and trusting learning community needs already to have been built up in the classroom in order for this strategy to be effective.

1. Read a story such as *Shiloh*, by Phyllis Reynolds Naylor, in which the central character takes in a mistreated dog and faces the dilemma of whether or not to return the dog to its cruel owner.

2. Encourage role-playing of central characters, so that the students can experience articulating the reasons behind the actions—"telling the moral story."

3. Invite students to tell their own moral stories in which they made a decision that was difficult. Invite supportive discussion from other students.

Tappan & Brown (1989) have successfully used the following interview protocol in helping students develop moral stories for an audience:

All people have had the experience of being in a situation where they had to make a decision, but weren't sure of what they should do. Describe a situation where you faced a moral conflict and you had to make a decision, but weren't sure what you should do.

1. What was the situation? (Be sure you get a full elaboration of the story.)
2. What was the conflict for you in that situation? Why was it a conflict?
3. In thinking about what to do, what did you consider? Anything else you considered?
4. What did you decide to do? What happened?
5. Do you think it was the right thing to do?
6. What was at stake for you in this dilemma? What was at stake for others? In general, what was at stake?
7. How did you feel about it? How did you feel about it for the others involved?
8. Is there another way to see the problem, other than the way you described it?
9. When you think back over the conflict you described, do you think you learned anything from it?
10. Do you consider the situation you described to involve a moral problem? Why/why not?
11. What does morality mean to you? What makes something a moral problem for you? (p. 195)

## Results

Children's storytelling results in authorship and ownership of their actions in facing moral dilemmas, and it contributes to the development of the moral sense. The audience must be responsive and the story must be about students' real experiences. Then, as students reflect on their experiences in the process of narrating those experiences, they are claiming authority and responsibility for their actions.

## Example

Tappan & Brown (1989) report this moral story from a seventh grader about an experience she had had as a fourth grader:

**In fourth grade I was in a big jam, okay. I was with these group of friends who weren't really my friends, but I didn't realize it then. And,**

I tried to fit in, but I just couldn't, you know. And then finally the time came when I had to make a choice of either staying with them and being miserable or finding a new set of friends, and you know, starting over with friends. And, I wasn't sure what to do. And . . . but I did . . . but then I realized that good things weren't happening. Let's put it that way. Because I wasn't happy, and I wasn't sure of myself, so I decided to find a new set of friends, and it worked.

*In thinking about what to do, what did you consider?*
I considered where I was at the moment, you know, which wasn't a great position, because I wasn't being honest with myself and I wasn't thinking about myself, I just wanted to have these group of friends.

*So what did you finally decide to do?*
Find a new set of friends.

*Do you think what you did was the right thing to do?*
Yeah, definitely.

*Why?*
My grades were dropping, and so I was always a straight A student, and then my grades started dropping, and I went down to Cs and Ds and stuff, and the teacher was really worried about me, and I think it was best for my education.

*Now how can that kind of thing affect your education?*
Because I was having trouble with my friends, and it seemed like they'd like me one day and they didn't like me the next, and I used to come home and I'd be like, "Oh, Mom, what am I going to do, they don't like me?" Then, "Oh Ma, they like me!" And my mom thought I was really confused, you know. I didn't know what was going on around me. So, she sort of pointed me in the right direction, and I started to take one step, you know, and then I took another, and they were bad for my education because I was losing confidence in myself. I was losing myself, really, and losing the kind of person I was. So, I just got back on track. (p. 193–194)

## ■ Strategy: *Be the Teacher/Choose the Task*
## Value: Initiative/Decision Making

### Objective

To help students make decisions about ways to teach something they know well.

- Discuss with your students your own daily life as a decision maker. How do you decide what to teach and which activities to use?
- Propose that your students make a list of the things that they would like to teach or share with the group. Examples: how to do origami, how to tell a story and lead a discussion, how to use a computer program, etc.
- Invite your students to sign up to teach at a particular time on a specified day. They decide what they will teach, how to arrange their teaching setting, and what size of group to plan for.
- Afterward, debrief with your student-teachers. Talk about the decisions they made about their teaching. What went well? What was difficult? What surprised them? What would they do differently next time? What would they like to teach next? Use this strategy often: The more they teach, they more they understand about learning.

### Outcomes

You can assess independence and decision-making growth in your students. They can assume responsibility for their actions and planning, thereby increasing their critical-thinking skills and sense of competence and autonomy.

### Example

Carol Turner's first-grade class engaged in active, reflective decision making both vicariously through literature and in their own daily school experiences. After several weeks, Carol thought that her students were ready to try a decision-making project in which they would make a number of connected decisions. To pull together a variety of aspects of the school day and place them in a decision-making context, Carol decided to invite her students to teach something they knew well to the rest of the class. They decided what to teach, when to teach, how to teach, how to arrange the classroom for teaching, and how many should be in a group. Their sign-up chart for teaching follows:

## Sign - up Teaching Sheet

| Name | What you will teach | Day |
|---|---|---|
| 1. Heqther | Goin to teach Book | VN Day |
| 2. Elissa | To rid a Hors | MUN Day |
| 3. Ullip | How To MAKE Ni NJA TURLE PICCHRs | To Day |
| 4. Kurt | How to cro LiKE ChicKEN | tomro |
| 5. Lauren | BUTRF (BUTTERFLY) | |
| 6. JoHN DAVID | MARIO → VOICES | TODAY |
| 7. EPhREN | TRAKT (TRACTOR) | tomro |
| 8. MiKe | | FE |
| 9. DAViD | tar PAL (NINJA TURTLES) | TODAY |
| 10. Will | #TOLCLICA PeN MATeS (How to look like a praying mantis) | TODAY |

First, the students who were teaching, presented to the class what they were going to teach and the rest of the class signed up for the session they wanted to hear. Four students at a time taught at centers. In this way, the whole class was divided into small groups of their choice. Carol said later:

**I was amazed. They were all so attentive, and they all learned what their peers were teaching. The children who were teaching were so organized and thoughtful in their presentations. They prepared materials ahead of time. One boy brought in his tape recorder. For his session on chickens, he had recorded his rooster crowing. Another child prepared materials for teaching the others how to**

make books. Another taught the children how to ride horses—dressage on the chairs in the classroom. Another taught his group about praying mantises and how to look like a praying mantis. He really did look like one!

I think this was successful for several reasons; first, because the children chose what to teach and what to learn; second, because their peers were teaching; third, because this was really important to them. We had discussed decision making for several weeks. The tone had been set for thoughtful choice, responsibility, consequences. A lot of thought went into both the teaching and the choosing of the learning center. They didn't just choose on the basis of "she's my friend." The children expended so much thought and effort in preparation, I was concerned that some might leave their groups if they found them uninteresting, and then someone's feelings would be hurt, but that didn't happen. They chose thoughtfully and then stuck by their decisions. They had ownership of this teaching/learning time.

If the teacher models making choices in the classroom and allows discussion of the decision making of characters in literature prior to using this strategy, the students satisfy their need to experience thinking through decisions before they jump into new decision-making territory on their own. If they have had some experience noting the motivations and consequences of decision making, they are more likely to consider the variety of possibilities and limitations in developing their own decision-making tasks.

---

## Theoretical Memo: Children Make Good Decisions about Their Own Learning

Children will usually choose to learn because that is the nature of healthy human curiosity. They may not always choose to learn what the teacher had in mind, and the children's discoveries will not always be right in any factual sense. Think of your students as little scientists, hypothesizing and testing. Like "negative results" in grown-up research, a "mistake" is as important as a good choice because it helps to determine the next step in learning. Frank Smith (1981) wrote the following about language learning:

*continued*

*There are only two kinds of mistakes . . . , those that make a difference and those that don't. A mistake that does not make a difference does not make a difference. A mistake that does make a difference becomes self-evident and is the basis of learning.* (p. 637)

In the same way that children, when given a choice, will choose a variety of foods (not all chocolate sundaes), they will competently choose to learn what they are *ready* to learn and what they *sense as important* to be learned. If they lack this readiness and this sense of the importance of what is being studied, they won't learn what is taught even by a teacher who makes their choices for them. Students operate at their own levels, in terms of their own readiness and curiosity, and they produce according to their abilities, when the classroom environment allows them to learn. Make it comfortable for your students to explore language, topics, questions, research issues, and do not view their partial results as deficient. Children need to ask their own questions and find their own answers in their own ways.

In the same way that a good reading teacher helps students develop strategies for *figuring out* an unknown word ("read the rest of the sentence, then come back, and see what makes sense there"), rather than *telling* the inexperienced reader the word, a democratic teacher facilitates processes, resources, and strategies for helping students to arrive at their own approximation of the knowledge base. Students then begin to trust the teacher and their peers to support them in their learning. They are naturally inquisitive, focused, and motivated when there is choice, ownership, and teamwork.[1] They will choose to learn different things and to express themselves in their individual ways.

What, then, is the teacher's role, if the students themselves are doing the teaching and learning? A growing body of professional literature on teaching presents the argument that the role of the teacher is to "lead from behind." In other words, the teacher is responsible for structuring environments and opportunities that support students in their self-motivated growth and self-directed learning. Those environments nurture choice, ownership, motivation, and curiosity.[2]

Teachers need to listen to their students, to kid-watch, to do action research, to watch for the learner to emerge and act, and then to support that action. Once students have experience in discussing choices and decision making in children's literature, and they feel competent and secure in making some curricular decisions for themselves, they are ready to join others in collaborative settings such as those that follow.

## ■ Strategy: *Roundtable Justice*

## Value: Peacemaking/Conflict Resolution

## Objective

Students will learn to accept responsibility for the consequences of their decisions.

## Procedures

- When there is a disagreement in the classroom among students, they are invited to the roundtable to adjudicate the issue.
- A group of peers not involved in the dispute joins the roundtable. This group of roundtable peers rotates monthly (or more often, depending on the group).
- Students involved in the dispute have an opportunity to state their point of view.
- The group of peers brainstorms ideas that may solve the problem. A secretary in the group (or you, the teacher) takes notes and reads back the ideas.
- Those involved in the dispute may choose a solution presented or offer their own.

Students, who usually have their own strong sense of right and wrong will likely want to assign blame for many incidents. You may want to agree or disagree with their judgments about the rightness or wrongness of their peers' actions. It is helpful to refer to classroom rules, your "democratic classroom list," in order to discuss the dispute in light of agreed-upon criteria for actions. One wise teacher had a simple classroom rule that covers a lot of moral ground: "I will not hurt anyone on the outside or the inside." Having established at the roundtable whether the actions in question are in accord with the rules, it is important to set the tone for reconciliation and peace; the parties must be reconciled and move toward solutions and restitution. The students in this way constitute the justice system within their limited school democracy, but the teacher is the enforcer.

## Results

Students will see that decisions have consequences, and that many factors can affect decisions. They will take responsibility for the results of their decisions. They will recognize that positive or negative consequences in the classroom can be traced to conscious or unconscious decision making.

## ■ Strategy: *Collaborative Learning Teams*

Encouraging and supporting group work and discussion in the classroom will go a long way towards fostering cooperation rather than competition, supportive critique of peers rather than criticism, and a sense of belonging to a working democracy. The current literature is full of talk about "cooperative" learning. I prefer to refer to this kind of grouping as *collaborative* because no idea fostered through group work belongs exclusively to one person. Learners are not merely working side-by-side; they are working together. They are mutually engendering new thoughts, plans, projects, and actions that could not come about if the individual were working alone, and would be different if the group members were merely working side-by-side. Although the specific idea may occur to one person who then shares it, the impetus and the environment for that idea is the group, and its working out and perfecting is the common property of all. Emphasis on the collaborative nature of the effort builds respect for group work and for the students themselves as they acknowledge and benefit from the ideas of their colleagues.

## Value: Collaboration/Teamwork

## Objectives

Students will learn to work together with consideration for, and patience with, others. They will acknowledge that many ideas are group generated and hence belong to the group.

## Procedures

### Forming teams

Students can be grouped in many ways.[3]

- Students sign up to read a book or do a project, and then they group themselves on the basis of interest.
- Teachers assign "study buddies" to work on skills or academic subjects.
- Teachers assign groups randomly.
- Teachers choose groups for specific reasons, e. g., low/high achievers, shy/outgoing students, and place students in different kinds of groups to have different kinds of learning experiences.
- After students have some experience at working in different kinds of groups, teachers may want to let them choose their own groups.
- Teams work in the elementary and middle grades work best for about two to four weeks.

### Building solidarity

- Have groups come up with team names, banners, T-shirts, and slogans; encourage them to display their tribal instincts in their team areas.

- Set aside bulletin-board space for each team to display projects, group-work, etc., to be decorated by the group.
- Discuss the kinds of tasks on which the groups will work so that they know in general what they will be doing.
- Assist your students to set their own criteria for group work, but don't do it for them. Ask: "What will make your team a great one? What will be important to remember in keeping your group on task and happy? Could you develop some rules for your groups so that you can check from time to time to see how you are doing?"

Suggest that they write down their rules and post them in a prominent team location. Group discussion of each team's rules will prove ongoing—before, during, and after their formulation. After every group has talked about their rules, ask your students to add any new rules for which they sense a need. Let them know what you yourself value in the team work, also.

- Help your students to realize that they are responsible for their own learning AND their group members' learning, too.
- Help students to see that they play different roles within their groups: reader, secretary, leader, observer, timer, organizer, and so on. Encourage them to rotate the roles among the several team members.

## Keeping Teams Going

Ask questions every so often to help students see what they are doing right.

- How did your group help you this week?
- What did you learn? Whom did you learn it from?
- Do you learn more by working with someone? Explain.
- Do you prefer to work alone? Explain.
- What did your partner/team do this week to let you know that they cared about your learning?
- Think about your group's rules. What did your group do best this week? What might you improve next week?
- Give an example of something that someone said that made you feel competent or important to your group.
- Give an example of something that someone said that made you think a new thought or understand a concept more clearly.
- Give an example of something that someone said that helped your reading and writing.
- What strategies did your group use to accomplish this project, task, paper, etc.?

## Don't give up!

Students who have had little experience with learning teams need time and support from you. Change teams often; let teams review their rules often; let teams evaluate themselves often; you ask the above questions often. By asking questions, you evoke thought, encourage reflection, and help students take responsibility for their actions.

## Results

Students will attain some measure of independence from the teacher. Peer support for decisions and actions related to the task stretches the students' confidence in themselves as learners and thinkers. Students also attain a measure of group interdependence and solidarity as they learn to work together towards common and individual goals. The most important outcome is that collaborative work—rule setting, in particular—allows the students to function on their own as moral thinkers and doers. Your trust in your students' ability to reason morally and to see the values underlying the rules, is an essential contribution that you, the teacher, make to these processes.

---

### *Theoretical Memo: Caring Partnerships/Compassionate Communities*

*The best and the deepest moral training is that which one gets by having to enter into proper relations with others. . . . Present educational systems, so far as they destroy or neglect this unity, render it difficult or impossible to get any genuine, regular moral training.* (Archambault, 1964, p. 341)

John Dewey

How do classrooms become communities in which people care about each other and their learning? Ought classrooms to function as free-for-alls where children read and write only when they want to, or finish work only when it suits them? Selfishness, rudeness, lack of effort, and resistance to learning can be eliminated when teachers learn how to structure the classroom organization and the curriculum for the sake of the students, rather than attempting to mold the students to the teacher's agenda and prepackaged curriculum. Graves (1991) wrote this useful perspective on today's multicultural classrooms:

*Children come from a variety of home environments. Some are autocratic, others democratic, permissive or interventionist. Some parents use physical punishment while others speak words that humiliate. In some homes, children see all property held in common—what is in the house can be used for play—but severe punishment may be meted out in another household if certain objects are not held in esteem. . . .*

*There may be more radical differences in the use of time. Some children eat with the family while others pick up food as they wish; some eat fast food*

*continued*

*while others sit down to a well-prepared meal with carefully defined customs and table manners. Other children are simply hungry or severely undernourished. . . .*

*Each morning children from all these backgrounds—which differ in family and ethnic customs, in their uses of space and time, in their patterns of negotiation, and in their understanding of the meaning of speech and print—enter the classroom.* (p. 33)

Graves goes on to say that teachers can deal with these differences in two ways:

1) By exercising total control of time and space, teachers make for a secure and predictable classroom in which children learn little about how to use space and time on their own or how to negotiate with each other. In others words, teachers become benevolent dictators.

2) By learning how to delegate and develop their classrooms as communities of learners in which all members take on many responsibilities, teachers become foster parents of little democracies. The limited democratic organization of the classroom gives students a sense of responsibility, trust, purpose, and initiative. All these values can be demonstrated as teachers and students learn how to become caring partners in communities of learning.

Part of dealing with conflicts within and without the learning community is to learn to recognize and appreciate similarities and differences within the group, as the following strategy demonstrates.

## ■ Strategy: *Same Circles, Different Circles*
## Value: Appreciation of Differences

### Objective

Students will see that underneath they may be different from those who seem to be like them on the surface, and like those underneath who appear on the surface to be different. Recognizing and valuing meaningful diversity and authentic sameness is the goal.

### Procedures

- Begin the lesson in a large open area—outdoors or in the gym.
- Be prepared with multiple sets of a variety of colored disks.
- Prepare trays or bowls labeled with distinctive characteristics or "difference markers." For example: gender, eye color, skin color, ethnic heritage, talents, religious affiliation, rural/urban, pets, family structure, clubs, hobbies, sports, favorite authors, favorite types of books—as many differences as you and your students can think of.

- One at a time, students will choose a disk from each tray of characteristics.
- Have large circles in the gym or on the playground marked with the colors of the disks.
- The students with a common color disk are to assemble briefly in the circle, see who is in their group, and talk about what they have in common.
- The whole class reassembles to talk about the similarities and differences.
- Possible discussion questions:
    1. Were you surprised at finding yourself in any groups?
    2. Did you know how much you shared with _____?
    3. We've seen some of the things that are different about us. Can you think of some things that are the same about all of us? List on chart paper.
- Develop a "we are the same, we are different" area in the classroom to celebrate diversity and similarity.
- Develop "Shoebox Autobiographies" or bulletin boards to celebrate individuality and diversity. Each student brings a box of artifacts/pictures/symbols that represent himself or herself for a show-and-tell event.

## Results

Students can appreciate the samenesses and differences among their classmates, broaden their views of classmates' talents, skills, and characteristics. They may begin to recognize that surface features of difference often have little bearing on people's talents and abilities, although individual interests and opinions are often shaped by group and cultural heritage. The cumulative effect of everyone's differences makes us culturally and individually what we are.

These ideas for easing into limited school democracies I have found to be workable and effective in every grade of elementary and middle schools. There are many additional materials available to the classroom teacher for democratic teaching practices, conflict resolution, grouping, and cooperative and collaborative learning practices.[4] Once some general democratic practices have been established, and students recognize by experience the ideas of choice, freedom, and responsible decision making, children's literature can provide the next powerful step in the pursuit of living values in the classroom.

While Giroux (1988) criticized the inculcation of "honesty, respect for law, knowing right from wrong, respect for parents and teachers, diligence, self-sacrifice, hard work, fairness, self-discipline, and love of country" as values that can oppress and disenfranchise as well as move us towards moral conduct, there is no doubt that stories written for children—particularly those found in basal readers—are a means of inculcating and transmitting traditional American democratic values. Giroux and other critics of

American schooling have further argued that schools do not encourage students to reflect and to examine values critically. To the contrary, I argue that we are all looking for a view of teaching and learning that moves us towards a vision of justice and compassion in our personal lives and in the larger society, even if we are not always successful in the attempt. The amount of traditional values teaching in public school textbooks has been reduced over two hundred years, but the basic core of mainstream values remains evident. Are there other worthy values to be considered? Undoubtedly. How, then, can we bring the discussion and acknowledgment of a multiplicity of values into the classroom?

First, students need a full range of classroom experiences that function as a context for lived values—cooperative and collaborative learning, choices in their reading and writing, opportunities to teach, and reflective telling of moral stories, as discussed above. Second, they need to do moral projects and develop inquiry studies such as those described in chapters one and two. Third, they need to discuss and work critiques stories written for children.

---

## Endnotes

[1] A number of researchers have talked about the social and academic benefits of choice, ownership and teamwork in the classroom. See Lev Vygotsky (1978), *Mind in Society*; Jerome Harste, Dorothy Watson and Carolyn Burke (1989), *Whole Language: Inquiring Voices*; Kenneth Goodman (1986), *What's Whole in Whole Language*; Johnson, Johnson and Holubec (1991), *Cooperation in the Classroom*.

[2] See Nancy Atwell (1992), *Living Between the Lines*, Judith Newman(1986), *Whole Language: Theory and Practice*, Kenneth and Yetta Goodman and Wendy Hood (1989), *The Whole Language Evaluation Book*, Jerome Harste, Kathy Short and Carolyn Burke (1988), *Creating Classrooms for Authors*, and Donald Graves (1991), *Building the Literate Classrom*.

[3] See Lickona (1991), Johnson, D. and Johnson, R., & E. Holubec (1991) for a discussion of ways to group children for learning and for building classroom cohesiveness.

[4] The headquarters for the Institute for Democracy in Education publishes *Democracy in Education: The Magazine for Classroom Teachers*. For information on the Institute and the magazine write to: IDE, College of Education, 119 McCracken Hall, Ohio University, Athens, OH 45701. See also the twice yearly *Teaching Tolerance*, published by the Southern Poverty Law Center. It is sent free of charge to educators. Write to: *Teaching Tolerance*, 400 Washington Avenue, Montgomery, AL 36104.

# 10 Using Children's Literature as a Context for Inquiry into Values

*[Storytelling] is international, transhistorical, transcultural: it is simply there, like life itself.*

Roland Barthes (1977): 79.

*A proverb, one might say, is a ruin which stands on the site of an old story and in which a moral twines about a happening like ivy round a wall.*

Walter Benjamin (cited in Rosen [1986]: 12).

**H**uman beings are storytellers—we "story" our lives. Narrative accounts of our own and others' experiences and our beliefs about them are a basic and essential mode of thought through which we endow experience with meaning and coherence. Hearing and reading stories is an age-old way of imparting, sharing, and reliving, in a personal and vicarious way, the meaningful experiences in the world imagined by the author. When we read stories, we are in essence enlarging and dramatizing our own lives—we are participating in a life-informing and life-transforming endeavor. We cannot tell good stories or read good stories—stories that are full of life and meaning for us—without constructing a parallel moral universe, one that either matches our own or is in conflict with it. It is out of this affirmation or conflict that our understandings of values are generated, in part, through contact with literature. Story is the most powerful means for understanding human experience and for assigning value to it; there is no more basic vehicle for values articulation than telling a story. To paraphrase Jerome Bruner (1986), we subjectivize experience by storytelling and render the realities of our moral lives changeable.

Storytelling in schools, however, has been held up in recent years as a way to encourage literacy—a vehicle for the "how-to" of reading and writing. The theory runs that if children hear and read wonderful stories, they will want to hear and read more stories, and their reading skills and attitudes will improve. I believe, however, that we need something of a reclamation project on children's literature. Great stories are not *primarily* for learning *how* to read, for causing children to become "strategic readers," for providing models of specific kinds of writing, or for obtaining free pizzas. Stories have always functioned to connect us to the worthy undercurrents and overriding moral imperatives of human life, and to explore and understand their opposites; storytelling and reading stories in school should accomplish the same purposes.

The wise use of children's literature is a step in the movement towards a broader vision of democracy. Books that recount the experiences of children in cultures parallel to the American mainstream culture give the teacher a tool for expanding students' sense of relationality—their recognition of their place in time, history, and in relation to other human beings. Literature allows vicarious experience and engagement with controversial issues on an emotional as well as on the intellectual level. We, students and teachers alike, construct our moral lives and our beliefs out of our experiences and social interactions with others. These interactions often take the form of storytelling. Stories about fictional or historical characters prepare students for the discussion of real experiences of their own classrooms and communities.

I suggest that rather than thinking, "How can I use this book to teach kids how to read?" teachers ought to ask different kinds of questions: Why are we reading stories in the first place? How do stories function in children's lives? How do we use literature to understand our lives? How do we use our lives to understand literature? How can stories provide us with a different "take" on topics of interest in history, the sciences, and current events?

We have long been grappling with the "how-to" questions: What makes a good reader? What method of teaching reading works best? Reading research has answered those questions in an abundant variety of ways. Decades of "good reader/poor reader" research helped us to focus on the skills necessary for effective and efficient reading. The next generation of reading research focused the field much more closely on the strategies of the good reader, reasoning that if we can figure out what a good reader does, and help the poor reader to do the same, we will have accomplished our goals as reading teachers. Do good readers identify the main idea, analyze characters, self-monitor, become strategic, predict, confirm, map, scaffold, web, reflect? Possibly.

But there are other, more interesting, more important questions: Do good readers love to read? Do good readers struggle with moral dilemmas in stories? Are good readers outraged by injustices recounted in stories? Do good readers outgrow themselves and expand their moral vision through good books? Not necessarily.
Large numbers of children and adults read perfectly well, but they choose not to read other than what is required for occupational functioning. I cite my undergraduate students as an example, Education majors whom I survey every fall. Among other questions, I ask: What did you read this summer? What did you write? Did you enjoy reading and writing in elementary school?

In the six years that I have been conducting these surveys, I have found that about two-thirds of these students read nothing beyond imposed textbooks but the newspaper and magazines, and even fewer write anything beyond grocery lists or notes in summer classes. Most of the students acknowledge that they did not like to read or write in elementary school, and many admit that they like neither reading nor writing now.

My mission as the instructor of these preservice teachers has been to reacquaint them with books. We begin slowly with children's literature—we read aloud and rejoice in the pictures and language of early-primary literature. Then, students choose their own books from a wide variety of adolescent novels available in our classroom, and they form literature circles for the discussion of their books. Many of the students have never discussed a novel of their own choosing with a peer. My goal is to socialize them into ways of reading that embody choice and critical thinking about issues and dilemmas in their books. Invariably, students' spontaneous discussions of stories center on experiences they have had that are conjured up by the story-talk surrounding their novel; they talk about their lives, their childhoods, their own children. Theorists such as Booth (1988), Coles (1989), MacIntyre (1981), and Rosenblatt (1938) have argued that because stories are organized around time as lived experience, stories allow us to interpret our pasts, understand better our current experiences, and see visions of our futures. I see evidence of this story-power in my students' talk.

We are all socialized into our ways of reading and our ways of thinking about reading. What we look for, attend to, comment on, and so forth, may well be determined by the context in which books are shared at home and at school. Think about the last time someone read to you, or discussed a story with you, or the last time you read to your children or your spouse. What was the purpose for that reading? To learn to use context better or to go on an adventure with a wonderful character? To get all the words right or to experience vicariously the dilemmas, decision making, and consequences of human experiences? To labor or to enjoy?

I am not suggesting that teachers abandon reading instruction—there is joy and purpose in learning *about* language in direct instruction as well as learning *through* language in story—but that they take another look at the literature they are using and the ways in which they use it in the classroom. If great books have become primarily a vehicle for teaching "main idea" and vocabulary, then look again. Our students' connections with stories are set in motion when two things happen: The writing rings true, and it touches them in some profound way. That's the essence of storytelling— that vicarious experience of the listener or the reader.

I have seen my students in language-arts and reading methods classes connect with stories. They work in learning teams in literature circles. They read novels, keep journals, and do a variety of strategies for exploring the novels and relating the authors' words and ideas to their own lives and experiences. Every so often, I ask the group to develop a couple of questions that they would like to ask the author. Invariably, students who are touched deeply by the writing want to know what motivated the writing. They want to ask the writer: Did this experiences happen to you or your family? Did you have to do a lot of research to write this book? These questions speak directly to the issue of **why** authors write. My students want to know what brought about this particular story. In other words, "We sense that you are a serious writer. You must have had some critical experiences in your own life to be able to write this. This came from your heart and touched my heart."

The written word has power over us. It speaks; it draws us; it takes us into other places and times. It is out of these moments of powerful connection with the author's message that discussion *about* language and story can naturally occur: What is the writing process? How do vocabulary, spelling, punctuation, and grammar contribute to a better dialogue between the reader and the writer? Can my own writing touch someone the way this book has touched me?

How does the teacher, the student, the parent, or the media specialist choose powerful stories that further the democratic, moral, and instructional goals that you and your classroom community have set? There are many resources for choosing books: journals and magazines such as *Book Links, Hornbook, Teaching Tolerance*; International Reading Association's "Children's Choice" lists published every year in *The Reading Teacher*; award-winning book lists; the bibliography at the end of this chapter; and others. While it is important to choose well-written books, I argue that teachers and parents need not be too quick to discount a book even though it is not politically correct or expresses an unacceptable ideology. Our current hopes and dreams for the envisioned classroom and the broader culture may make us discount books (ideas, people!) that seem unenlightened by our developing standards. We all need to examine our own thinking.

First, check your P.C.Q.—"political correctness quotient." I argue that in order for us to present children with choices and opportunities for moral growth, it is sometimes necessary to abandon our notions of political correctness if they determine our attitudes or cause us to adopt terminology and ideas that we have not made our own through experience. We need to acknowledge our current limitations and see ourselves and our students as would-be inhabitants of a metacultural future, coming to any piece of literature, any class discussion as learners-in-progress, with half-baked notions, ignorance, and bigotry. Those terms describe *everyone* who is willing to put him- or herself on the line as a learner and not merely to adopt a position and an ideological lexicon that appears to be savvy. No individual in this stage of our history can be so metacultural and so free of ignorance that they can understand the culture and beliefs of all others who may be present in the community and classroom culture.

Although there has always been a politically correct orthodoxy and a constantly changing accepted lexicon of "in" concerns, our lives can never be politically correct—not so long as we are learners, risk takers, people who are growing, knowing, and changing. We must refuse to see each other as unworthy, unenlightened, or beyond the ideals of justice and compassion. The moment we disagree, we have something to discuss and something to learn from each other.

Second, examine your own role in the classroom. Rethink your role so that you begin to function as a facilitator of literature groups, discussion, and research, one who is building a classroom context so that trust, compassion, healthy debate, and quest for understanding can surface and thrive.

Third, examine your own responses to children's literature. If we begin as teachers to examine our own responses to pieces of literature and to recognize that we bring many "selves" to our reading, then we can understand how others' interpretations can be quite different from ours. Here are two strategies that address multiple viewpoints on a topic and will help you to examine your responses to written material.

The first is the use of **text sets**. (See Harste, Short, & Burke [1988], pp. 358–365.) Teachers and students collect different genres of materials on a topic, including poetry, nonfiction, magazines articles, novels, photographs, music, and anything else that seems useful. Students choose a piece from this text set to read, and they return to the group ready to offer their insights on the topic based on their selections. The recording of information can be done on chart paper in list form and then categorized or webbed. The list can lead to further research in much the same way that the inquiry process described in chapters one and two developed. A text set functions as a mini-library in the classroom, but this library is a collection of "authentic texts," "real-world" items that you and your fellow-researchers have collected because you judged them informative and worthy. Inquiry method extends not only to selection of the topic but even to selections of the resources, authorities, texts, and literature.

A second strategy is **paired texts**.[1] Teachers and students collect pairs of books or other reading selections that provide contrasting viewpoints on a topic. The differing perspectives challenge students to acknowledge and grapple with multiplicity of beliefs and standards. As a way to introduce yourself to this strategy, I invite you and a reading partner to read *Words by Heart* by Ouida Sebestyen (a book that has, by turns, received glowing praise and blistering critique) and *Roll of Thunder, Hear My Cry* by Mildred Taylor.[2] Then do a little role-playing and invite discussion. Read from a variety of perspectives: as if you were a Christian minister or a Black Muslim or a professor of

African-American studies or the great-grandchild of plantation owners in a small town in the South. Gender, race and ethnicity, class, religion, locale, and a host of other individually defining and confining aspects of our identities play roles in our responses to literature and to each other. Think of these roles or aspects of a person's make-up as frames of reference that one can adopt and then temporarily set aside. As we change and exchange frames, the usefulness and validity of the frames may be challenged by the context in which we find ourselves. If that context is a classroom of diverse cultures and beliefs, then the frames can serve to explain various stances on knowledge and to explain and often to defuse conflict. I see both of these strategies as ways to begin the discussion of social issues, to unpack our values, and to improve critical thinking.

Fourth, set the tone for the interrogation of the knowledge base on an issue, i. e., become a classroom of researchers, debating and defending viewpoints based on a broad array of information. Because knowledge is individually and socially constructed, the interactions among group members in a learning context are important to the outcomes of the learning; moreover,they provide the context for the parallel goals in the classroom: understanding of others and knowledge of content. Ask yourself and your students: How useful is a scathing critique of others' opinions, no matter how unenlightened they may appear to you, if the recipients of that critique do not care what you think? Ask again: How useful is a scathing critique of another's opinions if that critique is based on hearsay, prejudice, and a lack of information? The building of trusting relationships and a full exploration of available information on an issue precedes the right to critique others' views in the classroom. The teacher can accomplish this through use of the democratic strategies discussed at the beginning of this chapter and an inquiry approach to curriculum demonstrated in chapters one and two. Inquiry curriculum and the strategies that lead to it fill the need for a methodology and a perspective on values teaching, not as a panacea but as a fruitful context for critical thinking. Then all those values that are deemed too religious, too secular, non-mainstream, together with the conflict they engender, may find a safe and meaningful context for exploration.

Can inquiry curriculum and wise use of children's literature take us to a better place than we have been? To a higher concept of democracy? A lot of rethinking about the current structures and frameworks of our social and academic lives will occur because we perceive that our current living out of our limited notions of schooling and democracy have not served to make us the just and compassionate society envisioned, though not yet realized, in our original charter. As a result of work on this book, I have many more questions than I have answers and many further studies to do. I want to learn about values consensus building and conflict resolution. I want to study students' discussions of paired texts. I want to understand more about the inquiry curriculum. I want to continue to test the hypothesis K + R = U— **knowledge** (derived through a social form of inquiry) *plus* **relationships** (built on trust and respect in classroom with a compassionate teacher) *equals* **understanding** (for a metacultural and just society).

All children need lives rich in the qualities that enable them to struggle for justice and to live compassionately—lives nurtured in a caring context, whether that context be a book, a home, or a classroom.

To all authors of children's books who are not afraid to put into the hearts and mouths of their characters the values that inspire worthwhile images of thought and action for children, I say: Thank you. Keep writing! To all the would-be authors of children's books who hold the seeds of untold stories that will touch the heart and inspire compassionate action, I encourage: Write your stories! Recognize their power.

To parents whose loving care and sharing of important books forges a bond of unity between parent, child, and book, you are providing a vicarious experience of choice and consequence, action and result: Keep reading! Find books that generate love and inspiration between yourself and your child.

To the many teachers who are seeking and finding the kind of literature that helps them to teach their students a high sense of values; to the teachers whose methods help students to learn democratic principles by living them in the classroom: Keep teaching! Yours is a classroom of living values and conscious reflection upon that which is worthwhile.

# Bibliography of Children's Literature for the Values Centered Classroom

The following is a bibliography of trade books that teach values which I recommend for book sharing among children and adults. The books have been classified according to the top twenty-five values identified in the readers of a hundred years ago and the top twenty-five identified values represented in readers in the 1990s. The following lists show these values in rank order, with the values most often taught listed first.

## Top Twenty-Five Values Taught in Readers at the End of the Nineteenth Century

1. Trust in God's presence and power
2. Value of home/family/family love
3. Work ethic
4. Consequences of right/wrong doing
5. Bravery/courage
6. Honesty
7. Obedience
8. Patience
9. Kindness
10. Generosity/Charity
11. Value of reading/writing/thinking
12. Temperance
13. Honor/respect for parents
14. Perseverance
15. Gentleness
16. Humility
17. Futility of war
18. Compassion
19. Unselfishness
20. Initiative
21. Self-sacrifice
22. Justice
23. Teamwork
24. Forgiveness
25. Freedom

## Top Twenty-Five Values Taught in Readers at the End of the Twentieth Century

1. Bravery
2. Appreciation of difference
3. Work ethic
4. Values of reading/writing/schooling
5. Self concept/identity
6. Familial love
7. Conservation of nature/animals
8. Perseverance
9. Gender role equity
10. Consequences of doing right/wrong
11. Initiative/self-reliance
12. Cooperation/teamwork
13. Kindness
14. Self-sacrifice
15. Wisdom
16. Forgiveness
17. Justice
18. Compassion
19. Freedom/patriotism
20. Honesty
21. Courtesy/manners
22. Generosity/altruism
23. Ingenuity/achievement
24. Service/social/political action
25. Humility

With these lists as our guides, I have developed the following bibliography of current children's trade books with the help of several children's librarians, children's bookstore owners, reading teachers, and classroom teachers. We have classified the books according to the major value thrust of the story. There may well be other strong values present. We have labeled each selection with "P" for "picture books" or "C" for "chapter book." We did not suggest reading "levels" per se, such as primary and intermediate, because our experience at all grade levels is that picture books provide a "hook" for bringing children into the topic. The use of literature circles (see Harste, Short & Burke, 1988) in place of basal reading groups, promotes *interest grouping* rather than *ability grouping* and encourages the use of books that present your topic for study from a variety of perspectives, without regard for reading levels.

Even though an author of a given children's book may not set out to demonstrate particular values in a book, it is the values component of a story nevertheless that makes it powerful and memorable. Many other children's books besides these have a strong values component, but we know the books in our bibliography and have used most of them with children; these are our favorites. The bibliography is organized beginning with the values from old readers; then are added the values from modern readers that did not occur in the old readers; then, a small list of values for the future. This list for the future needs a word of explanation: As we compiled this bibliography, we began to find that some of our own most dearly loved books did not seem to fit any of the categories from either new or old readers, and yet they embraced a strong values component. Through much discussion and debate on definitions of particular values (see the definitions where the values occur in the bibliography), we arrived at this small "futures" list that fits our sense of values important to the future:

- Hope
- Empathy
- Peacemaking
- Relationality
- Collaboration
- Individuality
- Spirituality

I hope teachers and parents will enjoy these books and use them with their children.

# Alphabetical Table of Values Contents for Bibliography of Children's Literature

## Children's Literature for the Values-Centered Classroom (P= Picture Book, C=Chapter Book)

### Value: Trust in God's presence and power.

Carlstrom, N. (1993). *Does God know how to tie shoes?* Grand Rapids, Michigan: Wm. B. Eerdmans Publishing Co. **P**

Goble, P. (1991). *I sing for the animals.* New York: Bradbury Press. **P**

Rylant, C. (1993). *The dreamer.* New York: Scholastic. **P**

Rylant, C. (1986). *A fine white dust.* New York: Bradbury Press. **C**

Spier, P. (1977). *Noah's ark.* Garden City, New York: Doubleday. **P**

Wood, D. (1992). *Old turtle.* Duluth, Minnesota: Pfeifer Hamilton Publishers. **P**

### Value: Home/family/familial love—an intense affection for another person based on familial or personal ties.

Boyd, L. (1990). *Sam is my half-brother.* New York: Viking. **P**

Clifton, L. (1978). *Everett Anderson's nine month long.* New York: Holt. **P**

Crews, D. (1991). *Bigmama's.* New York: William Morrow & Company. **P**

DePaola, T. (1981). *Now one foot, now the other.* New York: Putnam. **P**

Fox, M. (1988). *Koala Lou.* San Diego: Harcourt Brace Jovanovich. **P**

Hunt, I. (1976). *The lottery rose.* New York: Scribner's. **C**

Johnson, D. (1993). *Your dad was just like you.* New York: Macmillan. **P**

Joosse, B. (1991). *Mama, do you love me?* San Francisco: Chronicle Books. **P**

Jukes, M. (1984). *Like Jake and me.* New York: Knopf. **P**

Leach, N. (1993). *My wicked stepmother.* New York: Macmillan. **P**

MacLachlan, P. (1985). *Sarah, plain and tall.* New York: Harper & Row. **C**

Magnuson, J. (1978). *Orphan train.* New York: Dial Press. **C**

Miles, M. (1971). *Annie and the old one.* Boston: Little, Brown. **P**

Taha, K. (1986). *A gift for Tia Rosa.* Minneapolis, Minnesota: Dillon Press. **P**

Paterson, K. (1978). *The Great Gilly Hopkins.* New York: Crowell. **C**

Rylant, C. (1987). *Birthday presents.* New York: Orchard Books. **P**

Rylant, C. (1992). *Missing May.* New York: Orchard Books. **C**

Rylant, C. (1985). *The relatives came.* New York: Bradbury Press. **P**

Rylant, C. (1982). *When I was young in the mountains.* New York: Dutton. **P**

Sakai, K. (1990). *Sachiko means happiness.* San Francisco: Children's Book Press. **P**

Sharmat, M. (1977). *I'm terrific.* New York: Holiday House. **P**

Sharp, N. (1993). *Today I'm going fishing with my dad.* Honesdale, Pennsylvania: Boyd Mills Press, Inc. **P**

## Value: Work ethic—the principle that physical or mental effort or activity directed toward the production or accomplishment of something is good.

Bulla, C. (1975). *Shoeshine girl.* New York: Crowell. **C**

Bunting, E. (1994). *A day's work.* New York: Clarion. **P**

Medearis, A. (1990). *Picking peas for a penny.* Austin, Texas: State House Press. **P**

Mitchell, M. (1993). *Uncle Jed's barber shop.* New York. Simon & Schuster. **P**

Naylor, P. (1991). *Shiloh.* New York: Atheneum. **C**

Ray, D. (1990). *My daddy was a soldier.* New York: Holiday House. **P**

Schroeder, A. (1989). *Rag-time Tumpie.* Boston: Little, Brown. **P**

Taha, K. (1986). *A gift for Tia Rosa.* Minneapolis, Minnesota: Dillon Press. **P**

Warner, G. (1977). *The boxcar children.* Chicago: Albert Whitman. **C**

Williams, S. (1992). *Working cotton.* San Diego: Harcourt Brace Jovanovich. **P**

Williams, V. (1982). *A chair for my mother.* New York: Greenwillow. **P**

## Value: Consequences of right/wrong doing—the belief that there is a natural effect, result, or conclusion of doing right or wrong.

de la Mare, W. (1992). *The turnip.* Boston: David R. Godine. **P**

Fox, P. (1984). *One-eyed cat.* Scarsdale, New York: Bradbury Press. **C**

Myers, W. (1992). *Somewhere in the darkness.* New York: Scholastic. **C**

Naylor, P. (1991). *Shiloh.* New York: Atheneum. **C**

Soto, G. (1993). *Too many tamales*. New York: Putnam. **P**

Tsuchiya, Y. (1988). *Faithful elephants*. Boston: Houghton Mifflin. **P**

## Value: Bravery/courage—the state or quality of mind or spirit that enables one to face danger with self-possession, confidence, and resolution.

Cech, J. (1991). *My grandmother's journey*. New York: Bradbury Press. **P**

Coerr, E. (1993). *Sadako*. New York: Putnam. **P**

DeFelice, C. (1990). *Weasel*. New York: Macmillan. **C**

George, J. (1959). *My side of the mountain*. New York: Dutton. **C**

Hesse, K. (1993). *Letters from Rifka*. New York: Puffin Books. **C**

Higa, T. (1992). *The girl with the white flag*. New York: Dell Publishing Company. **C**

Lowry, L. (1989). *Number the stars*. Boston: Houghton Mifflin. **C**

Paulsen, G. (1987). *Hatchet*. New York: Bradbury Press. **C**

Paulsen, G. (1993). *Nightjohn*. New York: Delacorte. **C**

Ringgold, F. (1992). *Aunt Harriet's underground railroad in the sky*. New York: Scholastic. **P**

Sperry, A. (1940). *Call it courage*. New York: Collier Books. **C**

Wallace, B. (1987). *Red dog*. New York: Holiday House. **C**

Wells, R. (1988). *Shy Charles*. New York: Dial Books. **P**

## Value: Honesty—the qualities of truthfulness, integrity, and uprightness.

Bauer, M. (1986). *On my honor*. New York: Clarion. **C**

Bell, A. (1986). *The emperor's new clothes: A fairy tale*. New York: North South Books. **P**

Cohen, M. & Hoban, L. (1985). *Liar, liar, pants on fire*. New York: Greenwillow Books. **P**

Levy, E. (1976). *Lizzie lies a lot*. New York: Delacorte. **C**

Lexau, J. (1982). *I'll tell on you*. New York: Dutton. **P**

Ness, E. (1966). *Sam, Bangs, and Moonshine*. New York: Rinehart & Winston. **P**

## Value: Obedience—obeying or carrying out a request or command; dutifulness.

Mosel, A. (1968). *Tikki Tikki Tembo*. New York: Holt, Rinehart & Winston. **P**

Polacco, P. (1990). *Babushka's doll*. New York: Simon & Schuster. **P**

### Value: Patience—bearing affliction with calmness, tolerance, capacity of calm endurance.

Johnson, D. (1992). *The best bug to be*. New York: Macmillan. **P**

Kraus, R. (1971). *Leo the late bloomer*. New York: Simon & Schuster. **P**

Piper, W. (1986). *The little engine that could*. New York: Platt & Munk. **P**

Sharmat, M. (1991). *I'm the best*. New York: Holiday House. **P**

### Value: Kindness—of a friendly, generous, or warmhearted nature; showing sympathy or understanding.

Key, A. (1965). *The forgotten door*. Philadelphia: Westminster Press. **C**

McPhail, D. (1990). *Lost*. Boston: Little, Brown. **P**

Tusa, T. (1987). *Maebelle's suitcase*. New York: Macmillan. **P**

Uchida, Y. (1993). *The bracelet*. New York: Philomel. **P**

### Value: Generosity/charity—liberality in giving; an act or feeling of benevolence, good will, or affection.

Barker, M. (1991). *Magical hands*. Natick, Massachusetts: Picture Book Studio. **P**

Cooney, B. (1982). *Miss Rumphius*. New York: Viking Press. **P**

Luttrell, I. (1990). *Three good blankets*. New York: Atheneum. **P**

Silverstein, S. (1964). *The giving tree*. New York: Harper & Row. **P**

### Value: Reading, writing, schooling—valuing the stimulation or development of mental or moral growth.

Bunting, E. (1989). *The Wednesday surprise*. New York: Clarion. **P**

Duvoisin, R. (1950). *Petunia*. New York: Random House. **P**

Gregory, V. (1993). *Babysitting for Benjamin*. Boston: Little, Brown Company. **P**

Heide, F. & Gilliland, J. (1990). *The day of Ahmed's secret*. New York: Lothrop, Lee, and Shepard. **P**

Levine, E. (1989). *I hate English*. New York: Scholastic. **P**

Marshall, R. (1993). *I hate to read*. Mankato, Minnesota: Creative. **P**

Nixon, J. (1988). *If you were a writer*. New York: Four Winds Press. **P**

Paulsen, G. (1993). *Nightjohn*. New York: Delacorte. **C**

### Value: Temperence/moderation—exercising self-restraint.

Garland, S. (1992). *Song of the buffalo boy*. San Diego: Harcourt, Brace, Javonovich. **C**

### Value: Honor/respect for parents—a mark, token, or gesture of respect or distinction, regard with honor or distinction.

Leach, N. (1993). *My wicked stepmother*. New York: Macmillan. **P**

MacLachlan, P. (1980). *Mama one, mama two*. New York: Harper & Row. **P**

McDermott, G. (1974). *Arrow to the sun*. New York: Viking Press. **P**

Munsch, R. (1986). *Love you forever*. Scarborough, Ontario: Firefly Books. **P**

### Value: Perseverance—adherence to a course of action, belief, or purpose without giving way; steadfastness.

Bash, B. (1990). *Urban roosts*. Boston: Little, Brown. **P**

Bunting, E. (1991). *Fly away home*. New York: Clarion. **P**

Friday, B. & Friday, D. (1990). *Time to go*. San Diego: Harcourt Brace, Jovanovich. **P**

Fife, B. (1991). *The empty lot*. Boston: Little, Brown. **P**

Heinz, B. (1993). *The alley cat*. Garden City, New York: Doubleday. **P**

Hill, E. (1967). *Evan's corner*. New York: Viking. **P**

Hoffman, M. (1991). *Amazing Grace*. New York: Dial. **P**

Kiser, S. (1993). *The catspring somersault flying one-handed flip-flop*. New York: Orchard Books. **P**

Levine, A. (1993). *Pearl Moscowitz's last stand*. New York: Tambourine Books. **P**

Lyon, G. (1990). *Come a tide*. New York: Orchard. **P**

McCully, E. (1992). *Mirette on the high wire*. New York: G.P. Putnam Son's. **P**

MacGill-Callahans, S. (1991). *And still the turtle watched*. New York: Dial. **P**

Paulsen, G. (1992). *The haymeadow*. New York: Delacorte. **C**

Paulsen, G. (1990). *Woodsong*. New York: Bradbury Press. **C**

Piper, W. (1986). *The little engine that could*. New York: Platt & Munk. **P**

Rawls, W. (1976). *Summer of the monkeys*. Garden City, New York: Doubleday. **C**

Shelfelman, J. (1992). *A peddlar's dream*. Boston: Houghton Miflin Company. **P**

Steig, W. (1976). *Abel's Island*. Toronto: Collins Publishers. **C**

Williams, K. (1990). *Galimoto*. New York: Lothrop, Lee & Shepard. **P**

### Value: Gentleness—considerate or kindly in disposition; amiable.

Havill, J. (1993). *Sata and the elephants*. New York: Lothrop, Lee & Shepard Books. **P**

Martin, R. & Shannon, D. (1992). *The rough-faced girl*. New York: Putnam. **P**

### Value: Humility—meekness or modesty in behavior, attitude, or spirit.

Sharmat, M. (1977). *I'm terrific.* New York: Holiday House. **P**

Steptoe, J. (1987). *Mufaro's beautiful daughters: An African tale.* New York: Lothrop, Lee and Shepard. **P**

### Value: Futility of war—the uselessness of war.

Eco, U. (1989). *The bomb and the general.* San Diego: Harcourt, Brace, Jovanovich. **P**

Emberly, B. (1967). *Drummer Hoff.* Englewood Cliffs, New Jersey: Prentice-Hall. **P**

Houston, G. (1994). *Mountain valor.* New York: Philomel. **C**

McKee, D. (1990). *Tusk tusk.* Brooklyn, New York: Kane Miller. **P**

### Value: Compassion—to suffer with another; inclined to give aid or support or to show mercy.

Fox, M. (1985). *Wilfred Gordon McDonald Partridge.* Brooklyn, New York: Kane Miller. **P**

Fox, P. (1984). *One-eyed cat.* Scarsdale, New York: Bradbury Press. **C**

Fox, P. (1973). *Slave dancer.* Scarsdale, New York: Bradbury Press. **C**

Gray, L. (1993). *Miss Tizzy.* New York: Simon & Schuster. **P**

Innocenti, R. (1991). *Rose Blanche.* New York: Stewart, Tabori & Chang. **P**

Mills, L. (1991). *The Rag Coat.* Boston: Little, Brown. **P**

Paterson, K. (1990). *The tale of the Mandarin ducks.* New York: Scholastic. **P**

Polacco, P. (1992). *Mrs. Katz and Tush.* New York: Bantam. **P**

Thomas, J. (1981). *The comeback dog.* New York: Houghton Mifflin. **C**

### Value: Unselfishness—willingness to share, concern for the well-being of others.

Brodman, A. (1993). *The gift.* New York: Simon & Schuster. **P**

Burnett, F. (1911). *The secret garden.* New York: Lippincott. **C**

DiSalvo-Ryan, D. (1991). *Uncle Willie and the soup kitchen.* New York: Morrow. **P**

Nikly, M. (1982). *The emperor's plum tree.* New York: Greenwillow. **P**

Pfister, M. (1992). *The rainbow fish.* New York: North-South Books. **P**

Stevenson, S. (1987). *Do I have to take Violet?* New York: Dodd. **P**

Wilde, O. (1984). *The selfish giant.* Natick, Massachusetts: Picture Book Studio USA. **P**

**Value: Initiative—the power, ability, or inclination to begin or to follow through energetically with a plan or task; enterprise and determination.**

Baylor, B. (1986). *I'm in charge of celebrations*. New York: Scribner's. **P**

Gardiner, J. (1980). *Stone fox*. New York: Crowell. **C**

George, J. (1973). *Julie of the wolves*. London: Hamilton. **C**

Marshall, L. (1992). *The girl who changed her fate*. New York: Atheneum. **P**

Paulsen, G. (1991). *The river*. New York: Delacorte Press. **C**

Spinelli, J. (1990). *Maniac Magee*. Boston: Little, Brown. **C**

Williams. V. (1982). *A chair for my mother*. New York: Greenwillow Books. **P**

**Value: Self-sacrifice—sacrifice of one's personal interests or well-being for the sake of others for a cause.**

Brinckloe, J. (1985). *Fireflies*. New York: Macmillan. **P**

Buck, P. (1948). *The big wave*. New York: J. Day. **P**

Clements, A. (1988). *Big Al*. Saxonville, Massachusetts: Picture Book Studio. **P**

DePaola, T. (1983). *The legend of the bluebonnet*. New York: G.P. Putnam's Sons. **P**

Houston, G. (1983). *The year of the perfect Christmas tree*. New York: Dial. **P**

Luttrell, I. (1990). *Three good blankets*. New York: Atheneum. **P**

Tompert, A. (1988). *The silver whistle*. New York: Macmillan. **P**

Van Laan, N. (1989). *Rainbow crow*. New York: Knopf. **P**

**Value: Justice—moral rightness in action or attitude; the upholding of what is just, especially fair treatment and due reward in accordance to honor, standards, or law.**

Avi. (1991). *Nothing but the truth*. New York: Orchard Books. **C**

Harper, K. (1992). *Circle of gold*. New York: Dutton. **C**

Lasker, J. (1980). *Nick joins in*. Chicago: Whitman. **P**

Louie, A. (1982). *Yeh-Shen: A cinderella story*. New York: Philomel Books. **P**

**Value: Cooperation/teamwork—the principle of working or acting together toward a common end or purpose.**

Blaine, M. (1975). *The terrrible thing that happened at our house*. New York: Four Winds Press. **P**

Carris, J. (1982). *When the boys ran the house*. New York: Lippincott. **P**

*Using Children's Literature as a Context for Inquiry into Values*

Clever, V. & Clever, B. (1969). *Where the lilies bloom*. Philadelphia: J.B. Lippincott Company. **C**

Ernst, L. (1992). *Sam Johnson and the blue ribbon quilt*. New York: William Morrow & Company, Inc. **P**

Hayles, K. & Fuge, C. (1993). *Whale is stuck*. New York: Simon & Schuster. **P**

Speare, E. (1983). *The sign of the beaver*. Boston: Houghton Mifflin. **C**

### Value: Forgiveness—renouncing anger or resentment; refusing to impose blame.

Gray, L. (1993). *Dear Willie Rudd*. New York: Simon & Schuster. **P**

Jones, R. (1991). *Matthew and Tilly*. New York: Dutton Children's Books. **P**

Lioni, L. (1987). *Tiko and the golden wings*. New York: Knopf. **P**

Sebestyen, O. (1986). *Words by heart*. New York: Bantam. **C**

Whitt, A. (1984). *Suitcases*. New York: New American Library. **C**

### Value: Freedom/patriotism—the principle of liberty of a person from slavery, oppression or incarceration; political independence; love and devotion to one's country.

*(Note: In the old readers, these two values were embraced simultaneously in stories. Though there are distinctions in the modern readers and in today's children's literature, I have kept them in one category to maintain the comparison between old and new.)*

Bunting, E. (1990). *The wall*. New York: Clarion Books. **P**

Forbes, E. (1943). *Johnny Tremain*. Santa Barbara, California: ABC-Clio. **C**

Harris, D. (1993). *Sweet Clara and the freedom quilt*. New York: Knopf. **P**

Hopkisson, D. (1993). *Sweet Clara and the freedom quilt*. New York: Alfred A. Knopf. **P**

Monjo, F.N. (1970). *The drinking gourd*. New York: Harper & Row. **P**

Ringgold, F. (1992). *Aunt Harriet's underground railroad in the sky*. New York: Crown. **P**

# Modern Values

### Value: Appreciation of differences—recognition of the quality, value, significance, or magnitude of people who are different from oneself in a significant way.

**The Elderly**

Cooney, B. (1982). *Miss Rumphius*. New York: Viking Press. **P**

Daly, N. (1992). *Papa Lucky's shadow*. New York: McElderry Books. **P**

DePaola, T. (1973). *Nana upstairs & Nana downstairs*. New York: Putnam. **P**

DePaola, T. (1981). *Now one foot, now the other*. New York: Putnam. **P**

DiSalvo-Ryan, D. (1991). *Uncle Willie and the soup kitchen*. New York: Morrow Junior Books. **P**

Farber, N. (1979). *How does it feel to be old?* New York: E. P. Dutton. **P**

Fox, M. (1989). *Night noises*. San Diego: Harcourt Brace Jovanovich. **P**

Fox, M. (1985). *Wilfred Gordon McDonald Partridge*. Brooklyn, New York: Kane Miller. **P**

Gelfand, M. (1986). *My great-grandpa Joe*. New York: Four Winds Press. **P**

Johnson, A. (1990). *When I am old with you*. New York: Orchard Books. **P**

Kesselman, W. (1980). *Emma*. New York: Doubleday. **P**

Lasky, K. (1988). *Sea swan*. New York: Macmillan. **P**

Merriam, E. (1991). *The wise woman and her secret*. New York: Simon & Schuster. **P**

Peters, L. (1990). *Good morning, River!* New York: Arcade Publishing. **P**

Schwartz, D. (1991). *Supergrandpa*. New York: Lothrop, Lee & Shepard. **P**

Smith, R. (1984). *The war with Grandpa*. New York: Delacorte Press. **C**

Wild, M. (1989). *The very best of friends*. San Diego: Harcourt Brace Jovanovich. **P**

## People of Different Race or Ethnicity

Adoff, A. (1973). *Black is brown is tan*. New York: Harper. **P**

Banks, S. (1993). *Remember my name*. Niwot, Colorado: Roberts Rinehart Publishers in cooperation with the Council for Indian Education. **C**

Cannon, J. (1993). *Stellaluna*. San Diego: Harcourt, Brace, Jovanovich. **P**

Carlstrom, N. (1992). *Northern lullaby*. New York: Philomel Books. **P**

Davis, O. (1990). *Escape to freedom*. New York: Viking. **C**

Friedman, I. (1984). *How my parents learned to eat*. Boston: Houghton Mifflin. **P**

Mandelbaum, P. (1990). *You be me and I'll be you*. Brooklyn, New York: Kane Miller. **P**

Margolies, B. (1990). *Rehema's journey: A visit in Tanzania*. New York: Scholastic. **P**

Martin, B. (1987). *Knots on a counting rope*. New York: Henry Holt. **P**

O'Dell, S. (1970). *Sing down the moon*. Boston: Houghton Mifflin. **C**

Paterson, K. (1988). *Park's quest*. New York: Lodestar Books. **C**

Polacco, P. (1990). *Just plain fancy*. New York: Bantam Books. **P**

Ringgold, F. (1991). *Tar beach*. New York: Crown Publishers. **P**

San Souchi, R. (1987). *The legend of Scarface*. Garden City, New York: Doubleday. **P**

Speare, E. (1983). *The sign of the beaver*. Boston: Houghton Mifflin. **C**

Spier, P. (1979). *People*. Garden City, New York: Doubleday. **P**

Surat, M. (1983). *Angel child, dragon child*. Milwaukee, Wisconsin: Raintree. **P**

Swope, S. (1989). *The Araboolies of Liberty Street*. New York: Crown. **P**

Taylor, M. (1981). *Let the circle be unbroken*. New York: Dial. **C**

Taylor, M. (1990). *Mississippi bridge*. New York: Dial Books for Young Readers. **C**

Taylor, M. (1976). *Roll of thunder hear my cry*. New York: Dial. **C**

Taylor, M. (1975). *Song of the trees*. New York: Dial Press. **C**

Yashimo, T. (1955). *Crow boy*. New York: Viking Press. **C**

Yolen, J. (1988). *The devil's arithmetic*. New York: Viking Kestrel. **C**

Winter, J. (1988). *Follow the drinking gourd*. New York: Knopf. **P**

## People with Disabilities

Alexander, S. (1992). *Mom's best friend*. New York: Macmillan. **P**

Alexander, S. (1990). *Mom can't see me*. New York: Macmillan. **P**

Betancourt, J. (1993). *My name is brain/Brian*. New York: Scholastic. **P**

Booth, B. (1991). *Mandy*. New York: Lothrop, Lee & Shepard. **P**

Calvert, P. (1993). *Picking up the pieces*. New York: Scribner's. **P**

Clifteon, L. (1980). *My friend Jacob*. New York: Dutton. **P**

Coerr, E. (1993). *Mieko and the fifth treasure*. New York: Putnam. **P**

Cowen-Fletcher, J. (1993). *Mama zooms*. New York: Scholastic. **P**

DeAngeli, M. (1949). *The door in the wall*. Garden City, New York: Doubleday. **C**

Howard, E. (1984). *A circle of giving*. New York: Antheneum. **C**

Johnston, J. (1992). *Hero of lesser causes*. Boston: Little Brown. **P**

MacLachlan, P. (1980). *Through Grandpa's eyes*. New York: Harper & Row. **P**

Osofsky, A. (1992). *My buddy*. Henry Holt. **P**

Peterson, J. (1977). *I have a sister, my sister is deaf*. New York: Harper & Row. **P**

Ross, R. (1993). *Harper 'n Moon*. New York: Atheneum. **P**

## Value: Self-concept/identity—a person's sense of self, the set of behaviors and personal characteristics by which an individual recognizes him- or herself as her- or himself.

Archambault, I. & B. Martin (1990). *Knots on a counting rope*. New York: Henry Holt. **P**

Carlson, N. (1988). *I like me*. New York: Viking Kestrel. **P**

Teaching Kids to Care

DePaola, T. (1988). *The legend of the Indian paintbrush*. New York: Putnam. **P**

Glen, M. (1991). *Ruby*. New York: Putnam. **P**

Henkes, K. (1991). *Chrysanthemum*. New York: Greenwillow. **P**

Hoffman, M. (1991). *Amazing Grace*. New York: Dial Books. **P**

Howe, J. (1987). *I wish I were a butterfly*. San Diego: Harcourt. **P**

Johnson, D. (1992). *The best bug to be*. New York: Macmillan. **P**

Knowles, S. (1988). *Edward, the emu*. New York: Angus & Robertson. **P**

Kraus, R. (1971). *Leo the late bloomer*. New York: Simon & Schuster. **P**

Lasky, K. (1988). *Sea swan*. New York: Macmillan. **P**

Minarik, E. (1957). *Little bear*. New York: Harper. **P**

Paterson, K. (1988). *Park's quest*. New York: Lodestar Books. **C**

Shannon, G. (1981). *Lizard's song*. New York: Greenwillow. **P**

Sharmat, M. (1977). *I'm terrific*. New York: Holiday House. **P**

Steptoe, J. (1987). *Mufaro's beautiful daughters: An African tail*. New York: Lothrop, Lee & Shepard. **P**

Thomas, J. (1993). *Brown honey in broomwheat tea*. New York: Harper Collins. **P**

Waber, B. (1972). *Ira sleeps over*. Boston: Houghton Mifflin. **P**

## Value: Conservation of nature/animals—to protect animals and the natural environment from loss or depletion.

Allen, J. (1992). *Tiger*. Cambridge, Massachusetts: Candlewick Press. **P**

Arnold, C. (1983). *Pets without homes*. New York: Clarion. **P**

Baker, J. (1987). *Where the forest meets the sea*. New York: Greenwillow. **P**

Baker, J. (1991). *Window*. New York: Greenwillow. **P**

Brown, R. (1991). *The world that Jack built*. New York: Dutton. **P**

Burninghan, J. (1989). *Hey! Get off our train*. New York: Crown. **P**

Cherry, L. (1990). *The great kapok tree*. San Diego: Harcourt Brace Jovanovich. **P**

Cherry, L. (1992). *A river ran wild*. San Diego: Harcourt Brace Jovanovich. **P**

Clark, A. (1991). *In my mother's house*. New York: Viking. **P**

Cone, M. (1992). *Come back, salmon*. San Francisco: Sierra Club Books for Children. **P**

Cowcher, H. (1990). *Antarctica*. New York: Farrar, Straus & Giroux. **P**

Cowcher, H. (1988). *Rain forest*. New York: Farrar, Straus & Giroux. **P**

Fife, D. (1991). *The empty lot*. Boston: Little, Brown. **P**

Glimmerveen, U. (1989). *A tale of Antarctica*. New York: Scholastic. **P**

Havill, J. (1993). *Sato and the elephants*. New York: Lothrop, Lee & Shepard. **P**

Jeffers, S. (1991). *Brother Eagle, Sister Sky*. New York: Dial Books. **P**

Killilea, M. (1992). *Newf*. New York: Philomel. **P**

Locker, T. (1991). *The land of the grey wolf*. New York: Dial. **P**

Luenn, N. (1993). *Song for the ancient forest*. New York: Atheneum. **P**

McDonald, J. (1991). *Homebody*. New York: G. P. Putnam's Sons. **P**

Mendoza, G. (1990). *Were you a wild duck, where would you go?* New York: Stewart, Tabori, & Chang. **P**

Naylor, P. (1991). *Shiloh*. New York: Atheneum. **C**

Norman, L. (1983). *The paddock: A story in praise of the earth*. New York: Alfred A. Knopf. **P**

Rand, G. (1992). *Prince William*. New York: Holt. **P**

Seuss, Dr. (1971). *The Lorax*. New York: Random House. **P**

Seymour, T. (1983). *Pole dog*. New York: Orchard Books. **P**

Sharmat, M. (1991). *I'm the best*. New York: Holiday House. **P**

Tsuchiya, Y. (1988). *Faithful elephants*. Boston: Houghton Mifflin. **P**

Turner, A. (1989). *Heron street*. New York: Harper & Row. **P**

Van Allsburg, C. (1990). *Just a dream*. Boston: Houghton Mifflin. **P**

Yolen, J. (1992). *Letting swift river go*. Boston: Little, Brown. **P**

### Value: Gender role equity—valuing the state, ideal, or quality of being just, impartial, and fair without regard to traditional gender roles.

Ackerman, K. (1992). *When Mama retires*. New York: Knopf. **P**

Blane, M. (1975). *The terrible thing the happening at our house*. New York: Four Winds Press. **P**

Brown, A. (1986). *Piggybook*. New York: Alfred A. Knopf. **P**

DePaola, T. (1979). *Oliver Button is a sissy*. New York: Harcourt Brace Jovanovich. **P**

George, J. (1990). *On the far side of the mountain*. New York: Dutton. **C**

McGovern, A. (1987). *The secret soldier: The story of Deborah Sampson*. New York: Four Winds Press. **C**

Maury, I. (1975). *My mother the mail carrier*. New York: Feminist Press. **P**

Mills, L. (1993). *Tatterhood and the hobgoblins*. Boston: Little, Brown. **P**

Munsch, R. (1980). *The paper bag princess*. Toronto: Annick Press. **P**

Paterson, K. (1992). *The king's equal*. New York: Harper Collins. **P**

Zolotow, C. (1972). *William's doll*. New York: Harper & Row. **P**

### Value: Wisdom—understanding of what is interpersonally kind, right, and workable.

Franklin, K. (1992). *The old, old man and the very little boy*. New York: Atheneum. **P**

McGovern, A. (1967). *Too much noise*. Boston: Houghton Mifflin. **P**

Mendez, P. (1989). *The black snowman*. New York: Scholastic. **P**

Merriam, E. (1991). *The wise woman and her secret*. New York: Simon & Schuster. **P**

Shulevitz, U. (1993). *The secret room*. New York: Farrar Straus Giroux. **P**

Vigna, J. (1988). *I wish Daddy didn't drink so much*. Niles, Illinois: A. Whitman. **P**

Yolen, J. (1991). *All those secrets of the world*. Boston: Little, Brown. **P**

Young, E. (1992). *Seven blind mice*. New York: Philomel. **P**

### Value: Courtesy/manners—polite behavior; gracious, socially correct, and formal ways of acting.

Joslin, S. (1961). *What do you do, dear?* New York: Young Scott Books. **P**

Joslin, S. (1958). *What do you say, dear?* New York: Young Scott Books. **P**

Smith, R. (1984). *The war with Grandpa*. New York: Delacorte Press. **C**

### Value: Ingenuity/achievement—inventive skill or imagination; cleverness; something that has been accomplished successfully, especially by means of exertion, skill, practice, or perseverence.

Cleary, B. (1983). *Dear Mr. Henshaw*. New York: Morrow. **C**

Gilman, P. (1993). *Something for nothing*. New York: Scholastic. **P**

Polacco, P. (1993). *The bee tree*. New York: Philomel. **P**

### Value: Service and social/political action—the act of assistance, intervention, being of benefit to others.

Avi (1991). *Nothing but the truth*. New York: Orchard Books. **C**

Bunting, E. (1988). *How many days to America?* New York: Clarion. **P**

Everett, G. (1993). *John Brown: One man against slavery*. New York: Rizzoli International Publications. **C**

Havill, J. (1992). *Treasure nap*. Boston: Houghton Mifflin. **P**

Hewitt, M. and MacKay, C. (1981). *One proud summer*. Women's Press. **C**

Jacobs, W. (1990). *Ellis Island: New hope in a new land*. Charles Scribner's Sons. **P**

Leighton, M. (1992). *An Ellis Island Christmas*. New York: Scholastic. **P**

Oppenheim, S. (1992). *The lily cupboard*. New York: Harper Collins. **P**

## Future Values

### Value: Hope—a wish or desire accompanied by confident expectation of its fulfillment.

Gates, D. (1976). *Blue willow*. New York: Puffin. **C**

Ikeda, D. (1991). *The cherry tree*. New York: Alfred A. Knopf. **P**

Machizuki, K. (1993). *Baseball saved us*. New York: Lee and Low Books. **P**

Mitchell, M. (1993). *Uncle Jed's barbershop*. New York: Simon & Schuster. **P**

### Value: Empathy—sympathetic identification with, and understanding of, another's situation, feelings, and motives.

Byars, B. (1985). *Cracker Jackson*. New York: Viking. **C**

Estes, E. (1973). *The hundred dresses*. San Diego: Harcourt Brace Jovanovich. **C**

Innocenti, R. (1990). *Rose Blanche*. New York: Dell. **P**

Keller, H. (1987). *Lizzie's invitation*. New York: Greenwillow. **P**

Mills, L. (1991). *The rag coat*. Boston: Little, Brown. **P**

### Value: Peacemaking—causing conflict to cease, especially by settling the disputes of others; harmonious relations; stopping war.

Ackerman, K. (1990). *The tin heart*. Atheneum. **P**

Alexander, M. (1981). *Move over, twerp*. New York: Dial. **P**

Anzaldinua, G. (1993). *Friends from the other side*. San Francisco: Children's Book Press. **P**

Babbitt, N. (1969). *The search for delicious*. New York: Farrar. **C**

Blos, J. (1987). *Old Henry*. New York: William Morrow & Company, Inc. **P**

Bunting, E. (1992). *The wall*. New York: Clarion. **P**

Dolphin, L. (1993). *Neve shalom/wahat al-salem: Oasis of peace*. New York: Scholastic. **C**

Durrell, A. & Sachs, M., ed. (1990). *The big book for peace*. New York: E.P. Duttons Children's Books. **C**

Fradin, D. (1992). *Hiawatha: Messenger of peace*. New York: Macmillan/Margaret K. McElderry. **C**

Higa, T. (1991). *The girl with the white flag*. New York: Dell. **C**

Lowry, L. (1993). *The giver*. Boston: Houghton Miflin. **C**

Morimoto, J. (1990). *My Hiroshima*. New York: Puffin Books. **P**

Near, H. (1993). *The great peace march*. New York: Holt. **P**

Scholes, K. (1990). *Peace begins with you*. Boston: Little/Brown. **C**

Surat, M. (1983). *Angel child, dragon child*. Milwaukee, Wisconsin: Raintree Publishers**P**

Winthrop, E. (1989). *The best friends club*. New York: Lothrop, Lee & Shepard. **C**

## Value: Relationality—understanding and acknowledging one's place in history, community, and space.

Baylor, B. (1972). *When clay sings*. New York: Scribner. **P**

Burton, V. (1978). *The little house*. Boston: Houghton Mifflin. **P**

Fleischman, P. (1991). *The borning room*. New York: Harper Collins. **C**

Frasier, D. (1991). *On the day you were born*. San Diego: Harcourt Brace Jovanovich. **P**

Garland, S. (1993). *The lotus seed*. San Diego: Harcourt Brace Jovanovich. **P**

Hirst, R. (1990). *My place in space*. New York: Orchard. **P**

Johnston, T. (1988). *Yonder*. New York: Dial. **P**

Knight, M. (1993). *Who belongs here?: An American story*. Gardiner, Massachusetts: Tidbury House, Publishers. **C**

Knight, M. and Chan, T. (1992). *Talking walls*. Gardiner, Maine: Tilbury House. **C**

Lyon, G. (1993). *Dreamplace*. New York: Orchard. **P**

Lyon, G. (1992). *Who came down that road?* New York: Orchard. **P**

Precek, K. (1989). *Penny in the road*. New York: Macmillan. **P**

Pryor, B. (1987). *The house on Maple Street*. New York: W. Murrow. **P**

Rogers, P. & Rogers, E. *Our house*. Cambridge, Massachusetts: Candlewick. **P**

Shepard, J. (1993). *I know a bridge*. New York: Macmillan. **P**

## Value: Collaboration—working together, especially in a joint intellectual effort.

Cox, C. (1991). *Undying glory*. New York: Scholastic. **C**

Hammond, A. & Matunis, J. (1993). *This home we have made*. New York: Crown. **P**

Hill, E. (1991). *Evan's corner*. New York: Viking. **P**

Lionni, L. (1989). *Swimmy*. New York: Scholastic. **P**

Stanley, J. (1993). *Children of the dust bowl*. New York: Crown Publishers. **C**

Walsh, J. (1982). *The green book*. New York: Farrar, Straus, Giroux. **C**

### Value: Individuality/independence—being free, standing apart from the herd.

Arkin, A. (1976). *The lemming condition*. New York: Harper and Row. **C**

Baylor, B. (1986). *I'm in charge of celebrations*. New York: Scribner's. **P**

Gauch, P. (1971). *Christina Katerina and the box*. New York: Coward, McCann and Geoghegan, Inc. **P**

Hoffman, M. (1991). *Amazing Grace*. New York: Dial. **P**

Lowry, L. (1993). *The giver*. Boston: Houghton Miflin. **C**

Pinkwater, D. (1977). *The big orange splot*. New York: Scholastic. **P**

Shannan, G. (1981). *Lizard's song*. New York: Greenwillow. **P**

Swope, S. (1989). *The Araboolies of Liberty Street*. New York: Crown. **P**

### Value: Spirituality—perception and manifestation of a vital principle or animating force; relationship to the divine.

L'Engle, M. (1962). *A wrinkle in time*. New York: Dell. **C**

Lewis, C.S. (1986). *Chronicles of Narnia*. New York: Macmillan. **C**

Young, E. (1993). *Moon mother*. New York: Willa Perlman. **P**

---

# Endnotes

[1] "Paired Texts," as a strategy for critical reading, was developed by Carolyn Burke in the Language Education Department at the Indiana University (Bloomington) School of Education.

[2] More than a decade ago, Joel Taxel compared reactions to these two books in a paper entitled "Sensitizing Students to the Selective Tradition in Children's Literature," presented at the American Educational Research Association annual meeting in New York, March 19, 1982.

# References

**Alexander**, G. (1909). *Child classics: The first reader*. Indianapolis: Bobbs-Merrill.

**Alexander**, G. (1909). *Child classics: The fifth reader*. Indianapolis: Bobbs-Merrill.

**Allen**, C. (1889). *Fifth reader*. Indianapolis: Indiana School Book Company.

**Altwerger**, B. (in press). (Theme Cycles). Katonah: Richard C. Owen.

**Apple**, M. & L. Christian-Smith (eds.) (1991). *The politics of the textbook*. New York: Routledge.

**Archambault**, R. (1964). *John Dewey on education*. New York: Random House.

**Arons**, S. (1983). *Compelling belief: The culture of American schooling*. Paper presented at the Annual Meeting of the American Educational Research Association. ED231712.

**Association** for Supervision and Curriculum Development (ASCD) Panel on Moral Education (1988). Moral education in the life of the school. *Educational Leadership*, *45*, 4–8.

**Atwell**, N. (1992). *Living between the lines*. Portsmouth, New Hampshire: Heinemann.

**Baldwin**, J. (1897). *School reading by grades: Sixth and seventh years combined*. New York: American Book Company.

**Barthes**, R. (1977). Introduction to the structural analysis of narratives. In R. Barthes, *Image, music, text* (S. Heath, Trans.) Austin: University of Texas Press.

**Bohning**, G. (1986). The McGuffy Eclectic Readers: 1836–1986. *The Reading Teacher*, *40*, 263–269.

**Booth**, W. (1988). Pluralism in the classroom. *Critical Inquiry*, *12*, 468–479.

**Born**, P. (1993). Teaching values in school: A historical perspective. In *Insights on Global Ethics*, *3*, 7.

**Brown**, G. (1849). *The institutes of English grammar methodically arranged: With examples for parsing, questions*. New York: Samuel S. and William Wood.

**Bruner**, J. (1986). Life as narrative. *Social Research*, *54*, 11–32.

**Butler**, N (1857). *Goodrich's sixth school reader*. Louisville, Kentucky: Morton & Griswald.

**Buckelew**, S. (1888). *Practical work in the school room: A transcript of the object lesson on the human body*. New York: Lovell & Co.

**Clark**, S. (1875). *The normal grammar analytic and synthetic*. New York: American Book Co.

**Clark**, S. (1899). *Fourth reader*. Indianapolis: Indiana School Book Company.

**Cobb**, B. (1911). *A second reader. The Metcalf-Call Readers*. Boston, Chicago and New York: Thompson Brown Company.

**Cohen**, G. (1990). *Children of the mill: Schooling and society in Gary, Indiana, 1906–1960*. Bloomington: Indiana University Press.

**Coles**, R. (1989). *The call of stories: Teaching and the moral imagination.* Boston:Houghton Mifflin Company.

**Commager**, H. (1962). McGuffy and his readers. *Saturday Review, 45,* 50–15, 69–70.

**Criscuolo**, N. (1982). Effective ways to deal with the censorship issue. *NJEA Review, 56,* 18–19.

**Cuban**, L. (1984). *How teachers taught: Constancy and change in American classrooms 1890–1980.* New York: Longmans.

**Cuban**, L. (1986). Persistent instruction: Another look at constancy in the classroom. *Phi Delta Kappan, 68,* 7–11.

**Davidson**, I. (1922). *Fourth reader.* The Lincoln Reader. New York: Laurel Book Company.

**Davidson**, I. (1923). *Fifth reader.* New York: Laurel Book Company.

**de Charms**, R. & G.H. Moeller (1962). Values expressed in American children's readers. *Journal of Abnormal and Social Psychology, 64,* 136–142.

**Dewey**, J. (1902, 1966). *The child and the curriculum.* Chicago: The University of Chicago Press.

**Dewey**, J. (1916). *Democracy and education.* New York: Macmillan.

**Dewey**, J. (1938, 1963). *Experience and education.* New York: Collier Macmillan.

**Dewey**, J. (1968). *Problems of men.* New York: Greenwood Press.

**Dickinson, R.** (1815). *Columbian reader.* Boston: R. P. & L. Williams.

**Dolch**, E. (1934). *Teaching manual for the extension-reading work book.* Chicago: Scott, Foresman & Co.

**Down**, A. (1988). Preface to Harriet Tyson Bernstein, *A conspiracy of good intentions: America's Textbook fiasco.* Washington, D.C.: The Council for Basic Education.

**Eggleston**, E. (1915). *The Hoosier school master.* New York: Grosset & Dunlap.

**Eisner**, E. (1982). *Cognition and curriculum: A basis for deciding what to teach.* New York: Longman.

**Elam**, S. L. Rose, & A. Gallup (1993). The 24th annual gallup/Phi Delta Kappa poll of the public's attitudes toward the public schools. *Phi Delta Kapan, 74,* 41–53.

**Elam**, S. L. Rose, & A. Gallup (1992). The 25th annual gallup/Phi Delta Kappa poll of the public's attitudes toward the public schools. *Phi Delta Kapan, 75,* 137–52.

**Elson**, W. H. (1909). *Grammar school fourth reader for the eighth grade.* Chicago: Scott, Foresman & Co.

**Elson**, W. H. (1911). *Grammar school reader. Book one.* Chicago: Scott, Foresman & Co.

**Elson**, W. H. (1927). *The Elson readers: Book six.* Chicago: Scott, Foresman & Co.

**Elson**, W. H. (1911). *The story of the old world: A European background to the story of our country.* Boston and New York: Thompson Brown Co.

**Emerson**, C. (1928). *Physiology and hygiene: Book two.* Indianapolis: Bobbs-Merrill Co.

**Fleming**, D. (1987). Ethical issues in the classroom: Realism or happy talk? *Clearing House, 61,* 85–87.

**Flinders**, N. (1986). *Public school textbooks: Reflections of a shift in the philosophical foundations of American education?* Paper presented at the Annual Meeting of the Far Western Philosophy of Education Society. ED275058.

**Friere**, P. (1970). *Pedagogy of the oppressed* (Myra Bergman Ramos, Trans.). New York: Continuum.

**Gamberg**, R., W. Kwak, M. Hutchings., & J. Altheim (1988). *Learning and loving it.* Portsmouth, New Hampshire: Heinemann.

**Gardner**, H. (1983). *Frames of mind: The theory of multiple intelligences.* New York: Basic Books.

**Gardner**, H. (1987). *The mind's new science: A history of the cognitive revolution.* New York: Basic Books.

**Giroux**, H. (1988). *Teachers as intellectuals: Toward a critical pedagogy of learning.* Granby, Massachusetts: Bergin and Garvey.

**Giroux**, H. (ed.) (1991). *Postmodernism, feminism, and cultural politics: Redrawing educational boundaries.* Albany: State University of New York Press.

**Goble**, F. & B.D. Brooks (1983). *The case for character education.* Ottawa, Illinois: Green Hill Publishers.

**Goodlad**, J. (1984). *A place called school.* New York: McGraw-Hill.

**Goodlad**, J., et al. (1990). *The moral dimensions of teaching.* San Francisco: Jossey-Bass.

**Goodman**, K. (1986). *What's whole in whole language.* Portsmouth, New Hampshire: Heinemann.

**Gottschalk**, L. (1956) *Understanding history.* New York: Alfred A. Knopf, Inc.

**Graney**, M. (1977). Role models in children's readers. *School Review, 85,* 247–63.

**Graves**, D. (1991). *Build a literate classroom.* Portsmouth, New Hampshire: Heinemann.

**Gray**, W. (1932). *Teachers guidebook for the Elson basic readers. Book four.* Chicago: Scott, Foresman & Co.

**Gray**, W. (1956). *Fun with Dick and Jane. Basic readers: Curriculum and foundation program.* Chicago: Scott, Foresman & Co.

**Hamilton**, E. & H. Cairns (1971). *Plato: The collected dialogues.* Princeton, New Jersey: Princeton University Press.

**Harste**, J., K. Short. & C. Burke (1988). *Creating classrooms for authors: The reading-writing connection.* Portsmouth, New Hampshire: Heinemann.

**Harste**, J., D. Watson & C. Burke (1989). *Whole language: Inquiring voices.* Portsmouth, New Hampshire: Heinemann.

**Harvey**, T. (1869). *Harvey's Elementary Grammar.* Cincinnati: Van Antwerp, Bragg & Co.

**Hogan**, D. (1990). Moral authority and the antinomies of moral theory: Francis Wayland and 19th century moral education. *Educational Theory, 40,* 95–119.

**Howe**, W., M. Pritchard & E. Brown (1909). *The Howe Readers,* New York: Charles Scribner's Sons.

**Hubbard**, R. & B. Power (1993). *The art of classroom inquiry*. Portsmouth, New Hampshire: Heinemann.

**Illich**, I. (1971). *Deschooling society*. New York: Harper & Row.

**Jenkinson**, E. (1980). *Forty targets of textbook protesters*. Paper presented at the Annual Meeting of the Ohio Council of the International Reading Association, Columbus, Ohio, October 10–11, 1980.

**Johnson**, D. & R. Johnson (1988). Critical thinking through structured Controversy. *Educational Leadership, 45*, 58–64.

**Johnson**, D., R. Johnson & E. Holubec (1991). *Cooperation in the classroom*. Edina, Minnesota: Interaction Book Company.

**Kamhi**, M. (1981). Limiting what students shall read. Books and other learning materials in our public schools: How they are selected and how they are removed. ED210771.

**Kidder**, R. (1993). "Global ethics: A resounding "yes." *Insights on Global Ethics, 3*, 3.

**Kierstead**, F. & P. Wagner, (1993). *The ethical, legal, and multicultural foundations of teaching*. Madison, Wisconsin: Brown & Benchmark Publishers.

**Kohlberg**, L. & E. Turiel. (1971). *Moralization research: The cognitive-developmental approach*. New York: Holt, Rinehart, & Winston.

**Kohlberg**, L. (1976). *Assessing moral values: A manual*. Boston: Center for Moral Education, Harvard Graduate School of Education.

**Kohlberg**, L. (1984). *The psychology of moral development: The nature and validity of moral stages*. San Francisco: Harper & Row.

**Kohlberg**, L. (1985). The just community approach to moral education in theory and practice (pp. 27–87). In M. Berkowitz and F. Oser (eds.) *Moral education: Theory and application*. Hillsdale, New Jersey: Lawrence Erlbaum Associates.

**Kuhmerker**, L. (1992). Curriculum review: The Heartwood Project, and ethics curriculum for children. *Moral Education Forum, 17*, 17–19.

**Lickona**, T. (1991). *Educating for character: How our schools can teach respect and responsibility*. New York: Bantam Books.

**Livengood**, W. (1947). *Our heritage: Being a brief history of the American Book Company and an account of sundry textbooks and their authors*. Cincinnati: American Book Co.

**Lockwood**, A. (1991). Character education: The ten percent solution. *Social Education, 55*, 246–248.

**Lystad**, M. (1980). *From Dr. Mather to Dr. Seuss: 200 Years of American books for children*. Boston: G. K. Hall.

**MacIntyre**, A. (1981). *After virtue: A study in moral theory*. Notre Dame: University of Notre Dame Press.

**McClelland**, D. (1958). The use of measures of human motivation in the study of society (pp. 518–552). In J. W. Atkinson (Ed.), *Motives in fantasy, action, and society*. Princeton: Van Nostrand.

**McClelland**, D. (1975). *Power: The inner experience*. New York: John Wiley and Sons.

**McGuffey**, W. (1879). *First eclectic reader*. (Christian School Edition). Cincinnati: Van Antwerp, Bragg & Co.

**Mayher**, J. & Brause, R. (1986). Learning through teaching: Is your classroom like your grandmother's? *Language Arts, 63,* 617–620.

**Moshman**, D. (1989). *Children, education and the first amendment: A psycholegal analysis*. Lincoln: University of Nebraska Press.

**Mosier**, R. (1947). *Making the American mind: Social and moral ideas in the McGuffy readers*. New York: Columbia University, King's Crown Press.

**Nazario**, S. (1992). Right or wrong: Teaching values makes a comeback. *Wall Street Journal*, September 11, 1992, p. B6.

**Nemec**, L. (1940). *School friends*. New York: Macmillan.

**Newman**, J. (1986). *Whole language: Theory and practice*. Portsmouth, New Hampshire: Heinemann.

**Noddings**, N. (1992). *The challenge to care in schools*. New York: Teachers College Press.

**Norton**, D. (1991). *Through the eyes of children: An introduction to children's literature*. New York: Macmillan Publishing company.

**Osgood**, L. (1858). *Osgood's progressive fifth reader*. Pittsburgh: A. H. English & Co.

**Parker**, F. (1987). Textbook censorship and the religious right: Rise or decline? ED292715.

**Parker**, R. (1864). *The national fifth reader. Word-builder*. New York: Barnes & Burr Publishers.

**Parker**, R. (1869). *National first reader*. New York: Barnes & Co., Woolworth, Ainsworth.

**Parker**, R. (1875). *National third reader*. New York: A. S. Barnes & Co.

**Pennell**, M. (1929). *The children's own reader. Book two*. Boston: Ginn & Co.

**Perkins**, M. (1921) *Historical development of the moral element in American school readers*. A Dissertation Presented to the Faculty of Arts, Literature, and Science, of the University of Chicago, 54–55.

**Piaget**, J. (1965). *The moral judgment of the child*. New York: Free Press.

**Postman**, N. (1985). *Amusing ourselves to death*. New York: Penguin Books.

**Power**, C. (1991). Democratic schools and the problem of moral authority (pp. 317–333). In W. M. Kurtines & J. L. Gewirtz (Eds)., *Handbook of Moral Behavior and Development* (Vol 3: Application) Hillsdale, New Jersey: Lawrence Erlbaum.

**Pritchard**, I. (1988). *Moral education and character*. Washington, D. C.: U. S. Department of Education.

**Randall**, A. (1880). *Reading and elocution*. New York: Ivison, Blakeman, Taylor & Co.

**Richardson**, J. (1986). Paradigmatic shifts in the teaching of government publications. In *The Journal of Education for Library and Informational Sciences, 26,* 249–266.

**Rodrigues**, R. (1981). *Censorship: A multicultural issue*. Paper presented at the Annual Meeting of the Conference on English Education, Anaheim, California, March 19–21, 1981.

**Rosen**, H. (1986). *Stories and meanings*. NATE Papers in Education. Sheffield, England: The National Association for the Teaching of English.

**Rosenblatt**, L. (1938). *The reader, the text, the poem: The transactional theory of the literary work*. Carbondale: Southern Illinois University Press.

**Rothman**, D. J., & S.M. Rothman (1972). *The colonial American family*. New York: Arno Press.

**Sanders**, C. (1872). *New school reader. Fourth reader*. Sander's New Series. New York: Ivison, Blakeman, Taylor & Co.

**Sarason**, S. (1991). *The predictable failure of educational reform: Can we change course before it's too late?* San Francisco: Jossey-Bass Publishers.

**Schmidt**, W. (1983). Educational content of basal reading texts: Implications for comprehension instruction. ED228611.

**Searson**, J. (1923). *Studies in reading*. Chicago: University Publishing Co.

**Short**, K. & C. Burke (1992). *Creating curriculum*. Portsmouth, New Hampshire: Heinemann.

**Sidwell**, P. (1928). *Handbook of grammar*. New York: Charles Scribner's Sons.

**Smith**, F. (1981). Demonstrations, engagement and sensitivity: The choice between people and programs. *Language Arts, 58*, 634–642.

**Sullivan**. M. (1927). *Our times: The United States, 1900–1925, II, America finding herself*. New York: Charles Scribner & Sons.

**Tappan**, M. & Brown, L. (1989). Stories told and lessons learned: Toward a narrative approach to moral development and moral education. *Harvard Education Review, 59*, 182–205.

**Taxel**, J. (1982). Sensitizing students to the selective tradition in children's literature. A paper presented at the annual meeting of the American Educational Research Association, New York, March 19, 1982.

**Tenney**, S. (1887). *Young folks' pictures and stories of animals*. Boston: Lee & Shepard Publishers.

**Thomas**, C. (1880). *The frontier schoolmaster*. Montreal: John Lovell & Son.

**Thompson**, D. (1855). Locke Amsden, or the schoolmaster: A tale. Boston: Sanborn, Carter & Bazin.

**Thomson**, J. (1849). *Elements of algebra: Day & Thomson's Series*. New Haven & Philadelphia: Durrie & Peck, Loomis & Peck.

**Town**, S. (1857). *The progressive third reader for public and private schools*. Sanborn: Bazin & Ellsworth.

**Tschudi**, S. (1991). *Travels across the curriculum*. New York: Scholastic.

**Tyson-Bernstein**, H. (1988). *A conspiracy of good intentions: America's textbook fiasco*. Washington, D.C.: The Council for Basic Education.

U. S. Bureau of the Census. (1987). *Statistical Abstract of the United States: 1988 (108th edition)*. Washington, D.C.: U. S. Bureau of the Census.

U. S. Department of Labor. (1987). *Workforce 2000: Work and workers for the 21st century*. Washington, D. C.: U. S. Government Printing Office.

Vitz, P. (1986). *Censorship: Evidence of bias in our children's textbooks*. Ann Arbor, Michigan: Servant Books.

Vygotsky, L. (1978). *Mind in society*. Cambridge, Massachusetts: MIT Press.

Walker, A. (1924). *The study readers. Fourth year*. New York: Charles & Merrill Co.

Walker, B. (1976). *Curriculum evolution as portrayed through old textbooks*. Terre Haute, Indiana: Curriculum Research and Development Center, School of Education, Indiana State University.

Watson, J. M. (1876). *Independent fourth reader*. New York: A. S. Barnes & Co.

Webb, J. (1876). *Model fourth reader, in two parts, for intermediate and higher grades*. Chicago: George Sherwood & Co.

Webster, N. (1795). *The American spelling book: Containing an easy standard of pronunciation*. Boston: Isiah Thomas & Ebenezer Andrews.

Webster, N. (1829). *The American spelling book: Containing the rudiments of the English language*. New Brunswick, New Jersey: Terhune & Letson.

Webster, N. (1783). *A grammatical institute of the English language: Part I*. Hartford: Hudson & Goodwin (for the author).

Webster, N. (1784). *A grammatical institute of the English language: Part II*. Hartford: Hudson & Goodwin (for the author).

Webster, N. (1785). *A grammatical institute of the English language: Part III*. Hartford: Hudson & Goodwin (for the author).

Webster, N. (1807). *A philosophical and practical grammar of the English language*. New Haven: Oliver Steele & Co.

Wigginton, E. (1985). *Sometimes a shining moment: The Foxfire experience*. Garden City, New York: Anchor Press/Doubleday.

# Appendix: William Floyd and the Floyd Family Collection at Indiana State University

*William and Cletis Floyd*

**M**ost special collections have their genesis in either the occupations or hobbies of the individuals who assemble them. The Kirk Collection of sheet music and scores located in the Department of Rare Books and Special collections at Indiana State University, for example, reflects the life work of C. Weir Kirk. The Cordell Collection of Dictionaries began as the hobby of an alumnus, Warren Cordell, who spent his working life with the Nielsen Company as an account executive. The Floyd Family Collection was fostered by an amalgam of both kinds of involvement. The Collection is representative of William Floyd's work, an active life spent in the field of education either as a teacher, principal, or school superintendent in a career that started in 1927. The Collection of approximately 1,500 volumes of textbooks and related materials is indicative of Mr. Floyd's continuing interest as a collector of school textbooks, particularly those published in his home state of Indiana or used in its school rooms from about 1840 through the World War II era. Seeing himself as representative of a generation that was educated through use of these books, William Floyd has articulated their importance through this Collection. He sees his life as having been shaped by these books and he knows that he is not alone in this respect.

From 1927 until 1945, Floyd was an Indiana school teacher, first as an elementary teacher in the Washington County Schools. From 1945 to 1967, he was superintendent of education for the West Lafayette school system. Until his retirement, he was director of the Wabash Valley Education Center in West Lafayette, except for a year that he spent in France with his wife, Cletis, as a visiting high-school principal. Since his retirement, he has served frequently as a consultant to the Indiana Department of Education.

Floyd's own experiences as a young student, and then as an educator, colored his assessment of the probable importance of textbooks in the formation of the community of values among young people throughout the country. These were the books, like the family Bible, which had helped to form William Floyd's character and his views on life. He stated:

> **My own school experience played a part in the purpose envisioned in this collection. I was enrolled in Indiana public elementary and secondary schools from 1914–1926. The school textbook provided about ninety-eight percent of the reading matter available to me as a young scholar.**
>
> **I grew up in a middle-to-lower-middle-class small-farm family. I do not believe there were more than one dozen books other than school textbooks in my childhood home. My family subscribed to one weekly newspaper and one bi-weekly paper. Radio was not available in rural areas of southern Indiana until after 1920. The nearest town library was ten miles away with only a horse-drawn vehicle to reach it.**
>
> **The eight years of elementary school provided no more than a couple of dozen supplementary books for me to use. The four years in high school exposed me to less than one thousand library books. Hence, it was not until I arrived on a college campus in 1926 that I was able to view a library with a few thousand rather well-selected reference books and a librarian to give guidance to the use of books.**
>
> **I have injected this personal story with the intention of demonstrating the sparse learning facilities available to rural children in Indiana up through the first quarter of the 20th century. I believe my family represented a large segment of the greater community around us.[1]**

The Collection reflects a family whose members have been involved in public education. William and Cletis Floyd were both school teachers. Both of the Floyds' children, Iran G. and Ivan D., have followed them into careers closely related to the teaching profession. Other members of the family also have become involved in helping build the Floyd Family Collection.

The Floyd Family Collection was begun in 1979 with a first gift of 121 textbooks either published or used in the Indiana public schools. By chance or design, other members of the Floyd family and Cletis Floyd's family had kept some of their textbooks, and the Floyds added to these with selections garnered from bookshops and garage sales.

Although some of the holdings fall outside of the date guidelines, the focus of the Collection is largely books published between 1840 and about 1945, when textbooks played a central role not only in education but also as a means of conveying common values to Hoosiers. The beginning of this time period marks an era in which the large-scale publishing of textbooks began, increasing the influence of schoolbooks on large numbers of youths.

Unlike most other special collections, which generally retain only the best copy of a work, the Floyd Family Collection contains multiple copies of many texts. William Floyd reasons that annotations and even graffiti may provide keys to understanding the preoccupations of the developing minds of yesteryear's students. All areas of public-school curricula are represented, although textbooks on the "three r's" have the greatest representation. Because of their widespread use, examples remain extant.

Since providing the first gift in 1979, the Floyds have delivered ten gifts of books personally. By 1989, the Collection had reached 600 volumes through similar acquisitions. In slightly more than two years thereafter, the Collection more than doubled in size. As of 1994, the Floyd's remained actively interested in developing the Collection, scouring bookstores for books or beseeching friends and family members to part with theirs. In all, the Floyds' gifts to the Collection account for more than one-third of the approximately 1,500 volumes now housed in the Collection. Librarians in the Department of Rare Books and Special Collections concentrated on finding particularly scarce items on a *desiderata* list compiled by Mr. Floyd, and they have succeeded in finding some, though not all, of the titles.

Purchases account for only a small portion of the Collection. The most significant growth has occurred through gifts from many donors, some who were motivated to give a book when they read an article in the University's alumni magazine, and others by word of mouth. Some of the donors making substantial donations of books include the following individuals: Nathan Bridwell, the Crawford family, Mildred Pendergast, Dan Callahan, Mrs. Logan Miller, Harriette Miller, Edith Gertrude Dome, John W. Shonk, Vernon Cristee, and Benjamin Walker. (Benjamin Walker has also endowed the Cunningham Memorial Library with another collection of textbooks emphasizing hard-to-find titles.)

Edith Dome, a school teacher in Evansville, illustrates the wonderful degree to which some people preserve the things they value the most. In her home she had kept a copy of every school book she had used over nearly half-a-century of teaching. She donated several hundred volumes from the 1930s and '40s, and she would have gladly given the textbooks she had kept from the '50s and '60s, but these later books fell outside of the purview of the Floyd Collection. Ironically, Dome's husband had been a pioneer in the development of television, a medium that helped render textbooks less central to the conveyance of social values.

Two institutions that have made significant donations are the Lilly Library at Indiana University and the Indianapolis-Marion County Public Library (IMCPL). The Lilly Library does not collect school textbooks like the ones in the Floyd Family Collection; occasionally, therefore, it forwards textbooks to Indiana State University for inclusion in either the Floyd Family Collection or the Walker Collection. In the case of IMCPL, over 340 volumes were kept in storage in the main downtown library. The gift of these textbooks added many previously unidentified titles to the Floyd Family Collection.

Although the Collection contains many examples of textbooks across the spectrum of curricula and subjects taught from the 1840s to the 1940s, from grade school through high school, some key texts continue to escape acquisition.

A catalogue of the textbook collection of the Educational Research Library of the U.S. Department of Education, *Early American Textbooks*, 1775–1900, to appear in 1995, lists more than 12,000 volumes published in the eighteenth and nineteenth centuries. Although *Early American Textbooks* represents the largest collection of its kind, it is far from complete. It is difficult to say how many of these 12,000 textbooks were used in Indiana in addition to the 1,100 unique titles already housed in the Floyd Family Collection. Unfortunately, records of the books used in Indiana's schools were not maintained as a matter of routine in county courthouses until recent years. Many of the textbooks found both in the Floyd Family Collection and the Walker Collection are not listed in *Early American Textbooks*. These Indiana State University collections add, therefore, to the general record of textbooks used in public education.

Research continues, and there are many ways to verify that a book was used in Indiana. For example, individuals identify texts used by their forebears or a school ownership stamp provides evidence. A list of books compiled at the Indiana Historical Society Library adds further titles that will be acquired by the Collection when they can be located. Another list, compiled by William Floyd himself from his research on textbooks and their uses, contains names of other authors and titles of books desired for the Collection.

The quest for more books, although it continues, has slowed for a number of reasons. Like their Bibles, the textbooks of our forebears received rigorous use; books in good enough condition to preserve are difficult to find. Further, with the advent of rented books or school fees that included the use of textbooks, the disposal of old textbooks became routine; when an old textbook was replaced by a new one, the replaced works were taken away to be buried or burned. Prime examples of Indiana textbooks that might have been kept by adults, nostalgic for their school days, were often destroyed. Assembling collections of books that have received hard use is arduous, and it usually requires a lower standard of physical condition of the books. An imperfect book with, for example, a missing title page, yet identified by another means, will often be kept where there are few known copies surviving. Readers marks in well-used books, while detracting from the original beauty of the books, may suggest some interesting insights about their history and their users. Examples of such books must be kept, if not for their appearance, then for their worth as research materials.

As a teacher, William Floyd has known for a long time that some works are more important than others: he has gone to considerable pains to obtain some of the more important works. Some of these titles, like those in Benjamin Walker's collection of textbooks, are of greater importance in the history of education than others, regardless of where they were used. The following ten titles in the Floyds' Collection are considered to be among the most important textbooks of the bygone era, seminal to the development of American education:

Daniel Adams, *The Scholar's Arithmetic*: or, *Federal Accountant*, 1801.
Caleb Bingham, *The American Preceptor*, 1797. (reading instruction)
Nathan Daboll, *Schoolmaster's Assistant*, 1800. (mathematics)
William Holmes McGuffey, Readers, 1836–1920.
Jedidiah Morse, *Geography Made Easy*, 1784.
Lindley Murray, *English Grammar*, 1795.
Nicholas Pike, *A New and Complete System of Arithmetic*, 1788.
Joseph Ray, *Eclectic Arithmetic*, 1834. (subsequent editions issued in three parts with
    title variations)
Noah Webster, *An American Selection of Lessons in Reading and Speaking*, 3rd ed., greatly
    enlarged, 1787. (also known as *Grammatical Institute of the English Language, Part
    III*)
Noah Webster, *The Elementary Spelling Book: being an Improvement on the American
    Spelling Book*, 1829.

Besides acquiring important textbooks used in Indiana, William Floyd also wanted, when feasible, to include materials on which administrators and teachers would have relied to help them in their work. Mixed in among the textbooks, therefore, are a few examples of publishers' catalogues of textbooks and other offerings, and, in somewhat greater numbers, copies of teachers' manuals, teachers' editions, and similar instructional materials. Rare in themselves, these items augment the textbook collection by showing the relationship of schools and textbook materials to the commercial world around them, with which they shared many common values and interests. Whenever possible, the ISU Department of Rare Books and Special Collections has added to these holdings, in the realization that such materials increase our comprehension of the role of education both in the formation, and as a reflection, of American culture and values.

However important the books, pamphlets, and teacher-preparation materials may be in providing research materials, William Floyd's favorite acquisition is, to date, volume one of Conrad Malte-Brun's *System of Geography* (1828), a work pirated from the author's *Precis de la Geographie Universelle*, which revolutionized the teaching of world geography. In this instance, Floyd's role as a collector of books comes to the forefront. It is as much because of its scarcity and its curiosity as an "illegal" edition as its importance as a textbook that the Malte-Brun work intrigues him. Borrowing without attribution or permission among textbook writers and even publishers was

*The Floyds and David Vancil*

not uncommon, but this is an aspect of textbook history that has not been fully explored. The Malte-Brun is an example of another area in which the Floyd Family Collection makes possible further research.

The publication in recent years of scores of additional textbooks and other materials has placed an enormous burden on librarians to make the information available to scholars. At some point, compilation of a catalogue of the Floyd Family Collection needs to be undertaken. To have prepared a catalogue prematurely would create a false impression of the depth of the holdings; now, however, the Collection has become substantial. At this point, only a card catalogue arranged by main entry is available to help users of the Collection; other approaches are being explored, with plans underway to include the holdings in the main on-line database of ISU's library.

As a state normal school and then teachers' college, Indiana State University was the logical location for the Floyd Collection. Indiana State University is pleased to possess the Floyd Family Collection and plans to continue supporting it both with additions to the holdings and by other means. Its curators encourage its use and welcome inquiries from interested researchers.

**David Vancil, Curator**
**Rare Books Collection**
**Indiana State University**
**Terre Haute, Indiana**

# Endnotes

[1] All references to William Floyd's opinions or statements are from documents held in the administrative files of the Floyd Family Collection.

# Learning about Values at School:
# A Select Annotated Bibliography Drawn in Part from the ERIC Database

**Adams, Karen Irene,** *Multicultural Representation in Children's Books.* **1981. [ED 219 750]**

Fifty-seven children's books of accepted literary worth were evaluated for quantity and quality of multicultural representation. For evaluation, the cultural groups represented in books were arranged under nine headings: females, age, socioeconomic status, religion, handicaps, ethnic background, regional culture, language, and illustrations. The books were composed of two sets: 32 Newbery Award books from 1950 to 1981, and 25 children's classics ranging from 1697 to 1934 in original publication dates. First the books were read in random order by the researcher.

During this reading and evaluation process, an outside person read two books from the first third of the books read and evaluated, two from the middle third, and two from the final third. These outside evaluative findings were then compared with the researcher's to see if a change factor in the evaluative process had occurred. To avoid reader fatigue, the researcher read no more than 1.5 hours without a 10-minute break.

Findings showed that books of accepted literary worth did offer high-quality multicultural representation, though no books met the acceptable criteria levels for all nine categories. Of the 57 books examined, 21 proved acceptable. Broken into sets, 3 of the 25 classics and 19 of the 32 Newbery books were acceptable. The four categories with the highest percentages of acceptable responses were socioeconomic status, females, age, and regional culture. Comparing the two sets of books with one another, the pattern showed that acceptable multicultural representation increased with time—the acceptability percentages being consistently higher for Newbery books than for classics.

**Antell, Lee,** *Indian Education: Guidelines for Evaluating Textbooks from an American Indian Perspective.* **1981. [ED 209 051]**

Because most textbooks and instructional materials are designed to appeal to the majority market, they often are written from the ethnocentric viewpoint of the dominant White culture. American Indian viewpoints are either stereotyped, distorted, or omitted. To assist educators and publishers in developing awareness of American Indian heritage and culture and contemporary issues facing American Indians, general guidelines and a rating scale have been compiled by the Ethnic Heritage Project Advisory Council, to be used when evaluating textbooks and instructional materials.

The guidelines may be applied at all grade levels; they are focused on content, language, and illustrations. Content considerations include awareness of American Indians' perspective; contemporary as well as historical activities, contributions, and concerns; and avoidance of inferences that American Indians are "all the same" or that different lifestyles or customs are undesirable. Textbook language must explain that the term "Indian" is a misnomer, not use derogatory terms, avoid generalizations, be consistent when comparing activities of American Indians with other groups, reflect contemporary roles and life situations. Illustrations should avoid negative stereotypes and caricatures, be historically and culturally accurate, and depict American Indians in the same range of modern socioeconomic settings and occupational roles as other groups of Americans.

**Birchell, Gregory R. and Bob L. Taylor,** "Is the Elementary Social Studies Curriculum Headed 'Back-to-Basics?'" *Social Studies* 77/2 Mar-Apr 1986 p80-82. [EJ 336 690]

Reports the results of a study designed to determine whether eight widely used elementary basal social -tudies textbook series 1979–82 contain more "back-to-basics" content than did series from 10 years prior, during the rise of the "new social studies." The data show a marked influence of back-to-basics in all of these series.

**Brophy, Jere and others,** "Elementary Social Studies Series: Critique of a Representative Example by Six Experts," *Social Education* 55/3 Mar 1991 p155-60. [EJ 430 532]

Summarizes consensus points reached by three university professors and three elementary-school teachers who examined the Silver-Burdett-Ginn elementary textbook series. Explains the study's methodology. Finds textbooks constrained by the expanding environments framework, limited in multicultural coverage, and inadequate in developing themes around key ideas.

**Brouillet, Judith M.,** "West Meets East: A Study of Japan," *Social Studies Journal 19* Spr 1990 p18-21. [EJ 438 441]

Observes that elementary-school social-studies programs should broaden awareness of other peoples and cultures. Argues that commercial textbooks and programs seldom transmit the attitudes, respect, and feeling of humanness that comes from a child-centered, activity-oriented, interdisciplinary approach to the study of a country. Describes a first-grade unit on Japan.

**Buscaglia, Leo F.,** "Landmarks in Discovering the Human Dimension," *Childhood Education 60/3* Jan-Feb 1984 p154-65. [EJ 293 683]

Advocates teaching humanistic elements such as parents' history, individual uniqueness, potentiality, awareness, learning, new experiences, communication, and truth in discovery.

**Carlson, Kenneth,** "Academic Freedom in Hard Times," *Social Education 51/6* Oct 1987 p429-30. [EJ 358 604]

Reviews recent threats to academic freedom and examines the tendencies that either undermine or bolster the individual's willingness to exercise that freedom. Concludes that those who would curtail academic freedom are receiving support from a conservative federal judiciary and a national administration that identifies closely with fundamentalist Christianity.

**Clouse, Bonnidell,** *Teaching for Moral Growth: A Guide for the Christian Community— Parents, Teachers, and Pastors.* **Wheaton, Illinois: Victor Books, 1993.**

Addresses children's growth into responsible, honest, caring adults. Discusses questions regarding the use of such strategies as behavior modification, Kohlberg's stages of moral reasoning, and values clarification by examining 1) the basic assumptions of the psychology that emphasizes the technique, 2) the consequences to self and society if the technique is implemented, and 3) the extent to which each method is in accord with Christian theology. Psychological answers to moral growth offered by learning, cognitive, humanistic, and psychoanalytic approaches are among the contemporary issues addressed and critiqued.

**Coles, Robert,** *The Call of Stories: Teaching and the Moral Imagination.* **Boston, Massachusetts: Houghton Mifflin, 1989.**

**Comber, Geoffrey and others, "The Touchstones Project: Discussion Classes for Students of All Abilities,"** *Educational Leadership* **17/3 Mar 1989 p39-42. [EJ 385 278]**

Through lively discussions of specially selected texts, students of diverse abilities often discover that they can learn a lot from one another. The Touchstones Project in a Baltimore (Maryland) middle school features group discussion of classical texts.

**DeRosa, Bill, "Game Plan: Concentrate on Kindness,"** *Children and Animals* **13/2 Feb-Mar 1989 p13-15. [EJ 391 112]**

Describes a learning game in which students will find about 40 different ways they can help animals, learn more about animals' needs and people's responsibilities for animal welfare. Provides directions, suggested activities, and two copyable pages of game cards.

**Epstein, Kitty-Kelly and William F. Ellis, "Oakland Moves to Create Its Own Multicultural Curriculum,"** *Phi Delta Kappan* **73/8 April1992 p635-38. [EJ 441 214]**

Oakland, California, has launched a protracted campaign against the purchase of a state-approved K-12 social-studies-textbook series published by Houghton Mifflin. Numerous organizations, parents, and teachers voted against adopting these texts, which portray U.S. society as an immigrant culture but shortchange African-American, Latino, and Asian contributions to U.S. history. Oakland opted, instead, for its own curriculum.

**Feldmesser, Robert A. and High F. Cline, "To Be or Not to Be: Moral Education in the Schools,"** *New York University Education Quarterly* **13/3 Spr 1982 p11-20. [EJ 265 367]**

Discusses developmental, values clarification, actionist, and rationalist strategies in moral education and the problems associated with each strategy. Explores the question of whether schools should offer moral instruction. Outlines criteria for selecting a moral education program and emphasizes that moral issues raised in the classroom are related to everyday life.

**Field, Carolyn W.,** *Values in Selected Children's Books of Fiction and Fantasy.* **Hamden, Connecticut: Library Professional Publications, 1987.**

**Fleming, Dan, "Ethical Issues in the Classroom: Realism or Happy Talk?"** *Clearing House* **61/2 Oct 1987 p85-7. [EJ 359 242]**

Discusses the problem school system have in selecting textbooks that do not offend special interest groups but still address pertinent, possibly controversial, issues.

**Garcia, Jesus and others,** *Multicultural Textbooks: How To Use Them More Effectively in the Classroom.* **1990. [ED 320 262]**

Although the minority content of textbooks has increased and improved over time, its purpose and application are seldom discussed. Various approaches that promote multicultural principles, such as films, intergroup contact, curriculum innovation, multi-ethnic readers, and literature packages, are outlined in this review of the effective application of multicultural textbooks in the classroom. The review of literature indicates that favorable information about minority groups has a positive modifying effect on racial attitudes. Preliminary findings of a study conducted by one of the authors indicate that students became more knowledgeable about Afro-Americans; they changed their attitudes as a result of the teachers' use of multicultural materials.

The results suggest that the problem may not be the textbooks, but in the ways in which they are used in the instructional process. The teacher's role is crucial: books can be thought of as the tools, and teachers as the catalysts. The more effective teachers use a variety of materials, make effective use of curricula, are aware of textbook limitations, and recognize the importance of interaction between teachers, students, and resources.

Gorn, Cathy, "The Columbian Voyages and Primary-Grade Learners," *Social Studies and the Young Learner 4/4* Mar-Apr 1992 p17-18. [EJ 453 719]

Encourages educators to rethink approaches to teaching about Columbus' "discovery" of the Americas. Recommends that teachers examine textbooks for balance of presentation about Columbus. Suggests using children's literature and primary sources in addressing the topic. Underscores the need to present a balanced, multicultural explanation of the voyages of Columbus.

Graves, Donald, *Build the Literate Classroom*. Portsmouth, New Hampshire: Heinemann, 1991.

Provides a handbook for democratic classroom practice (though he doesn't particularly emphasize democratic principles) and focuses on teacher change and decision making. Includes a process for introducing decision making to children. The theoretical aspects of process curriculum go hand-in-hand with "actions," as the teachers implement specific strategies designed to support changes in their own and their students' thinking.

Gutherie, John T., "Research: Learning Values from Textbooks," *Journal of Reading 26/6* March 1983 p574-76. [EJ 276 220]

Responds to the challenge of textbook censors that content is critical to the process of value formation by presenting other determinants: the theme of the text, the values of the reader as related to that theme, and the teaching strategies implemented.

Harste, Jerome, Kathy Short, and Carolyn Burke, *Creating Classrooms for Authors*. Portsmouth, New Hampshire: Heinemann, 1988.

Promotes independent, social "authoring" in the broadest sense of the word. The authors discuss the theoretical underpinnings of process curriculum and the step-by-step structure (though they would not want it implemented rigidly) for helping children to become readers and writers. Though the authors do not directly address the issue of values development in the classroom, the democratic processes are evident. The second half of the book is devoted to reading/writing strategies.

Hogan, David, "Moral Authority and the Antinomies of Moral Theory: Francis Wayland and Nineteenth-Century Moral Education," *Educational Theory 40/1* Win 1990 p95-119. [EJ 406 310]

Wayland wrote what is arguably the most influential nineteenth-century moral philosophy text. This article examines the Calvinist tradition, from which Wayland diverged; explores his views as they relate to the home and school; and describes his impact on the formation of the middle class of his day.

Kahn, Elizabeth A. and others, "Making Small Groups Work: Controversy in the Key," *English Journal 73/2* February 1984 p63-65. [EJ 293 042]

Describes the use of value analysis exercises to promote small-group and class discussion.

**Kane, Frank,** "The Controversy over Civic Education," *Social Studies Review 22/3* Spr 1983 p4-8. [EJ 281 945]

Because of the unpopularity of the inquiry method, most new government texts are of the straight narrative type. Many educators believe that civics curriculum materials are subject to censorship by special interest groups. Regarding goal achievement, many believe that civics education has not trained students to accept their civic responsibilities.

**Kaplan, Joseph H.,** *Values Education: A Response to Moral Relativism.* 1989. [ED 315 360]

There is a growing agreement that the moral relativism or values-neutral education of the 1970s has been a failure, and many groups and individuals are calling for values education to become part of school curriculum. This paper focuses on the administration of values education and discusses the public policy debate surrounding it. Several institutions, through publications, conferences, and curriculum guides, advocate bringing values education back into the classroom.

Most notable is People for the American Way, a public interest organization that sponsored a 1987 national conference on values educations, and addressed some of the common concerns aroused by values education. The American Jewish Committee, the Center for Civic Education, and many other groups also advocate values education. A number of religions tend to back values education, as do many not-for-profit groups that advocate good citizenship. Several reviews have found the treatment of religion and values in textbooks to be unsatisfactory. A coalition of fourteen organizations from across the political and religious spectrum sponsored a brochure offering guidelines for teaching about religion in schools. They felt the need for more clarification of the appropriate place of religion in the schools, since it has played a significant role in history and society, but has been ignored in U.S. history textbooks. Many public figures also advocate values education, and several state and local governments have instituted programs for their schools. As more citizens learn about values education and as the mass media gives it more attention, the debate will increase and become more public.

**Kazemek, Frances E.,** "Literature and Moral Development from a Feminine Perspective," *Language Arts 63/3* Mar 1986 p264-72. [ED 331 137]

Explores the relationships between children's literature and moral development. Discusses characteristics of a "female morality" and why such a perspective is important. Describes some children's books that exemplify this perspective and offers suggestions for their use to help children develop morally as well as cognitively and socially.

**Kilpatrick, William,** *Why Johnny Can't Tell Right from Wrong.* New York: Simon and Schuster, 1992.

Argues for a return to authoritarian "traditional character education model" because children, in his view, are not ready for true democratic participation. Asserts that values clarification is alive and well in today's classroom, though many authorities in character education have long since abandoned it. Cooperative learning models and democratic classroom environments are given only a cursory examination in this book.

**King, Joyce Elaine,** "Diaspora Literacy and Consciousness in the Struggle against Miseducation in the Black Community," *Journal of Negro Education 61/3* Sum 1992 p317-40. [EJ 453 900]

Examines ideological representations of how slavery began and a slave's trip to America (the Middle Passage) as depicted in classroom texts in California public schools. Explores the controversy over the adoption of these supposedly multicultural textbooks through interviews with eight African-American parents and four multicultural education specialists.

L'Engle, Madeleine, *Trailing Clouds of Glory: Spiritual Values in Children's Literature*. Philadelphia, Pennsylvania: Westminster Press, 1985.

Lamme, Linda Leonard, *Literature-based Moral Education: Children's Books and Activities for Teaching Values, Responsibility, and Good Judgement in the Elementary School*. Phoenix, Arizona: Oryx Press, 1992.

Larkins, A. Guy, "Hero, Place, and Value: Using Biography and Story in Elementary Social Studies," *Georgia Social Science Journal 19/*1  Win 1988 p6-10. [EJ 375 591]

States that because of an unclear rationale for instructional goals, the expanding environment organizational scheme results in trivial course content. Recommends that elementary social studies be guided by a citizenship education rationale. Two illustrative lessons, using story, biography, and historical narrative, are provided: Sojourner Truth and "Knots on a Counting Rope."

Larkins, A. Guy and Michael L. Hawkins, "Trivial and Noninformative Content in Primary-Grade Social Studies Texts: A Second Look," *Journal of Social Studies Research 14/*1 Winter 1990 p25-32. [EJ 431 915]

Criticizes the prevalence of trivial and noninformative content in two primary grade social studies expanding environment textbook series. Extends earlier study, adding three additional analytical categories to its framework. To teach citizenship effectively, recommends (1) eliminating redundant, superfluous, and text-inappropriate content; (2) abandoning impotent approaches to affective goals; and (3) designing textbooks with structural integrity and imaginative writing.

Lee, Ger Bei, "Moral Education in the Republic of China," *Moral Education Forum* 15/3 Fall 1990 p2-14. [EJ 422 025]

Examines Taiwanese moral education, which has traditionally developed moral themes from Confucian ethics found in Chinese literature. Emphasizing altruism and self-discipline, lists moral values that primary and middle-school students encounter in "Chinese Readers," the predominantly used texts. Questions how industrialization and commercialization will influence moral education and textbook content.

LeMahieu, Bethene, "Learning to Choose," *Theory into Practice* 20/4 Fall 1981 p273-77. [EJ 255 786]

When children choose their learning experiences, they learn the emotional states that accompany decisions. They also learn to choose according to their potential, to identify strengths and interests, and, ultimately, to determine their lifestyles. Such a program in Montclair, New Jersey, is described.

Lickona, Thomas, *Educating for Character*. New York: Bantam, 1991. [ED 337 451]

Investigates strategies and supporting research on the development of character in school children. Shows how to develop a responsible and caring classroom environment for both academic and moral development. Deals with controversial social issues and their wise and humane address in the school setting.

Lickona, Thomas, "Character Development in Elementary-Grade Children," *Religion & Public Education* 6/3 Fall 1989 p409-17. [EJ 417 424]

Identifies goals of character development for elementary school children. Offers four processes that promote positive social growth and moral maturity: (1) building self-esteem and a sense of community; (2) learning to cooperate and help others; (3) reflecting on moral choices; and (4) participating in decision making. Suggests how teachers have implemented these processes.

**Lickona, Thomas, "Four Strategies for Fostering Character Development and Academics in Children,"** *Phi Delta Kappan 69/6* **February 1988 p419-23. [EJ 365 989]**

Discusses three goals of character development for elementary school children: promoting (1) cooperative relationships and mutual respect; (2) moral agency; and (3) a moral community based on fairness, caring, and participation. Explores teaching strategies for building self-esteem and fostering cooperation, moral reflection, and participative decision making.

**Lystad, Mary H.,** *From Dr. Mather to Dr. Seuss: 200 Years of American Books for Children.* **Cambridge, Massachusetts: Schenkman Publishing Co., 1980. [EJ 147 008]**

Traces children's literature from Colonial times to the present. Emphasizes the changing social and cultural influences that it reflected and the differential treatment given to the genders and races.

**Morrow, S. Rex, "Values and Moral Education: Revisited,"** *Councilor 47* **Oct 1987 p31-33. [EJ 365 349]**

Discusses the increasing need for inquiry and inductive-learning teaching techniques in the social studies. Encourages the use of values clarification, moral education techniques, and experiential learning to assist students in clarifying and constructing a positive belief system. Challenges social-studies teachers to work actively toward solutions to the problems facing students.

**Nucci, Lary, "Synthesis of Research on Moral Development,"** *Educational Leadership* **44/5 Feb 1987 p86-92. [EJ 350 658]**

In an attempt to clarify the confusion about the teaching of morality in the classroom, the author discusses the distinction between the concepts of morality and convention. Young children can distinguish between rules and moral principles, and successful moral discussion is more likely to occur in classrooms employing cooperative goal structures.

**Oppewal, Donald,** *Religion in American Textbooks: A Review of the Literature.* **1985. [ED 260 018]**

This section of a larger report describing a project designed to investigate systematically the presentation of religious and traditional values in today's public school curricula, presents a review of the literature focusing on studies that have analyzed the treatment of religion and values in elementary and secondary textbooks. This survey is supplemented by an examination of a sampling of literature anthologies used in upper elementary and secondary English classes, health/sex education textbooks, secondary biology texts, elementary social studies texts and textbooks used in civics/government and history classes. Using a table categorizing types of sex and ethnic bias (McCune, Matthews and Gall) and the "Humanist Manifesto" developed by the author, texts were analyzed to determine whether religious and traditional values and beliefs are accorded equitable treatment.

Findings indicate that the literature anthologies contain materials that expose students to traditional religious values, with amounts varying from negligible to significant depending upon whether the texts contain writings from earlier periods. The examination of three health/sex education textbooks and four secondary biology texts revealed from the traditional focus on biological concepts to controversial socio-moral issues in the secondary biology texts. Analysis of social-studies texts also revealed an underrepresentation of the role of religious belief and the church in society as well as a misrepresentation or underrepresentation of traditional values.

**Page, Homer and Jesse Liles**, *Experiential Plus: A Multiple Purpose Foundations Course.* **1981. [ED 230 486]**

A description is given of a course, oriented towards traditional foundations of education concepts, designed to prepare regular teachers for teaching handicapped students in their classrooms. The course's underlying philosophy is that education students should have an opportunity to apply concepts and relationships drawn from other disciplines to current educational challenges. The course places emphasis on experiences that can be related to fundamental philosophical questions about the purpose of education in society and the achievement of equal educational opportunity. Following a statement of the objectives, an outline of the course is presented. A listing of experiential learning activities is provided with brief annotations pointing out their significance in accomplishing affective objectives of the course. Procedures for evaluating the course's effectiveness in achieving desired student outcomes are described. Required readings are suggested, and sample tests outlined. A summary is offered on the fundamental concepts of equality of educational opportunity and values clarification.

**Palmer, Frank**, *Literature and Moral Understanding: A Philosophical Essay on Ethics, Aesthetics, Education and Culture.* **Oxford: Clarendon Press, 1992.**

**Parr, Susan Resneck**, *The Moral of the Story: Literature, Values, and American Education.* **New York: Teachers College Press, 1982.**

**Phillips, Carla R. and William D. Phillips, Jr., "The Textbook Columbus: Examining the Myth,"** *Humanities 12/5* **Sep-Oct 1991 p27-30. [EJ 442 191]**

Surveys U.S. historiography dealing with Christopher Columbus from the eighteenth century to the present. Traces the changes in interpretation—treating Columbus as hero, victim, visionary, genius, and mariner. Discusses past textbook treatments of Columbus and the portrayal of minorities in descriptions of his expeditions.

**Power, Clark, "The Just Community Approach to Moral Education,"** *Journal of Moral Education* **17/3 Oct 1988 p195-208. [EJ 382 988]**

Discusses Lawrence Kohlberg's theory of moral education through the structure of the just community. Evaluates experimental programs designed to implement this theory. Indicates that these programs establish cultures conducive to the development of socio-moral reasoning and action. Suggests ways to use these programs in the traditional school structure.

**Rylance, Dan,** *Reading, Writing, Arithmetic and Recitation: The Curriculum of the One Room School. Country School Legacy: Humanities on the Frontier.* **1981. [ED 211 254]**

The state superintendent, the county superintendent, and the one-room school teacher each contributed to classroom instruction in North Dakota. In 1895, the "School Text Book Law" provided for free text books and school supplies for all pupils; however, the law was not mandatory. Specific courses of study and elaborate handbooks on all subjects became common publications of the State Department of Public Instruction by the 1920s. Long periods of adjustment were necessary to balance grades, classes, and time when students in one-room schools were divided into classes one through eight (daily programs for 1901, 1908, 1918, and 1928 are included). Efforts of county superintendents of schools like Mattie Davis (1896) to initiate programs for teachers and students resulted in improved education. Teaching of patriotism and moral values was integral to the curriculum. In 1927, the state legislature passed a law requiring the conspicuous posting of the Ten Commandments where classes convened. Great emphasis was placed on phonics and penmanship. A former student, Ross Bloomquist, recalled that teaching materials he remembered from his school days included a dictionary, a globe, and a case of maps. Leila Ewen, a former teacher, recalled some unexpected teaching aids derived from the farm character of the land.

**Shwalb, David W. and Barbara J. Shwalb,** *Cooperation and Competition in Japanese Schools: A Mirror for American Educators.* **1984.**

Provides a foundation for research on socialization in Japanese schools, identifying types of cooperative and competitive student behavior as seen by teachers. The first of two surveys (each using two questionnaires) asked teachers to list examples of cooperative or competitive behavior. The second, designed from the responses to the first, asked a different sample to rank the tope 10 of 30 behavior items; through factor and cluster analysis, these items were reduced to composite indexes. Of eight cooperation indexes, six changed ranking between school levels; "harmony" and friendliness were most important overall. Evidently, specific standardized activities foster cooperation, some particular to school level. Though it is unproven that such activities comprise a grand scheme for teaching cooperation, the Japanese school system clearly states goals for socialization. Of nine competition indexes, all changed ranking between school levels; in contrast to cooperative activities, few were sanctioned or formal. Issues raised include, first, the degree to which cooperative and competitive behavior stem from nonschool factors and from explicit or implicit curricula; second, the interplay and social meaning of cooperation and competition in schools.

**Schwartz, Donald, "'Who Will Tell Them after We're Gone?' Reflections on Teaching the Holocaust,"** *History Teacher 23/2* **Feb 1990 p95-110. [EJ 429 259]**

Explores the rationale for including the Holocaust in the social-studies curriculum and analyzes how aspects can be introduced at elementary-grade levels. Outlines course objectives for studying the Holocaust that are relevant to major issues in social studies. Notes that 34 States do not require world-history courses, and that textbook content is uneven.

**Smith, Ben A. and Guy A. Larkins, "Social Studies Textbooks, Grades 1-4: A Review of Literature,"** *Journal of Social Studies Research 11/1* **Win 1987 p22-30. [EJ 372 664]**

Reviews literature, published between 1930 and 1985, concerning general content of social studies textbooks for grades 1-4. Notes that scholars, legislators, publishers, and authors have tended to criticize different aspects of these textbooks but that surprisingly few reviewers have criticized their trivial content.

**Stanley, William B., "Training Teachers to Deal with Values Education: A Critical Look at Social Studies Methods Texts,"** *Social Studies 74/6* **Nov-Dec 1983 p242-46. [EJ 292 244]**

Of the 36 texts examined, only two did not deal with values education in any significant way. The remaining 34 provided inadequate coverage. Almost all of the texts failed to discuss criticisms of the various approached used to teach values and issues related to the imposition of values.

**Sullivan, Emilie P. and Carol Yandell, "What Are the Religious/Spiritual Values in Children's Books? Do Children Get the Values Messages?" Paper presented at the Annual Meeting of the American Reading Forum, 1990. [ED 328 884]**

Reports one study of the religious and spiritual values in selected children's books and a second study of children's comprehension of the values messages. Thirty realistic fiction books which won, or were honor books for, the John Newbery Medals for 1974-1988 were studied. A modified version of the Values Category Scale was developed and included five categories: negative religious, nonreligious,

humanistic, Christian-Judeo religious, and other religious. A panel of 5 experts in children's literature, 3 educational library media specialists, and 2 children's literature professors read and indepen-
dently evaluated all 30 books. Results indicated that 24 of the books had nonreligious content while
only 7 of the books had Christian-Judeo content exceeding 25%. Results also indicted that historical
fiction works were more likely to contain religious values than contemporary fiction works. In the
second study, 8 children's librarians in northwest Arkansas selected a total of 29 Newbery Award
books and identified specific spiritual values in those books. Thirty-five third- through sixth-grade
students voluntarily read a total of 21 of the titles chosen by the librarians. The students were then
interviewed to discover what spiritual values they recognized and whether they identified the same
values as the librarians. Results indicated that (1) the librarians and the children were able to identify
a wide range of spiritual values in the books; (2) librarians chose stories emphasizing family relationships, love of parents, family unity, or the need for children to experience a loving and supportive,
traditional or nontraditional, family unit; and (3) in those books conveying spiritual values which
adults interpret as having religious significance, child readers focused only on the value in a nonreligious connotation.

**Taylor, Bob L. and Gregory R. Birchell,** *Has the "Back-to-Basics" Movement Influenced Elementary Social Studies Textbooks?* **1983. [ED 237 432]**

To test whether elementary social-studies texts have changed in response to the back-to-basics
movement, a content analysis was made of selected basal texts series published between 1969-1972
and reissued between 1979-1982. Quantitative data, anecdotal data, and educational criticism were
used to compare eight matched text series for knowledge base, skills base, values base, and recommended teaching strategies. Results indicate that the back-to-basics movements has effected a return
to traditional content and methods in social studies textbooks at all elementary levels. Findings
included an increased emphasis on reading development; an increased emphasis on American history,
geography, map and globe skills, citizenship education, and traditional American values; use of
simpler vocabulary, shorter sentences and fewer concepts; a de-emphasis on innovative teaching
suggestions; and increased testing of factual recall.

**Tuer, Andrew White,** *Stories from Old-fashioned Children's Books, Brought Together and Introduced to the Reader.* **Detroit: Singing Tree Press, 1968.**

An anthology of short stories and poetry, particularly stories with morals, collected from the literature read by children of the late-eighteenth and early-nineteenth centuries.

**Tyson, Harriet, "The Values Vacuum: A Provocative Explanation for Parental Discontent,"** *Religion & Public Education 16/3* **Fall 1989 p381-93. [EJ 417 422]**

Describes the public school bias toward objectivity that has produced a values-neutral education.
Reviews literature on textbook content and examines textbooks and curriculum to assess the impact of
the denatured curriculum on history, literature, home economics, and science instruction. Advocates
strengthening the humanities so that students can encounter complexities of life and fundamental
philosophical issues.

**Vitz, Paul and others,** *Equity in Values Education: Do the Values Education Aspects of Public School Curricula Deal Fairly with Diverse Belief Systems?* **New York University, Department of Psychology, 1985. [ED 260 017]**

Intended to examine equity in values education in public school curricula, this comprehensive report
is organized into two major sections. Section 1 is empirically oriented and presents evidence describ-

ing the representation of religion and traditional values in the nation's public school textbooks. Part 1 of section 1 (by Donald Oppewal) is a review of the already published literature on this topic. Part 2 of section 1 reports on the current portrayal of religion and traditional values in a large and representative sample of the nation's textbooks. Four appendices, making up approximately half of the report, provide tables showing the 60 social-studies books in the sample listed by publisher, grade, and title, followed by general summaries of major sections and emphases for each text. The books analyzed are social-studies, grades 1-6; American history, grades 11 or 12; and basal readers, grades 3 and 6.

Section 2 addresses the question, whether values should by taught, and if so, what rationale for teaching values is most defensible. Part 1 of section 2 (by Henrietta Schwartz) argues on the basis of anthropology that values are an inescapable part of any culture or subculture, such as schools. Part 2 of section 2 (by Edward A. Wynne) describes and extensively critiques the two most common rationales in the public schools for teaching values today—values clarification and Kohlberg's model of moral development. This part also presents a newly revived alternative approach to teaching values—an approach explicitly aimed at the development of character.

**Vitz, Paul C., *Religion and Traditional Values in Public School Textbooks: An Empirical Study*. 1985.**

This section, from a larger report describing a project designed systematically to investigate the representation of religious and traditional values in today's public school curricula, presents seven studies intended to examine the presentation of religion, religious values, and family and family values in typical textbooks used in the nation's public schools. Studies 1 through 5 deal with how religion and some social and political issues are represented in social studies texts for grades 1-6. Study 6 deals with the same topics as portrayed in high school American history books. Study 7 investigates how religion and certain traditional values are portrayed in the books used to teach reading, in grades 3 and 6.

The analyses were based on 60 commonly used social studies texts produced by the following publishers: Allyn and Bacon (1983); D.C. Heath (1982); Holt, Rinehart, & Winston (1983); Laidlaw Brothers (1983); Macmillan (1982-83); McGraw-Hill (1983); Riverside (1982); Scott Foresman (1983); Silver Burdett (1984) and Steck-Vaughn (1983). The books were read and scored by the principal investigator; all results were verified by independent evaluators. The general finding of the studies is that public school textbooks present a biased representation both of religion and of many traditional values.

Appendices (80% of report) include (1) a list of the 60 social-studies books listed by publisher, grade, and title; (2) adoptions of textbooks listed by State; (3) a text-by-text, page-by-page analysis of the presentations of religious values in text and in images and family values in text; (4) analysis of the treatment of selected religious topics such as the Pentecostal movement, Martin Luther King, and fundamentalism; and (5) summaries of 670 stories and articles analyzed in the study.

**Wurdinger, Scott, "The Ethics of Teaching Virtue," *Journal of Experiential Education* 10/1 Spr 1987 p31-33. [EJ 376 755]**

Attempts to answer the question "Can virtue by taught?"—the heart of what many experiential educators try to do. Argues that virtue exists but cannot be inculcated through any pedagogical methods because freedom is a necessary condition for learning virtuous action.

**Wynne, Edward A. and Paul C. Vitz, "The Major Models of Moral Education: An Evaluation. Section 2, Part 2" of "Equity in Values Education: Do the Values Education Aspects of Public School Curricula Deal Fairly with Diverse Belief Systems? Final Report," New York University, Department of Psychology. July 1985. [ED 260 021]**

This section, from a larger report describing a project designed systematically to investigate the representation of religious and traditional values in today's public school curricula, presents a critical evaluation of the two most discussed and influential models of moral education operating in the United States today. Both of these models have been developed in the last 20 years or so by education theorists at American universities and research institutes. The first model is known as "values clarification"; the other is based on the theory of moral development proposed by Lawrence Kohlberg. A third and oft-applied alternative, referred to as the "character education" model, is described. This alternative approach to teaching values involves articulation of such traditional moral aims as promptness, truthfulness, courtesy, and obedience. Whereas the first two approaches aim to shape patterns of moral reasoning, the third approach aims at shaping conduct. Concludes that as American education revives its concern for basic disciplines, educators should also return to the direct and indirect teaching of morality found in the traditional model.

## Teaching Values through Teaching Literature

by Margaret Dodson

Presents over forty teaching strategies to develop students' thinking abilities through exploration of ethical and moral dilemmas. Proven ideas for literature instruction use powerful novels, folk literature, poetry, and ethnic literature. Specific titles include "The Pied Piper," *The Pearl, The Catcher in the Rye, Huckleberry Finn, Things Fall Apart*, and *1984*.

Activities explore such topics as "Race and Class Tolerance," "How to Choose a Leader," "Native American Values," "The Mentally Retarded in Literature and Fact," "Values Declaration through Writing," and "Clarifying Values through Teenage Problem Novels." (Middle and Secondary)

Softcover, 8½ x 11 in., 168 pp.
**AT13**; $16.95

## Teaching Literature by Women Authors

by Carolyn Smith McGowen

This collection of exceptional lesson ideas from the ERIC database focuses on two purposes: (1) building a respect for, and awareness of, gender equity issues, and (2) expanding literature-based learning to include the works of 29 women authors.

Interesting, classroom-tested strategies explore the novels, short stories, and poems of Maya Angelou, Emily Brontë, Pearl S. Buck, Anne Frank, Toni Morrison, Joyce Carol Oates, Anne Tyler, Eudora Welty, Laura Ingalls Wilder, and many other great writers of the past and present. Ideas for elementary through college-level classrooms. (Elementary, Middle, and Secondary)

Softcover, 8½ x 11 in., 224 pp.
**AT14**; $16.95

## Critical Thinking, Reading, and Writing

by Mary Morgan and Michael Shermis

Encourages reading, writing, and thinking in a critically reflective way for students at all levels. Practical classroom activities make critical thinking an achievable goal.

Elementary activities include "Learning Styles: Developing Students' Self-Awareness," "Language and Thinking Skills: Science and Social Studies Activities," and "Folk and Fairy Tales: Analyzing Traditional Literature." Secondary activities include "Author Influences: Identifying Frames of Reference," "Critical Reading: Newspapers, Junk Mail, and Television," and "Study Guides: Examining Moral Issues." (Elementary and Secondary)

Softcover, 8½ x 11 in., 96 pp.
**AT03**; $14.95

## Peer Teaching and Collaborative Learning in the Language Arts

by Elizabeth McAllister

Six real-life scenarios illustrate how teachers have successfully implemented peer teaching and collaborative learning in the classroom. By sharing and cooperating, students gain more knowledge and sharpen their skills, and they learn from one another how to learn.

Describes four ways of organizing a peer-teaching program, offers suggestions on how to train tutors and design tutoring lessons, and explains how to evaluate the effects of a program in cooperative learning. Includes sample evaluation and accomplishment forms and an illustrated "Indiana Jones" map of peer-tutorial progress. (Elementary and Middle)

Softcover, 8½ x 11 in., 65 pp.
**AG13**; $15.95

## Celebrate Literacy! The Joy of Reading and Writing

by Jerry L. Johns, Susan J. Davis, June E. Barnhart, James H. Moss, and Thomas E. Wheat

Turn your elementary school into a reading-and-writing carnival with literacy slumber parties, book birthdays, and battles of the books! Proven lesson ideas cover the full range of language-arts outcomes and literature. Features a cross reference of classroom activities found across various lessons, such as reading, oral language, parent involvement, writing, drama, games, and cloze procedures. (Elementary)

Softcover, 8½ x 11 in., 92 pp.
**AT11**; $14.95

## Reading Strategies for the Primary Grades

by Kim and Claudia Kätz

Presents a store house of clever ideas to begin reading and writing, and to build vocabulary and comprehension. Uses stories, poems, response logs, oral reading, Whole Language, and much more! (Elementary)

Softcover, 8½ x 11 in., 102 pp.
**AT08**; $14.95

## Language Arts for Gifted Middle School Students

by Susan J. Davis and Jerry L. Johns

Supplies challenging lessons in a variety of language arts areas: communication skills, literature, mass media, theater arts, reading, writing. Activities designed for gifted students also work for others. (Middle)

Softcover, 8½ x 11 in., 74 pp.
**AT07**; $14.95

## Teaching the Novel

by Becky Alano, edited by Mary Morgan

**O**ffers strategies for teaching many novels, including *To Kill a Mockingbird*, *The Color Purple*, *The Scarlet Letter*, and other oft-taught works of interest to middle school and high school students.

Softcover, 8½ x 11 in., 65 pp.
**AG13**; $15.95

## Teaching Values in the Literature Classroom: A Debate in Print

by Charles Suhor and Bernard Suhor

**C**harles Suhor writes, "The question . . . is not 'Should values be a part of literature instruction?' but 'What is the role of the teacher in dealing with the moral elements in works under study?'"

*Teaching Values in the Literature Classroom* is a written debate between two brothers: Charles Suhor, Deputy Executive Director of NCTE, who strongly states a neutralist "Public School Perspective," and Bernard Suhor, a teacher of literature in the Roman Catholic schools of Louisiana, who represents with equal vigor a "Catholic School Perspective."

Both contestants in this debate describe their own styles of clarifying values in their respective classrooms. By discussing the moral and ethical contents of numerous pieces that are typically read in English literature classrooms, they offer teachers several options in the approach to teaching values through teaching literature.

Softcover, 6 x 9 in., 245 pp.
**AG31**; $16.95

## Whole Language: The Debate

moderated by Carl B. Smith

**W**hole Language advocates and detractors debate the highly touted, but still controversial, language arts instructional paradigm. The evidence for Whole Language claims is questioned and defended.

Important questions are raised and responded to in this volume which includes proceedings from a debate held at the National Reading Conference in San Antonio. Writing for Whole Language in the debate are Susan Ohanian (a freelance writer) and Patrick Shannon (a professor at Pennsylvania State University). Writing caveats about Whole Language are Michael McKenna (Georgia Southern University), Richard Robinson (University of Missouri at Columbia), and John Miller (Florida State University). Comments from Jerome Harste, Shelley Harwayne, Michael Pressley, and Stephen Stahl are included.

Essential reading for teachers, scholars, and policymakers on either side of the Whole Language fence.

Softcover, 6 x 9 in., 320 pp.
**AG51**; $24.95

**T**o order any of these excellent books from ERIC / EDINFO Press, complete the Order Form on the next page, or call 1-800-925-7853.

# Order Form

| Order No. | Qty. | Description | Unit Price | Total |
|---|---|---|---|---|
| AG56 | | *Teaching Kids to Care* | $19.95 | |
| AT13 | | *Teaching Values through Teaching Literature* | 16.95 | |
| AT14 | | *Teaching Literature by Women Authors* | 16.95 | |
| AT03 | | *Critical Thinking, Reading, and Writing* | 14.95 | |
| AG13 | | *Peer Teaching and Collaborative Learning* | 15.95 | |
| AT11 | | *Celebrate Literacy! The Joy of Reading and Writing* | 14.95 | |
| AT08 | | *Reading Strategies for the Primary Grades* | 14.95 | |
| AT07 | | *Language Arts for Gifted Middle School Students* | 14.95 | |
| AT02 | | *Teaching the Novel* | 14.95 | |
| AG31 | | *Teaching Values in the Literature Classroom: A Debate in Print* | 16.95 | |
| AG51 | | *Whole Language: The Debate* | 24.95 | |

| | |
|---|---|
| Subtotal | |
| Add 10% for S&H (minimum $3.00) | |
| IN residents add 5% sales tax | |
| TOTAL | |

Prices subject to change.

## To Order:

**By Mail:** **ERIC/EDINFO Press**
**Indiana University**
**P.O. Box 5953**
**Bloomington, IN 47407**

**By Phone:** **1-800-925-7853**
**(M-F, 8 a.m. – 5 p.m. EST)**

**By FAX:** **1-812-331-2776**

## Method of Payment:

❑ check  ❑ money order  ❑ P.O.#_____

❑ MasterCard  ❑ Visa

Cardholder_____

Card no._____

Expiration date_____

Cardholder's signature_____

## Ship to:

_____  _____
Name                                Title

_____  _____
Organization                        Phone

_____  _____
Address                             City/State/ZIP

## SATISFACTION GUARANTEED

If for any reason you are not completely satisfied with a product or publication you purchase from us, simply return the item within 30 days and we will refund your money and any postage costs.

ERIC®
EDINFO Press